# *Earthing the Gospel*

An inculturation handbook for pastoral workers

## Gerald A. Arbuckle, SM

ORBIS BOOKS

Maryknoll, New York 10545

The Catholic Foreign Mission Society of America (Maryknoll) recruits and trains people for overseas missionary service. Through Orbis Books Maryknoll aims to foster the international dialogue that is essential to mission. The books published, however, reflect the opinions of their authors and are not meant to represent the official position of the Society.

Copyright © Gerald A. Arbuckle 1990

Published in the United States of America by Orbis Books, Maryknoll NY 10545
Published in Great Britain by Geoffrey Chapman, an imprint of Cassell
Publishers Ltd, London

Typeset by Colset Private Limited, Singapore
Printed and bound in Great Britain by
The Bath Press, Avon

**Library of Congress Cataloging-in-Publication Data**
Arbuckle, Gerald A.
  Earthing the Gospel: an inculturation handbook for pastoral workers
  / Gerald A. Arbuckle.
        p.  cm.
  Includes bibliographic references.
  ISBN 0-88344-643-X
  1. Christianity and Culture.  2. Missions—Theory.  3. Evangelistic
  Work—Philosophy.  4. Ethnology—religious aspects—Christianity.
  I. Title.
  BR115.C8A67  1990
  266'.001  dc20
                                                            89-77599
                                                            CIP

# Contents

# Acknowledgements

The writing of this book has been a co-operative venture, involving many hundreds of people of the First and Third Worlds. In my twenty-five years of anthropological fieldwork, people have generously shared their personal stories with me, some of which are recorded in the text. Participants of countless workshops/lecture programmes have provided their experience, challenging questions and pastoral enthusiasm, all of which have helped to mould my own insights.

In particular, I thank Robert Kelly and Ruth McCurry, editors of Geoffrey Chapman, London, for their patient and stimulating encouragement; Terence Gleeson, FMS, for stylistic guidance. I thank the editors of *Human Development*, *The Jurist*, *Theological Studies*, *Review for Religious* and *Worship* for permission to use material that I had originally published in their reviews.

Extracts from W. H. Auden, 'I am not a Camera' and 'Archaeology', from *Collected Poems*, are reprinted by permission of Faber and Faber Limited, and Random House, Inc.

Quotations from the Jerusalem Bible, published and copyright 1966, 1967 and 1968 by Darton, Longman and Todd Ltd, and Doubleday, a division of Bantam, Doubleday, Dell Publishing Group, Inc., are reprinted by permission of the publishers.

Very specially, I thank Tom O'Gorman, SJ, and the staff of the East Asian Pastoral Institute, who generously gave me the time and the fine research facilities for the writing of this book.

East Asian Pastoral Institute
Ateneo de Manila University
Manila
Philippines                                                        December 1988

# Introduction

The Word was made flesh and dwelt among us (Jn 1:14).

A Gospel which has not permeated a culture is a Gospel not fully proclaimed (John Paul II).

Inculturation is the interaction or dialogue between the Gospel and cultures. Volumes have been written on the importance of the fact that the Gospel must permeate cultures, but little on *how* in practice this is to take place. The reason is simple. We know a lot about the Gospel and theology, but there is so little readily available for the evangelizer about the other pole of the dialogue—culture or cultures. This book is a response to this lack of resource material on the culture side of inculturation.

An ancient Oriental fable illustrates the unsuspected dangers that await the evangelizer who has little grasp of the complexity of culture(s). Once upon a time a monkey and a fish were in a huge flood. The agile monkey was able to save itself by grasping a tree branch and pulling itself to safety. Happy at last, the monkey noticed a fish fighting against the massive current and, deeply moved by its plight, he bent down to save it. The fish was not happy, for it bit the monkey's hand. Whereupon the monkey, being terribly annoyed at the fish's ingratitude, threw the fish back into the water.[1]

As water is to the fish, so culture is to the human person—a truth so difficult to grasp unless, like the fish, we experience the trauma of suddenly being without a culture, a sense of belonging. We evangelizers and theologians can act very much like the monkey—full of goodwill, but with little sensitivity to what culture is or how it 'operates'. The results of our amateurish, half-hearted efforts at inculturation can consequently be pastorally disastrous. To be thoroughly involved in the dialogue between the Gospel and cultures, we need a lot more than the goodwill of a monkey!

Culture is a 'silent language'.[2] Traditions, values, attitudes and prejudices are silent, like the stillness of water for fish, in the sense that people are most often unconscious of their presence and influence. The unique task of the cultural (or social) anthropologist[3] is to unearth, and articulate clearly and objectively, what is hidden from the consciousness of people about how they interact with one another.

This book provides analytical instruments from cultural anthropology to help evangelizers grasp what is happening to cultures within the First World (and also within many parts of the Third World). With the aid of these instruments, evangelizers can sit down with people from all levels of society to listen, with more understanding than ever before, to their griefs, hopes and joys. As a result of this dialogue there may well emerge new local theologies that are earthed in the symbols, myths and rituals of people's lives (see Chapters 1 to 3).

In the latter part of this book I claim that the confusion or sense of pastoral chaos that the Churches feel, when confronted with a world in rapid cultural change, can paradoxically be a positive experience. Henry Adams is right: chaos often breeds life, when order breeds habit. Chaos forces us to look for new ways to teach the Gospel, for the old ways no longer work. I argue that the chaos is so great in fact that we now must speak of 'refounding the Church itself'. (The meaning of this expression is clarified on p. 209.) The term 'renewal' can no longer convey the immensity of the challenge we face. If refounding is to occur, however, the Churches desperately need people of imagination and creativity to translate the Gospel into today's language (see Chapter 12).

This book is the result of over twenty years of fieldwork and lecturing in several parts of the First and Third Worlds. For example, I have researched into the problems of socio-economic change in villages in Fiji and Papua New Guinea; at times I have tried to listen to migrant and dispossessed peoples in Britain, the USA, New Zealand and Australia tell of their loss of cultural and personal roots. I have felt the crippling power of racial and cultural prejudice among the dominant cultures in several rich nations and how Christians can be totally insensitive to its presence. And several major studies have been made of the effectiveness of evangelizers when faced with the chaos of rapid cultural change. I am especially indebted to those participants from all around the world who have attended my courses in the East Asian Pastoral Institute, Ateneo de Manila University, Philippines, since 1977. Their questions and experience have helped shape this book and keep it rooted in the contemporary pastoral needs of people.

# Explaining the title: 'Earthing the Gospel'

## 1. 'Earthing'

Jesus is a masterful teacher. He catches his listeners' attention by telling a story or by referring to objects they are familiar with. Since Jews are agricultural people, Jesus quite naturally uses the earth, ground and seeds to convey some basic truths, e.g.:

### The symbolism of the seed: the word of God

A seed has the potential to become something huge. 'The kingdom of heaven', Jesus says, 'is like a mustard seed which a man took and sowed in his field. It is the smallest of all the seeds, but when it has grown it is the biggest shrub of all' (Mt 13:31f.). 'The seed', he says, 'is the word of God' (Lk 8:11).

### The symbolism of the earth: giving and receiving

The earth has life that the seed needs if it is to sprout and grow. If the earth is too dry, seeds shrivel and die, but the seed that falls into rich soil grows and produces 'its crop a hundredfold' (Lk 8:8).

For growth there must be a giving and a receiving. Both the earth and the seed change. The earth gives of its richness to the seed and receives in return the shell of the seed which helps to refertilize the soil: 'Whatever you sow in the ground has to die before it is given new life' (1 Cor 15:36). There is an interchange.

## The symbolism of the sower

The sower of the kingdom of heaven is first Jesus himself (Mt 13:37). Christ is the wheat grain *and* the sower. He must die if there is to be life: 'Now the hour has come . . . unless a wheat grain falls on the ground and dies, it remains only a grain; but if it dies, it yields a rich harvest' (Jn 12:23f.). All who listen to Jesus will have the power also to be a Gospel wheat grain *and* sower at the same time; yet one cannot be an effective grain or sower unless there is a death of one's own false attachments.

Together, these symbols of seed, earth and sower used by Jesus dramatically convey precisely what is meant by the dynamics of inculturation:

- Inculturation is a process of exchange: the culture receives, but actively in return affects the Gospel, e.g. through people's questions we come to see new insights in the familiar stories of Christ's life and message.

- The evangelizer as the sower offers the seed of the good news to a people. Like all good sowers, he or she must prepare the ground, seek advice from knowledgeable people about the best time and methods to sow the seed of the Gospel, nurturing it when growth emerges, but avoiding too much care lest the young plant becomes overly dependent.

  As the Gospel and cultures are both modified or changed through interaction, so also is the evangelizer as the sower. The good gardener is affected through contact with the earth, for there is joy and grief at the success and failure of earthing seeds. The evangelizer is no different; the more he or she gives to the earthing process, the more he or she is enriched through faith contact with both the culture and the Gospel.

- Earthing the Gospel is a team effort—evangelizers, those being evangelized, and the Lord himself: 'After all, what is Apollos and what is Paul? . . . I did the planting, Apollos did the watering, but God made things grow. It is all one who does the planting and who does the watering. . . . We are fellow workers with God' (1 Cor 3:5-9).

The biblical/pastoral set of relationships involved in the inculturation process is set out in Figure I.1.

# 2. 'The Gospel'

What is meant by 'the Gospel' will differ in each Christian tradition. For example, for Roman Catholics the one source of revealed truth is divine Tradition, that is, the body of revealed truth passed down from the apostles through the centuries and contained in the doctrine, teaching and practice of the Church. Tradition thus includes the Scriptures, but the ultimate interpreter of how these Scriptures are to be understood is the Church's teaching authority.

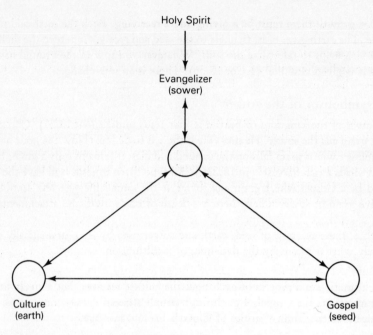

Holy Spirit

Evangelizer
(sower)

Culture
(earth)

Gospel
(seed)

**Figure I.1**   Inculturation: fourfold relationship

For many Protestant Churches, 'the Gospel' means the Scriptures. As the 1982 Seoul Evangelical Declaration states: 'We unequivocally uphold the primacy and authority of the Scriptures'.[4] The final authentic source of how the Scriptures are to be interpreted may well be the individual believer or the faith community.

# Objectives

This book particularly aims to serve:

## 1. Evangelizers/pastoral workers

The handbook is primarily for evangelizers who have little or no knowledge of anthropology, but are keen to find out how this subject can help them be more effective in preaching the word of God today. It is for people who have an unselfish desire to come to the aid of others, not in the well-meaning but bungling manner of the monkey who attempted to help the fish, but in ways that are founded on a solid grasp of what culture and culture change/conflict mean to people today.

Though the book is written with the needs of First World evangelizers directly in mind, pastoral workers in the Third World will nonetheless find in it issues that deeply concern them also.

## 2. Academic/pastoral theologians

In recent years theologians have become increasingly interested in the need to begin theological reflection not with abstract thinking, but at the level of people's lives or cultures—their anxieties, hopes, frustrations, joys, e.g.:

- Liberation theology has pioneered this approach. Theology is the uncovering of the injustices being suffered by oppressed people for the purpose of alleviating their inhuman plight. Pastoral theologians turned to the social scientists to help them not just to discover *why* the oppression exists, but also *how* to become involved in removing it. Thus, liberation theology has been effectively shaped in response to the conditions of cultural oppression within South America.

  Karl Rahner, especially in his later studies, felt that theology may discover 'its most significant dialogical partner not in philosophy but in the natural, psychological, and social sciences which shape people's self-understanding in the present'.[5] David Tracy asserts that theology will grow and be able to relate to what people are really concerned about, if theologians investigate not just texts, but also a culture's 'symbols, rituals, events, witnesses'.[6] However, despite these comments, few Western theologians so far have turned to the social sciences to help them grasp the nature and power of contemporary Western cultures.

In the First World, while liberation theology can offer helpful pastoral insights into the evangelization of cultures, it simply cannot provide theologians and evangelizers with the instruments to grasp the enormous variety of cultures and pastoral challenges within the Western world. Poverty and oppression are not the *immediate* experience of the majority of people within the First World.

What the majority of all ages and cultures in the First World do experience today, however, is a dramatic loss of meaning—understood as order, predictability and certainty—in their lives. People feel overwhelmed by an elusive sense of chaos (see Chapter 4). There is a yearning for belonging in a world that is changing at faster and faster rates. Many find the mainline Churches confused and directionless and unable to respond to the need people have for meaning in their lives. Some attempt to find meaning in more and more material goods, in religious or secular sects/cults, or in drugs (see Chapters 7 and 8).

This book provides analytical instruments to help theologians and others grasp what is happening to cultures within the First World. It is then that theologians can sit down with people from all levels of society to listen, with more understanding than ever before, to their griefs, hopes and joys. From these reflections, hopefully, we will have the beginnings of new local theologies that are earthed in the symbols, myths and rituals of people's lives (see Chapters 1 to 3).

## 3. Church leaders

That great Christian social critic, R. H. Tawney, reflects on why the Church of England in the eighteenth century failed to respond to the needs of people in the emerging age of industrialization: 'The social teaching of the Church had ceased to count, because the Church had ceased to think. . . . The social theory . . . turned its face from the practical world.'[7] Does Tawney's criticism apply to the Churches today?

Certainly, there is no lack of official documents about the Gospel rights of the poor and abandoned. But these documents are simply *not* getting through to the grassroots of the Churches, e.g.:

- Sociologist Michael Hornsby–Smith concludes that in Britain the powerful can rest easily for there will be 'no prophetic uprising of five and a half million [Roman] Catholics determined to bring the Good News to the poor'.[8]

- In the USA it is estimated that less than 2 per cent of American Roman Catholics have an evangelizing commitment;[9] 8 per cent of the Spanish Roman Catholic population, claims Andrew Greeley, have already drifted to other religious sects mainly because the Church is not responding to 'the emotional, communal and religious needs of some of the new Hispanic middle-class'.[10]

This book is of service to Church leadership, since it highlights:

- the fact that inculturation does not occur by decree or documentation from on high; it results from the free decisions of individual men and women within the faith community (see Chapter 11).

- the need to grasp the power of culture in people's lives if the Gospel is to permeate the heart of a culture (see Chapters 2 to 4).

- the *absolute* urgency to search for, and place in positions of influence, people who have apostolic creative *imagination*. There simply cannot be any movement out of chaos without imaginative persons. We *desperately* need these people to translate the Gospel into today's language so that through their creative example and teaching others may come to know and love the Lord. Official Church leaders will find these people uncomfortable to work with, for prophets in any era upset the 'tried and true ways' of the past. But the Church cannot survive and grow without them. They are the Church's refounding agents (see Chapter 12).

## 4. Religious congregations

This book aims to help religious read with more apostolic accuracy the 'signs of the times'. It also reinforces the insight that the chaos we face within the Church and religious life today demands that there be refounding persons within religious congregations. These people have the qualities of the original founding persons, e.g. courage, and an enormous creative, pastoral imagination.

## 5. Ecumenists

As is described in Chapter 1, Christians view inculturation in ways that reflect their different traditions.

Roman Catholics see inculturation as an *exchange* or *dialogue* between the Gospel and cultures in which both are affected in some way or other. The World Council of

Churches tends to stress the political and social liberation dimension of inculturation. Roman Catholics and many Evangelical Protestants agree that the aim of 'inculturation is to make local Christians congenial members of the Body of Christ', that evangelizers 'must avoid all cultural imperialism'.[11] But Evangelicals would not go as far as Roman Catholics and assert that inculturation must involve an in-depth *exchange* between the Gospel and cultures.

Each tradition can learn from the others. For example:

- Roman Catholics could learn from those Evangelical Protestants who insist on highly professional anthropological expertise in the study of cultures to be evangelized. Within the Roman Catholic Church there is considerable rhetoric about the need to know cultures better through the assistance of the social sciences. In reality, many theologians and evangelizers remain unconvinced. They either distrust the social sciences, or in practice consider them irrelevant to their needs.[12]

- Some Churches have produced in recent years analyses of socio-religious issues that are of value to all, e.g. the 1977 Irish Roman Catholic Bishops' pastoral letter on justice; the 1980 document *The Easter People* by the Roman Catholic Bishops' Conference of England and Wales; the 1985 Archbishop of Canterbury's report on social and pastoral conditions within the inner cities; the US Roman Catholic Bishops' document on national poverty; John Paul II's 1987 encyclical on world poverty; the World Council of Churches' pronouncement on human rights. This handbook uses and comments on key issues of these documents.

# Using the handbook

## Structure of the book

The book is divided into three parts:

- In Part 1, 'Theoretical considerations', key concepts are defined, e.g. inculturation, culture (i.e. symbol, myth and ritual), culture change.

- In Part 2, 'Pastoral issues', anthropology is applied to particular contemporary pastoral issues, e.g. cults, fundamentalism, prejudice, youth subcultures.

- And in Part 3, 'The pastoral agent', guidelines are given about how the imaginatively creative evangelizer is to relate personally to cultures and culture change.

Anthropology is about how people feel and communicate with one another. The best way to appreciate the power of human communication is to hear people actually speaking. Hence, examples/case studies are given throughout the text to illustrate the theory. To protect the privacy of people, however, personal comments/case studies have at times been edited.

## Suggested reading and questions

Readers wishing to go beyond the text may like to consult particular references listed in the notes or the Suggested Reading lists. Sometimes these lists allow readers from different parts of the world—e.g. the UK, the USA, Australia—to look more closely at the issues within their respective countries.

## Prayer and reflection

No matter how perfect our combined theological and anthropological information may be, our decision to act in this or that way remains a 'mere human judgment' without the act of faith (2 Cor 5:16). There can be no inculturation without faith in the risen Lord.

Thus, while there are personal and group questions at the end of each chapter, I suggest that before you start to reflect, you turn to the Lord in prayer for enlightenment and the courage to do his will. Prayer reminds us that 'the surpassing power' of inculturation 'comes from God and not from us' (2 Cor 4:7).

# PART 1
## Inculturation: theoretical considerations

# 1 Understanding mission, evangelization and inculturation

In order to evangelize effectively, it is necessary to have resolutely an attitude of *exchange and of comprehension*. The power of the Gospel must penetrate to the very heart of different cultures (John Paul II).

## Introduction

The Great Commission of Christ—'Go, therefore, make disciples of all the nations' (Mt 28:19)—at first sight looks uncomplicated. As the Father sent the Son into the world, so the Son is missioning his followers to carry on his work. *Mission* connotes a sending of persons, with authority, to preach the salvation of Christ in accordance with the text, 'they will never have a preacher unless one is sent' (Rom 10:15). *Evangelization* describes the actual proclamation, by word and example, of the Good News of Christ to the nations.

However, when it comes to the implementation of the mission, that is, evangelization, we are confronted by a theological and pastoral problem that has caused division within Christianity in the past, and continues to have a significant, though lessening, role in dividing Churches today. The various traditions within Christianity do not always agree about just how evangelization should relate to cultures. Should evangelization be concerned *directly* with the cultural needs of people, i.e. their socio-economic and political needs? Or should the *primary* emphasis in evangelization be on the salvation of souls? The aim of this chapter is to identify briefly the responses to these questions according to the traditions of:

- the Church up to the Reformation;
- the Roman Catholic Church since the Reformation;
- the World Council of Churches;
- the Evangelical Churches.

I will consider each tradition in turn.

# The Church and cultures

The Church has related to cultures in a variety of ways over the centuries. Sometimes, it has fostered a dialogue relationship. But, more frequently, it has demanded of cultures that they conform, not just to the heart of Christ's message, but to the dominant, Western, cultural way of expressing the Good News. To aid the understanding of how the Church has interacted with cultures, the topic will be divided into two periods:

- Evangelization and cultures to Vatican II: from flexibility to inflexibility

- Evangelization and cultures since Vatican II: 'inculturation' re-emerges

## Evangelization and cultures to Vatican II: from flexibility to inflexibility

At the risk of oversimplification, it is possible to distinguish three historical emphases in the Church's relationship with cultures up to the time of Vatican II. During the historical reflection, which will help refine the meaning of inculturation, other important pastoral terms, e.g. 'functional substitution', 'acculturation' and 'adaptation', will be explained.

## 1. Relative openness to cultures until the fourteenth century

### Functional substitution: a pastoral method

Up to the Peace of Constantine (Emperor 306–337), evangelizers faced periods of considerable hostility, either from the Jewish people or from Roman officials. But evangelizers during this time, despite the opposition, successfully used the *functional substitution* technique in the teaching of the faith. This is a process whereby, over a period of time, a Christian meaning is substituted for a non-Christian understanding of an action or expression.[1] The emphasis is on *process*. It is assumed in this process that symbols change their meanings only slowly. While people may accept intellectually a new understanding of a rite, it takes a very long time for their hearts to feel comfortable with it.

Jesus himself uses functional substitution. He preaches in the synagogue and shows himself to be a good Jew by frequenting the temple. At the same time, however, when he uses traditional religious customs, he endows them with new meanings, e.g. at the Last Supper the traditional Passover meal is given a much richer meaning. This is a perfect example of *inculturation*, that is, a dynamic and critical interaction between the Gospel and cultures. Jesus helps his listeners to discover what is good and what to retain in traditional Jewish life, and what needs to be changed because of his message by the introduction of new meanings.

When it comes to relating the new faith to the cultures of Gentiles, we see yet another way in which the faith is related to different cultures: Gentiles must not be expected to take on Jewish culture in order to accept the faith. St Peter, at the Council of Jerusalem, expressed this basic pastoral principle that was to guide St Paul's work among the Gentiles:

> It would only provoke God's anger now, surely, if you imposed on the disciples the very burden that neither we nor our ancestors were strong enough to support? Remember, we believe that we are saved in the same way as they are: through the grace of the Lord Jesus (Acts 15:10f.).

The religio-cultural demands of circumcision and the following of the law of Moses were not to be considered part of the new faith. The lesson will be a hard one to learn: evangelizers must discover what is of the essence of the faith, and invite people to accept it, and not this or that foreign cultural expression of it.

In the second and third centuries there are intriguing examples of evangelizers using functional substitution. Tertullian, in the third century, uses Roman juridical language to explain aspects of the faith; for example, baptism is the breaking of a contract with the world and the entering into a new contract with God in Christ. His listeners, attuned to juridical language, would have understood what baptismal renunciation and the profession of faith in Jesus means.[2] Pope Gregory the Great (540–604) provides a fascinating example of functional substitution. He writes to Abbot Mellitus, a fellow missionary of St Augustine of Canterbury:

> Tell Augustine not to destroy the temples of the gods, but only the idols housed therein. Tell him . . . to set up altars and place relics of the saints [in those same temples]. . . . The people will see that their places of worship have not been destroyed and will, therefore, be more inclined to renounce their error and recognize and adore the true God for the places to which they will come will be familiar to them and highly valued.[3]

## Fourth century: acculturation to secular symbols

With the Peace of Constantine, the Church went out to embrace all within the then civilized world. Constantine himself felt obliged, even called by God, to direct all peoples towards what he considered to be the true religion. The atmosphere was so positive for the Church, however, that at times it fell victim to uncritical *acculturation* of the imperial culture. That is, evangelizers accepted the symbols of the hierarchically structured imperial system, but failed to measure these symbols sufficiently by the standards of Gospel values. Hence, bishops adopted the power or authority symbols of royalty; the priest accepted authority *over* people and downplayed the role as servant *within* the community. Worship left the home and entered the basilica.[4] Negative aspects of Roman legalism began to have a deep impact on Christian living. For example, sin, which had earlier been thought of as a fracturing of the relationship of love and trust between members of the community, and as a violation of the covenant relationships between the community and God, was now seen in legal terms as a breaking of a divine or ecclesiastical *law*.[5]

Whenever the Church became uncritically involved in the local culture, it lost its evangelical flexibility. Evangelizers found it hard to distinguish what was of faith and what pertained to its particular cultural expression. As Yves Congar commented:

> There existed an imperialism which tended to confuse unity and uniformity, to impose everywhere the Roman customs and rites, in a word, considering the

universal Church as a simple extension of the Church of Rome. . . . We find in
Pope Siricius in 385, in Innocent I in 416 . . . the astounding affirmation that no
one can truly have the faith of Peter unless he desires the customs and rites of
Peter, that is, of Rome.[6]

# 2. Period of inflexibility: the Roman Catholic Church from the fifteenth to the twentieth century

## Euro-centric Church: firmly established

Many factors were involved in this new inflexible emphasis. In particular, the new age
of European colonial expansion deeply affected missionary activity. As one
commentator notes: 'The missionaries—true children of their times—shared the
intolerant and prejudiced views of the conquistadores on the native cultures and
religions'.[7] The Church, in the eyes of many evangelizers and ecclesiastical authorities,
had become so intertwined with European culture that no distinction could be made
between them. Conversion meant accepting the European cultural expression of the
faith, the very evil that the Council of Jerusalem had condemned centuries before.

The establishment of the Congregation for the Propagation of the Faith in 1622
was an effort on the part of the Church to stop this foolish cultural imposition. In 1659
the Congregation pleaded, with remarkable practical and anthropological precision,
for the process of inculturation and condemned ecclesiastical and cultural *ethnocentrism*,
that is, the point of view that one's own European way of life is to be preferred to all
others:

> Do not for any sense of zeal attempt to . . . persuade those people to change
> their rites, customs, and ways unless they are most obviously contrary to Faith
> and good morals. For what could be more absurd than to carry France, Spain, or
> Italy, or any other part of Europe into China? It is not this sort of thing you are
> to bring in but rather the Faith.[8]

After warning about the stupidity of exalting one's own customs and blinding oneself
to the values of other cultures, the Congregation urged evangelizers not to force
changes on people, but to respect their dignity: 'Admire and praise the customs that
merit praise. . . . Do not rashly and excessively condemn the unworthy. Let customs
that prove to be depraved, be uprooted more by hints and by silence . . . gradually
without jolting.'[9]

Fine and courageous words! But they were ignored, as is quickly evident in the
condemnation of Matteo Ricci's approach to evangelization in China in 1742. Ricci, a
Jesuit with extraordinary pastoral insight and cultural sensitivity, had attempted with
growing success to enter into a dialogue with Chinese culture. For example, he and his
companions had used Chinese words to express Christian ideas. They also had given
permission to their converts to perform, under certain conditions, the rites in honour
of Confucius and their ancestors. They were condemned by the Roman authorities for
encouraging what the latter wrongly thought was idolatry. In reality, this meant that
the Jesuits had refused to impose on the Chinese the faith mixed in with European
cultural values and customs.[10] Sadly, the condemnation meant that the lesson of the
hard-won victory at the Council of Jerusalem in favour of inculturation had been
forgotten. The evangelizing thrust of the Church would consequently suffer for
centuries to come.

## Primary concern: individual soul

This Eurocentric vision of the world, while an important tragic factor, is not sufficient in itself to explain the style of the evangelizing in this period. Particularly in the early centuries of Christianity, evangelization was directed to the individual, but *in* and *through* the community or congregation of believers. The faith of the individual had to be nurtured and sustained through the support of the community. But, particularly in reaction to the Reformation, the primary theological stress moved away from community evangelization to the salvation of the individual soul. The overall goal of evangelization became the implantation of the Church as an institution, as a monarchical and hierarchical entity, as the sole instrument of individual salvation and welfare. The strongly clerical Church was depicted as the visible vehicle of salvation—a boat that ferries its members across the 'turbulent seas of life', or as a 'cable-car that lifts them over the abyss into which they otherwise would fall'.[11]

According to this model of evangelizing and Church, there was little need for evangelizers to understand culture(s). Only the soul mattered. Christians were to show compassion, for example, through medical and educational services, but such efforts were accidental to the main evangelizing thrust—namely, the conversion of the individual soul to God. Culture had little or nothing to do with this salvation.

An insight into this approach is evident in the reason given by a Roman Catholic archbishop for why Maoris (indigenous New Zealanders) were leaving the Church in the 1860s, a period during which the Maoris were being severely oppressed by British colonial forces. The archbishop is insensitive to this cultural oppression and its impact on Maoris. It is as though Maoris were disembodied souls: 'From 1868 the Maoris were unwilling to listen to their pastors, and the latter, called away to minister to the rapidly increasing Europeans, left the Maoris to their insubordination, and attended to the souls of the Europeans'.[12]

# 3. Efforts at flexibility frustrated: 1900–1965

## New terms: 'adaptation', 'accommodation', 'indigenization'

In the late nineteenth century, there were efforts to replace this European-centred cultural and individual/soul-oriented model of missionary action. Under Pope Leo XIII, the approach of the thirteenth-century theologian St Thomas Aquinas was reintroduced into the Church. Aquinas had developed his theology with the assistance of the non-Christian philosophy of Aristotle.

People were now encouraged to reflect on human nature and society as a way of discovering key insights about life and culture, even about the divine nature itself. The soul and the human body are in partnership and this interrelationship had to be investigated. Just as Aquinas also used non-Christian sources to help him, so evangelizers must be prepared to do the same if it could aid them in their work of teaching the faith.[13]

Sadly, however, this officially sponsored, renewed concern for the totality of the person (and thus indirectly for cultures) had little effect on evangelization. While missionary exaltation of their own culture was strongly condemned, no action was taken at the same time to break down the all-pervasive emphasis of Eurocentric culture in ecclesiastical administration, in worship and in seminary and religious-life formation.

During this period, the terms 'adaptation', 'accommodation' and 'indigenization' became familiar in missionary writings, together with vigorous written support for the rights of people to maintain their own cultures. Pope Pius XII claimed that 'the rights to one's culture and national character . . . are exigencies of the law of nations dictated by nature itself'.[14] He also insisted that 'the Catholic Church is supranational by her very nature. . . . She cannot belong exclusively to any particular people, nor can she belong more to one than to another.[15]

In fact, of course, the Church belonged very intimately in its expression of life and administration to Europe, even exclusively so. In 1951, the same Pope spoke enthusiastically of the value of adapting the faith to local customs. The Church 'grafts a good scion upon the wild stock that it may bear a crop of more delicious fruit . . . [The evangelizer's] office does not demand that he transplant European civilization and culture, and no other, to foreign soil, there to take root and propagate itself.'[16]

## The Eurocentric Church remains

These were challenging words. But little could be done to obstruct the transplanting of 'European civilization and culture', as long as the theology of the local Church remained underdeveloped. A theology (and administrative structures) did not exist to allow the freedom necessary to foster the localized earthing of the Gospel. The term 'adaptation', or its equivalent 'accommodation', still connoted a ready-made European-centred way of living Christianity or of worshipping. The term meant that evangelizers could *use*, as a good practical or pastoral tactic to make the Eurocentric expression of the faith more acceptable, this or that custom of the culture being evangelized. It did not alter substantially the barriers to genuine evangelization, simply because *adaptation*, as defined and understood, did not allow evangelizers to enter into a genuine dialogue or exchange with cultures.

Finally, whenever expressions like *adaptation* were used, it was always in reference to the so-called mission countries. It was wrongly assumed that, in some way or other, the Church was fully adjusted to the cultures of Europe. Pastoral workers did not need to 'adapt the faith to them'.

## 'Indigenization' reinforced

In the 1940s and 1950s the expression 'indigenization' became increasingly common. It meant little more, however, than the recruitment of local people of different cultures as priests and religious. 'The final goal', wrote Pius XII in 1951, 'towards which we must strive and which must ever remain before our eyes is the firm establishment of the Church among the peoples, each [local Church] having its own hierarchy chosen from the ranks of the native clergy.'[17] As long as priestly and religious-life formation remained Eurocentric in emphasis, uninterested in the insights of the social sciences and situated in institutions isolated from contact with people, there was little hope of the Church being able to sink its roots deep within the symbols of different cultures.

In the years from 1945 to Vatican II the gap between the missionary rhetoric on the one hand, and the actual reality on the other, became increasingly marked as nationalism intensified during the decolonization years. Church worship and institutions looked more and more foreign.

In 1959 the enthusiastic optimism of Pope John XXIII seemed unreal:

The [Church] does not identify herself with any particular culture, not even European and Western culture . . . [The] Church is ever ready to recognize, to welcome and indeed to encourage all things that honour the human mind and heart even if they have their origin in places of the world that lie outside this Mediterranean basin.[18]

Within a short period of time, however, this same Pope initiated the Council that would permit, at least in theory, this vision to become at last a reality.

---

## Evangelization and cultures since Vatican II: 'inculturation' re-emerges

---

# 1. Vatican II: foundation for inculturation

The Council laid the foundation for the re-emergence of a more flexible, apostolic relationship between the Gospel and cultures, the type of openness that had characterized the missionary life of the early Church. Within ten years of the closing of the Council, a new theological word, *inculturation*, would be invented to define this relationship, which is to exist not just in the Third World but in the First World, that is, wherever the Gospel is being preached.

In the following summary of the relevant conclusions of the Council, note, apart from the emphasis on the exchange relationships that must exist between the Church and cultures, the marked stress on the community, rather than on the individual aspect in evangelization:

---

1. The whole person—soul *and* body—is the object of evangelization.[19]

2. Evangelization, while concerned with individual salvation, is essentially community-oriented: 'It has pleased God . . . to make people holy and save them not merely as individuals without any mutual bonds, but by making them into a single people, a people which acknowledges Him in truth and serves Him in Holiness';[20] evangelizers 'must raise up congregations of the faithful', who 'everyday must become increasingly aware and alive as communities of faith, liturgy and love'.[21]

3. The Church is not to be a huge, uniform monolith of Eurocentric cultural characteristics, but a fraternity of local Churches, each of which seeks to give life to the universal Church, in accordance with the native genius and traditions of its own members.[22]

4. God has been, and continues to be, active in every culture, even before evangelization; his presence is experienced in the virtues of people; evangelization discovers these virtues and further enhances them through the people's knowledge of Christ.

5. There must be 'a living exchange between the Church and the diverse cultures of people'.[23] Through a process of dialogue and exchange between the Gospel and cultures, local expressions of worship and theology should emerge.[24]

15

6. For a dialogue or exchange to occur, people must feel free from all physical or moral coercion to accept the Gospel.[25]

7. Genuine dialogue requires that people be open to listen to one another. It means taking every means possible to learn about the culture of the people with whom one wishes to dialogue.[26]

8. Involvement in social justice must not be used as an *instrument* to win converts to the Church; the concern for justice must rather come from the desire to present a sign of the perfect justice, to be realized in the fullness of the Kingdom to come.[27]

---

In the early years after the Council, two events particularly influenced the Catholic Church's understanding of evangelization: the emergence of liberation theology, and the publication by Pope Paul VI of the document *Evangelii Nuntiandi* (On Evangelization) in 1975, which followed the 1974 Bishops' Synod on Evangelization of the Modern World.

## The emergence of liberation theology

In 1968 the Latin American bishops met at Bogota and Medellín and laid the foundations for the Church's first, major, contemporary, local theology, the 'theology of liberation'. It is a theology elaborated in dialogue, not with the non-believer, but with *non-persons*, that is, with people denied their rightful dignity by oppressive structures.

While other theologies seek an understanding of revelation, this theology actually seeks to bring about the kingdom of God—a kingdom of peace and justice. It requires that evangelizers totally immerse themselves in the culture of the poor, otherwise dialogue and action is impossible. The Church belongs to the culture of the elite, or oppressing class, and it is for this reason that the first act of liberation must be to liberate the Church itself.[28]

## *Evangelii Nuntiandi* 1975: inculturation is to be universal

In this document, which is rightly called the *Charter of Inculturation*, Paul VI sharply defines just what evangelization means:

what matters is to evangelize human culture and cultures (not in a purely decorative way as it were by applying a thin veneer, but in a vital way, in depth and right to their very roots). . . . The transposition has to be done with discernment, seriousness, respect and competence.[29]

This is the first significant Roman document to use contemporary, cultural anthropological terminology in describing culture, e.g. signs and symbols are at the heart of a culture and evangelization must penetrate deep within them. And the call for the evangelization of cultures makes no distinction between the First and Third Worlds; it is an imperative for effective evangelization *everywhere*.

The document also insists that:

• concern for social justice is an integral part of the Church's mission;[30]

- but evangelization must 'include the prophetic proclamation of a hereafter, our profound and definitive calling'. Hence, the Church's contribution to 'liberation is incomplete, if she neglects to proclaim salvation in Jesus Christ';[31] salvation is not to be thought of as *only* the struggle for, and achievement of, political justice.

- the ultimate evil is sin, which is at the root of all injustice in cultures.[32]

## 2. Defining inculturation

How and when the term 'inculturation' was invented is uncertain, except that it seems to have been used publicly in the early 1970s. In 1977 the term received wide official approval, when it was used in the message of the Fifth World Synod of Bishops. Particularly under the influence of the central administration of the Jesuits, the expression was never associated only with the local churches in the Third World. 'The need for inculturation', wrote Fr Pedro Arrupe, Jesuit Superior General, 'is universal.'[33]

### Definition

---

Inculturation is the 'dynamic relation between the Christian message and culture or cultures; an insertion of the Christian life into a culture; an ongoing process of reciprocal and critical interaction and assimilation between them'.[34]

---

### Comments

1. Inculturation is NOT the same as:

a. *enculturation* or *acculturation*, which are purely sociological terms; *enculturation* is the process of learning, from childhood onwards, that enables an individual to become an integrated part of his or her culture. *Acculturation* is the acquiring by one society of the cultural qualities of another society (e.g. as noted above, the Church uncritically acculturated the symbols of the imperial culture at the time of Constantine).

b. *adaptation*; as explained above, 'adaptation theology' assumes that Eurocentric theology and worship have nothing to learn from other cultures; some local customs could be used, however, to convey the Eurocentric message. A culture is thought to be like a machine. Unnecessary and visible 'pieces of machinery' (e.g. rituals in worship) are to be removed, and isolated 'pieces of other machines' (some customs of a local culture) inserted in their place. The act of worship, or Eurocentric theological expression, would then 'appear', it was hoped, to local people as *their* worship, *their* theology. The technician in the adaptation is to be the evangelizer; he or she is to choose the 'pieces' to be inserted. (See Figure 1.1.)

c. *contextualization* or *localization*; both expressions, as used in the Roman Catholic tradition, may be considered too similar to the superficiality and paternalistic

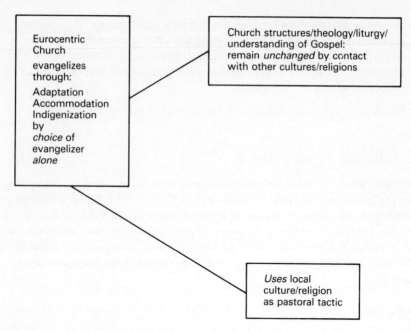

**Figure 1.1** Eurocentric evangelization

qualities of adaptation. *Contextualization* has been defined as 'the process of making evangelism and the new lifestyle relevant in the specifics of time and space'.[35] This definition, however, connotes that the interaction between the Gospel and cultures is something external and superficial, without the dialectical, depth interaction demanded by inculturation. One further criticism of the term is that it has been too frequently used by Western theologians with reference to the Third World, without sufficient sensitivity to the fact that what is conveyed by contextualization, is as urgent in the West as in other parts of the world. The term is seen as just another form of Eurocentric domination.[36]

*Localization* (or *indigenization*) historically connotes little more than the recruitment of local people of different cultures as priests and religious.

d. a merely *pastoral tactic*, that is, as a method *only* to make the Gospel and theology better understood in a local culture. Inculturation is an *exchange*, that is, through the interaction with a local culture, new insights will emerge into the Gospel itself; inculturation is not a one-way process.

e. a mere *translation* of liturgical/theological books produced by official ecclesiastical sources.

2. Inculturation IS:

a. strictly a *theological* word and is synonymous with evangelization. It aims to emphasize the fact that evangelization, as a process of reliving the incarnation itself, demands the *insertion* of the Gospel within the very heart of a culture. This point was reinforced by the Extraordinary Synod of 1985, when it warned against 'mere external adaptation' efforts by evangelizers.[37]

18

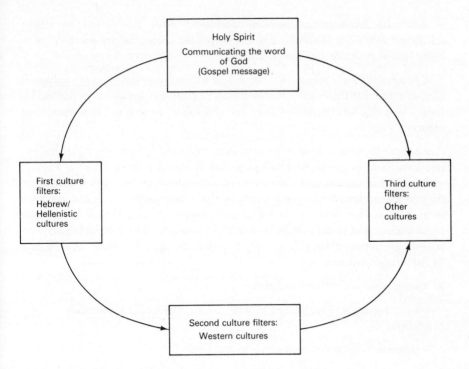

**Figure 1.2** 'Filtering' the Gospel message

b. an interaction between *two* cultures. It is not a simple encounter between the Gospel and a culture, because the Gospel comes to our times as already embedded in a particular culture of the time of the evangelists. There must be an ongoing discernment to discover what is at the heart of Christ's message, and what belongs to Hebrew/Greek cultures of his time and that of the evangelists. (See Figure 1.2.)

c. a process of *exchange*; for example, new insights can be achieved into the message of Christ as the evangelizer listens to, and is questioned by, the people being evangelized. Not only is there a giving to a culture, but there is also a receiving in return. (See Figure 1.3.)

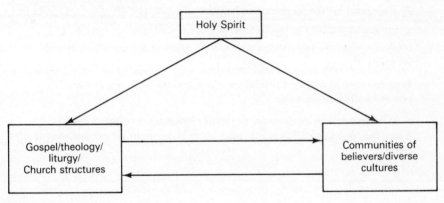

**Figure 1.3** Inculturation process

d. first and foremost, a *converting* encounter with the person of Christ (cf. Acts 9:3–9; 22:6–11; 26:12–23); the deeper the union, the greater the urge to bring him alive within one's own culture.[38]

e. a process of *critical interaction*, that is, the ultimate measure of every culture is Christ; cultural attitudes and structures must be measured against his justice and his love. There will be rejection of some cultural values, as well as the acceptance of others.

f. a *dialogue* between a community of faith and cultures. Inculturation is, therefore, not something designed by theological and liturgical experts in some kind of ecclesiastical laboratory and then imposed from above on the faith community. Experts are necessary for they help to refine what Christ and his Church would wish us to believe. But their intellectual actions, important though they be, are not inculturation. The moment individuals and a community believe in the Lord and act accordingly in this or that culture, only then does inculturation occur. (See Chapter 11 for a fuller explanation.)

g. taking place under four conditions:

—a lucid grasp by evangelizers of what Gospel mission/evangelization involves;

—personal/community conversion to the Lord;

—an understanding of the culture(s);

—the interaction between the believing people and culture(s), resulting in action.[39]

Understood, therefore, in the above sense, inculturation 'presupposes a long and courageous process . . . in order that the Gospel may penetrate the soul of living cultures'.[40] It is a never-ending process, because cultures are constantly changing. In summary, the Roman Catholic approach to inculturation assumes that:

---

1. salvation is individual *and* corporate; the commitment to social justice is an *integral* aspect of the Church's mission.

2. there must be 'the prophetic proclamation of a hereafter'.[41]

3. sin is at the root of all human evil; structures are unjust, i.e. 'sinful', as a result over time of many individual acts of injustices or the neglect to struggle for justice.[42]

4. the removal of injustices demands not just structural changes, but also personal attitudinal conversion.[43]

5. inculturation *is* evangelization; the word emphasizes the *depth* of the interaction/dialogue/exchange that must occur between the Gospel message and cultures.

---

# The World Council of Churches and cultures

Three major identifiable views outside the non-Roman Catholic tradition about how Christianity is to relate to cultures are:

---

1. Personal conversion is *the* aim of evangelization.

2. Personal conversion *and* the just restructuring of cultures are *equally* important aspects of evangelization.

3. Evangelization *is* synonymous with *only* the struggle for the just restructuring of cultures.

---

Many contemporary Evangelicals, e.g. Billy Graham, tend to accept the first view; concern for social justice within cultures is important, but it is not a priority of evangelization. The third view, e.g. as explained by some theologians in the late 1960s (such as Gibson Winter and Harvey Cox), eliminates the transcendent aspect of evangelization entirely and simply makes salvation synonymous with social justice.[44]

The second view is emphasized in the official documents of the World Council of Churches (WCC); their position seems over all to be close to that of the Roman Catholic Church, as explained above. The WCC approach has changed over the years; during the 1960s there was a tendency to come close to the third option above. A preparatory statement for the WCC's Fourth Assembly at Uppsala, in 1968, stressed the secularized approach to salvation: 'We have lifted up humanization as *the* goal of mission'.[45] At times, the official statements seem to underplay the reality of personal sin, the call to radical conversion and the final fulfilment of salvation in the world to come.

On *indigenization* and *contextualization*, a 1972 WCC document comments:

> Indigenization tends to be used in the sense of responding to the Gospel in terms of a traditional culture. Contextualization, while not ignoring this, takes into account the process of secularism, technology and the struggle for human justice, which characterizes the historical moment of nations in the Third World.[46] (See Table 1.1.)

However, in a 1982 document on mission and evangelism from the WCC, the emphases—e.g. on sin and conversion, liberation of people from unjust structures—resemble *very* closely the themes of *Evangelii Nuntiandi* of Paul VI summarized above. The one notable exception is the lack of *strong* emphasis on the life to come. The document is explicitly in support of inculturation:

> The planting of the Church in different cultures demands a positive attitude towards inculturation of the Gospel. . . . Inculturation has as its source and inspiration the mystery of the incarnation. . . . Inculturation should not be understood merely as intellectual research; it occurs when Christians express their

**1. Pre-Vatican II 1900–1965:**

*Terminology*:
  adaptation
  indigenization
  accommodation

*Meaning*:
  tactic for implanting Eurocentric Church in Third
  World
  *cultures*:
  no dialogue; missionary
  chooses customs to be used

| Roman Catholic Church | World Council of Churches | Evangelical Churches |
|---|---|---|
| **2. Vatican II impact 1965–73:**<br>• theology of local Church<br>• stress on dialogue between Church and all cultures<br>• pursuit of justice constituent part of evangelization<br>• liberation theology | **1960s:** *Indigenization*:<br>• concern to give power to locally based Third World organizations<br>• tactic to make Gospel understood in the Third World | **1960s/1970s:** *Contextualization*:<br>• tactic to make Gospel understood in Third World cultures |
| **3. 'Inculturation' emerges: 1974–77:**<br>• evangelization of cultures<br>• exchange between Gospel and cultures<br>• process within communities | **1970s:** *Contextualization*:<br>• term stresses challenge of contemporary movements in Third World, e.g. secularism<br><br>**1980s:** *Inculturation*:<br>• close to Roman Catholic tradition | **1980s:** *Homogeneous Churches*:<br>• identification with local cultures |

**Table 1.1** Evolution of terminology: summary

faith in the symbols and images of their respective culture. The best way to stimulate the process of inculturation is to participate in the struggle of the less privileged for their liberation. Solidarity is the best teacher of common cultural values.[47]

Concern with local cultures in this text tends to be concentrated on the socio-political context, that is, on how evangelizers can work with people for their liberation from injustices. The Roman Catholic meaning of inculturation is far broader than this, as explained above.

# The Evangelical Churches and cultures

As with the World Council of Churches, it is very difficult to summarize precisely the various theological views on evangelization and cultures within the Evangelical tradition. However, several different emphases can be identified within this tradition over the last forty years:[48]

## Emphasis on the Great Commission, 1940–1955

The emphasis was on sharing with others, especially with those who have not heard the Gospel before, one's personal, liberating encounter with Jesus in response to the Great Commission (Mt 28:18–20). Individual souls were to be saved and nothing should interfere with the implementation of this mandate. According to this theology, evangelists had no need to be concerned with the cultures of the people to whom they are preaching.

## Church growth and contextualization, 1955–1960s

The 'church growth' movement began in 1955, that is, 'the multiplication of churches, not of evangelists'. It was increasingly recognized that people needed not just to be taught about Jesus, but they needed to be baptized and nurtured in their new-born faith. This required congregations. There also developed at this time a growing awareness of the need to have a more sensitive knowledge of the cultures being evangelized. Thus, there emerged the principle of *contextualization*. Contextualization is a communication tactic. It is an effort to understand, through high-quality cultural anthropological research, just how cultures function; with this knowledge, evangelizers will know how best to communicate the Gospel message within the Third World.[49]

## Debate over social action, 1970s

During the 1970s there raged an extremely sharp and heated debate over whether or not evangelism should be *directly* involved with social justice. According to Billy Graham and many others, the vital mission of the Church is to call people to Jesus for the salvation of their souls. While Christians do have a responsibility to work for social justice, it was not seen as *the* priority task; the salvation of souls and evangelism are the priorities.

Back in 1964, an Evangelical preacher, Jerry Falwell, wanted Christians out of all social justice/political action. Thus, he condemned the civil rights activism of liberal preachers: 'Preachers are not called to be politicians but to be soul winners. Our only purpose on this earth is to know Christ and to make him known.'[50]

## Commitment to social action/contextualization, 1970s–1980s

Under the influence of the Charismatic/Pentecostal revival movement, many Evangelicals recognized that there are divers gifts of the Holy Spirit. Consequently, it was then seen as wrong to stress only the gift of calling souls to salvation, without also directly attacking, at the same time, unjust structures.

Every congregation will include, therefore, people with various gifts, e.g. those gifted to call individual souls to salvation, others with the grace to be involved directly in the struggle for social justice within and between cultures. Jerry Falwell changed his mind in 1979 claiming that for certain issues, e.g. the fight against abortion, Christians must become involved in political action.

Some Evangelicals now use *contextualization*, not as a tactic, but as a process in some ways like inculturation, as defined according to the Roman Catholic tradition. However, because primacy is given to the biblical word in the Evangelical tradition, and not to liturgical or sacramental life, these Evangelicals would possibly prefer the term *contextualization*, as defined above, not *inculturation*.

Theologian Donald McGavran has argued for what he calls 'homogeneous' churches. He believes that Christ's intention was the formation *exclusively* of culturally/linguistically, or class-centred, separate Churches.

People will, in these Churches and within their own particular culture or class, wrestle with biblical revelation: they will not only translate the Bible into their own language, but will express its revelations in their own thought forms.[51] This translation is impossible, he claims, if the Church tries to embrace, in one worshipping community, peoples of different cultures or classes. Others, however, consider that his understanding of the word 'nations' in the Great Commission is far too narrow. The words 'all nations' mean the whole inhabited world or the entire world created by God.

# Reflection questions

## To the reader

1. How does *inculturation* differ from *enculturation*, *adaptation*?

2. Apart from the example of the Last Supper, do you think that Jesus Christ used the pastoral technique of *functional substitution* at other times? If so, when?

3. How does *contextualization* differ from *inculturation*?

## To a discussion group

1. Why do you think that conversion to Jesus Christ is an essential precondition for inculturation to take place?

2. Within your parish boundaries, there may be several different Christian denominations. Try to organize a small study group, so that together you have a chance to share what evangelization means to each participant.

3. Imagine that St Peter and St Paul are to visit your parish today to explain the decisions of the Council of Jerusalem (Acts 15:1–12). What would they say about how you teach and live the Christian faith?

# Suggested reading

Atherton, A., *Faith in the Nation: A Christian Vision for Britain* (London: SPCK, 1988).

Boff, L. and C., *Salvation and Liberation: In Search of a Balance between Faith and Politics* (Maryknoll, NY: Orbis, 1984).

Boyack, K. (ed.), *Catholic Evangelization Today: A New Pentecost for the United States* (New York: Paulist, 1987).

Dorr, D., *Option for the Poor: A Hundred Years of Vatican Social Teaching* (Maryknoll, NY: Orbis, 1983).

'The Evangelical–Roman Catholic Dialogue on Mission, 1977–1984: A Report' in *International Bulletin of Missionary Research*, vol. 10, no. 1 (1987), pp. 2–21.

Gremillion, J. (ed.), *The Church and Culture since Vatican II: The Experience of North and Latin America* (Notre Dame, IN: University of Notre Dame Press, 1985).

Hiebert, P. G., 'Critical Contextualization' in *International Bulletin for Missionary Research*, vol. 11, no. 3 (1987), pp. 104–112.

Luzbetak, L. J., *Church and Culture: New Perspectives in Missiological Anthropology* (Maryknoll, NY: Orbis, 1988).

Pieris, A., *An Asian Theology of Liberation* (Maryknoll, NY: Orbis, 1988).

Shorter, A., *Toward a Theology of Inculturation* (London: Geoffrey Chapman, 1988/Maryknoll, NY: Orbis, 1989).

Song, C. S., *Theology from the Womb of Asia* (Maryknoll, NY: Orbis, 1986).

Stott, R. W., and Coote, R. (eds), *Down to Earth: Studies in Christianity and Culture—Papers of the Lausanne Consultation* (Grand Rapids, MI: W. B. Eerdmans, 1980).

World Council of Churches, *Your Kingdom Come: Mission Perspectives—Report on the World Conference on Mission and Evangelism: Melbourne, 1980* (Geneva: WCC, 1980).

# 2 The world of meaning: culture

Any human experience that is to be communicated to others and preserved over time must be expressed in symbols (Peter Berger).[1]

Evangelization loses much . . . effectiveness . . . if it does not use the people's language, their signs and symbols (Paul VI).[2]

## Introduction

On one occasion three friends, an Englishman and two Nigerians, were walking down the Strand, an intensely busy and noisy street in the heart of London. The two Nigerians were trying to converse with the Englishman, but though the latter could see their lips moving, he could hear little of what they were saying. He shouted above the traffic noise that it would be only possible to carry on a conversation when they were in a quieter side street. Then someone dropped a coin on the pavement. The Englishman bent down to pick it up, for he alone of the three had heard the coin hit the concrete.

Why did only the Englishman hear the coin fall, but he was unable to follow the conversation of his companions because of the traffic sounds? The answer is simple. The Englishman, from early childhood, had become accustomed to hear the 'all-important' sound of coins clicking together or into money boxes, but not so the Nigerians. They had been trained to hear quite different sounds. Culture has such power that it dramatically influences what we see, hear and smell. Its power enters into every fibre of our being, without us ever being fully conscious of its influence.

As was explained in Chapter 1, inculturation is the dynamic, evaluative interaction between the Gospel/tradition and cultures. This chapter is about culture—its nature and power, its components: symbols, myths and rituals.

## Incident: discovering culture

Several years ago, on my first visit to Japan, I was carefully following instructions on how to get to the hotel where a friend was staying. All went well on the underground train system until unexpected disaster hit. I got off the train at the wrong station. Crisis! I was stunned. I seemed to be surrounded by thousands of people moving with determination and obvious know-how from platform to platform, while I did not know what to do. The signs were totally in Japanese. They made no sense to me whatsoever. I was utterly lost. Panic struck me. I became angry with everything Japanese. A law should be made, I quite irrationally said to myself, to demand that all Japanese signs had English subtitles, for, after all, all sensible people speak English! I yearned for the less packed rail system of my own country, New Zealand.

In a miserable state of mind, I accidentally turned to a shop window behind me. By an extraordinary coincidence, the small shop was selling blankets made from New Zealand wool. And there at the bottom of one blanket was a symbol of New Zealand—a small stylized kiwi (the kiwi is a flightless bird to be found only in New Zealand).

I was quite overcome by this discovery. Warm, secure memories of my family, friends and the magnificent countryside came to me. I had discovered in that kiwi the security, identity and sense of belonging that I had lost in this fear-creating subway station in the heart of Tokyo. How would other New Zealanders react in my situation, I asked myself. The answer was simple: not with self-pity, but with resourcefulness, initiative and courage. Right, I said to myself, I will do the same. I turned and immediately asked, in English, the first Japanese I spotted to give me directions. No luck. He could not understand me. Then the second, the third; and finally the fourth could answer my plea for direction with ease.

## Reflecting on the incident

This simple incident contains several important lessons of this book: the nature and power of culture and its component elements—symbols, myths and rituals.

I panicked when I could not understand the world around me in that subway station simply because I had temporarily lost my sense of identity, belonging, security. I could not grasp the *meanings* of things around me. And that is what culture is all about. Culture gives us what we so desperately need in human life: a set of meanings. Once we know the meaning and significance of things, we are able to develop that comfortable sense of belonging, or the feeling of 'being at home' in one small section of the world, a sense of identity and security. If we lose this crucial set of meanings, we are in a state of chaos or the world of non-meaning. And that can be an intensely frightening experience. In fact, culture is so much part of life that we do not realize its power and its role until we are suddenly deprived of it, as was the case in the above incident. Recall the fable about the monkey and the fish in the Introduction. The fish did not 'know' the importance of water until it was suddenly out of it!

Notice what happened when I discovered the small, stylized kiwi at the bottom of a simple blanket. I experienced, in a brief period, the power of the three elements of all cultures:

### Symbol

Immediately I *re*-discovered my identity. The small, apparently insignificant, object became for me my country, my culture, my friends, my identity. That is, it became a powerful *symbol* for me. In a symbol, the object becomes the thing it signifies.

## Myth

It sparked off memories of great culture heroes and heroines—New Zealanders who had triumphed over all kinds of challenges through the power of their initiative, creativity and courage. If they had shown such courage, so could I face the strange world around me. I was thus identifying with the creation *myth* or story about the origins of a large section of my own country.

## Ritual

The actual movement from self-pity to action, that is, the move to go out and ask people for direction is what we call *ritual*. I had been energized to do this because of my identification with a creation story of my culture.

---

In summary:

1. People belong to the same culture if they share a common set of meanings about life. As anthropologist Clifford Geertz writes, culture is:

> an historically transmitted pattern of meanings embodied in symbols, a system of inherited conceptions expressed in symbolic forms by means of which people communicate, perpetuate, and develop their knowledge about and attitudes toward life.[3]

2. A subculture describes those special worlds of interest and sense of belonging that set apart some individuals and groups from the wider culture, e.g. youth subculture, drug subculture, ethnic subculture. Subcultures may differ according to various measures, e.g. the rigidity of separation or distance from the main culture; the level of exclusivity; the degree to which they overlap with other subcultures.

3. All cultures have some forms of repeated, *symbolized* behaviour that is tied by some form of explanation to their fundamental way of understanding the meaning or purpose of life. The repeated symbolic behaviour is what we call *ritual*. The explanation of the ritual's meaning is the *myth*. In the case above, the myth was about the creation story of the white section of New Zealand culture. (See Figure 2.1.)

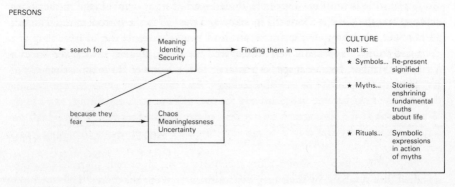

**Figure 2.1**  The source of culture

I will now explain in more detail each of the three components of culture: symbol, myth and ritual, giving particular emphasis to the first two and leaving ritual until Chapter 6.

# Understanding symbols

The poet W. H. Auden pinpoints a fundamental fact of human life:

> What we have not named
> or beheld as a symbol
> escapes our notice.[4]

We swim in a symbolic world like fish who never need to be taught how. Symbols are as important to us as water is to the fish. Without them we cannot think nor can we communicate with other people. But when we come to try to give a precise definition of what symbols are, and how they work—that is, to be fishermen rather than the fish—it escapes through the holes in the net.

*Defining symbols*

A symbol is any reality that by its very dynamism or power
leads to (i.e. makes one think about, imagine, get into contact with, or reach
out to) another deeper (and often mysterious) reality through a sharing in the
dynamism that the symbol itself offers (and not by merely verbal or
additional explanations).

To explain the definition. There are three aspects to any symbol: the meaning, the emotive and the directive levels. The *meaning* aspect allows a symbol to make a statement about something. For example, the kiwi symbol I saw in the Japanese shop window said to me: 'You are a New Zealander!' Secondly, there is the *emotive* aspect or level. The symbol, because it speaks primarily to the hearts or the imaginations of people, gives rise to positive or negative feelings. And this is why symbols have dynamic power. The kiwi became imaginatively for me, my country, my family, my friends. When I look at the photograph on my desk of my deceased mother, she becomes present to me in a very real way. I do not say 'this is a *picture* of my mother', but 'this *is* my mother'.

So, this is why a symbol is more than just a sign. Signs only point to the object signified, but symbols, by their very dynamism, *re*-present the object. The stop notice down the road used to be just a sign indicating that I must stop the car to allow other traffic to pass. This week, however, it became for me a symbol because I accidentally hit it to avoid a major collision with another car. Every time I see the notice, I *relive* the accident.

Thirdly, a symbol *directs* me to do something as a result of its meaning and its emotional impact on me. In my case, the impact of the kiwi symbol was to make me express joy and courage because I was once more in touch with the heart of my culture. And at the stop notice, I now definitely *stop*!

The effect of symbolic activity, therefore, is the achievement of emotionally experienced meaning. Symbols must speak for themselves. If people try to explain the meanings of this or that symbol, they eventually prevent us from personally experiencing the meanings emotionally. The symbols are reduced to mere signs. They lose their mysterious dynamism. Parishioners once complained to me that a particular pastor spent far too long trying to give us the meaning of the Sunday Gospel before he read it: 'We are tired of the explanations. If only he would cut down on the efforts to explain the Gospel, read it slowly, deliberately, and let it speak to our hearts and our experience!'

## Particular qualities of symbols

In addition to the aspects I have just described, symbols have three important qualities:

*Multivocality*:
Symbols gather layers of meaning over time. The cross I wear recalls Christ crucified, but it also reminds me of the Solomon Islands in the South Pacific where it was made, and of my deceased friend to whom it once belonged.

*Polarization*:
A symbol can enshrine opposite meanings at precisely the same time, e.g. the cross symbolizes both the death *and* resurrection of Christ.

*Timelessness*:
I do not recall the year my friend died, but his cross still *re*-presents for me the vivid experience of his death. Because of their emotive aspect, symbols have power to grip the allegiance of people over a long period of time. Logical or rational attacks on symbols do not necessarily destroy them.

*Example*:
A pastor in an Italian parish explained at length to his parishioners that their devotions to the statues of the saints in the church were 'superstitious and theologically contrary to Vatican II'. He threatened to remove the statues if the people did not stop praying before them during the Mass. His logical condemnation and warning had not the slightest effect on the people. The following Sunday they were doing exactly what he had forbidden them to do the week before! The pastor misunderstood the power of symbols.

# Types of symbols

The following are some important types of symbols to be found in all cultures. Notice, as you reflect on them, just how relatively unimportant verbal symbols are; in fact, *non-verbal* symbols tend to be far more powerful in communication than the spoken word.

## 1. Public/private

National symbols are *par excellence* public, e.g. a flag, an anthem. They connote values cultivated and shared by the nation; they also *re*-present the nation. Hence, this accounts for the power of the respect or disrespect that can be shown to such symbols. For example, when people want to express their anger against a nation or its authority, they commonly publicly burn the nation's flag. Private symbols lack the universality of acceptance that characterizes public symbols.

## 2. Sacred/profane

Sacred symbols refer to that which is protected specifically against violation, intrusion, or defilement, and which the profane should not touch with impunity. Most nations have sacred symbols or sites, e.g. the Lincoln Memorial in Washington, DC, for Americans, Westminster Abbey for English people, and the tomb of Napoleon for French citizens.

## 3. Structural/antistructural

Structural symbols are those that reflect the ordinary, everyday life of rules or status. To facilitate the smooth running of society, people need to know the roles individuals play, e.g. I need to know that this man is a medical doctor, not a butcher, so I expect there to be symbols outside a surgery clearly indicating that this is his official role in society.

There are periods in daily life, however, in which these structural roles in society become quite deliberately unimportant. For instance, at the beginning of a religious service, a pastor will begin this way: 'Sisters and brothers in the Lord'. No matter who is in the church—politicians, doctors, lawyers, butchers, teachers—during this service they are reminded by the symbols 'Sisters' and 'Brothers' that before the Lord all are equal. Societal roles are deliberately stripped away and this is achieved through the *antistructural* symbols, 'Sisters' and 'Brothers'.[5]

## 4. Dominant/instrumental

Dominant symbols are those that obviously stand out in a social situation; they have meanings that are generally constant and consistent over time. Instrumental symbols aid the dominant symbols to realize their function.

Within technological cultures, human happiness, understood in a materialistic

31

sense, is often a dominant symbol. More and faster cars, deodorants, even bigger and more elegantly designed coffins or caskets are instrumental symbols.

## 5. Order/disorder

People feel the need for some order both for themselves and for the conduct of social life. Recall the key point above: we humans desperately fear chaos or loss of meaning in our lives. Hence, there will be some level of orderliness or predictable patterns of behaviour within all cultures. Whatever is not ordered correctly will be considered 'dirty', 'polluting', or even 'dangerous' to the welfare of the culture. For example, in Japan the wearing of shoes within the house is considered 'dirty' or 'not at all decent'; in Western countries this is not the case, but to place used shoes on the table is definitely regarded as 'dirty' or 'polluting'.[6]

Not surprisingly, therefore, whoever questions the accepted order in a culture, e.g. a prophetic person, is seen as dangerous or as a symbol of 'pollution'. Thus, when Martin Luther King was alive, he was considered thoroughly dangerous by many middle-class white Americans because he was interfering with the established order of society. Their feeling of where blacks and whites belonged in American society was being severely challenged. And this they did not like.

## 6. Cognitive–normative/oretic–physiological[7]

In the former, the stress is more on intellectual than on experiential knowledge, e.g. 'God' as a theological symbol. The oretic–physiological symbol relates more especially to experiential knowledge, e.g. the experience of God's presence in prayer. Jesus uses both types of symbols in his teaching of the disciples. He offers them a theological analysis of his role in salvation as redeemer; he then *lives* this analysis, e.g. through his suffering and death.

## 7. Body-control/non-body-control

Cultures that stress vigorous control over the freedom of their members have strict rules about how people should dress and use their bodies. In the Soviet Union, body movements that result from loose control—e.g. wild or ecstatic movement, trances, unconventional appearance—are rigorously excluded from all government rituals and public life generally. In contrast, symbols that express careful control of the human body and precise co-ordination of many people are officially valued and widely encouraged, e.g. the precisely co-ordinated mass military parades on May Day.

In cultures where freedom of movement is valued, however, such symbols of body control do not exist.[8] Hence, we have the toleration within the USA, and generally within Western nations, of hippie cults, communes, and religious sects and movements (e.g. Pentecostal groupings) that exhibit all kinds of ecstatic expression.

Within the Roman Catholic Church prior to Vatican II, body control symbols in liturgy were most evident, e.g. in the highly detailed rubrics about how ministers were to celebrate Mass or when people in the congregation should stand or kneel. With the emphasis in the Council on the responsible use of freedom, body control symbols are far less obvious.

# 8. Oppositional

A highly distinctive feature of many cultures is the division of life into a number of separate sectors, each sector being marked by powerful, distinguishing symbols, e.g. home/workplace; work/leisure; white collar/blue collar; public sector/private sector; Church/State; left hand/right hand; public morality/private morality.

We are likely, as anthropologist Claude Lévi-Strauss points out, to order our experience and life according to a system of pairing.[9] Any breaking of these dichotomies can suggest disorder, danger, or pollution. Not surprisingly, therefore, unisex hairstyles and clothing disgust or anger some people within Western cultures. Boundaries are blurred. This creates uncertainty or fear of chaos.

# 9. Power/powerless

I was once being driven by a very clearly marked police car, with its blue light periodically flashing, several hundred miles in order to lecture to police officers. The traffic became very orderly, and cars ahead of us slowed down once the drivers noticed the police car. I had never before had such a thoroughly enjoyable journey! Later, with a sense of shame, I realized why. I was right inside a power or authority symbol of my culture and I rejoiced to see people embarrassed by it: they slowed their speed, they looked afraid. They felt powerless in the presence of such a dominant cultural symbol.[10]

## Decoding symbols

Thinking symbolically is not pure rational reasoning. Nor is it fully conscious thought. Hence, it is difficult at times to be precise about the many meanings of symbols. It is difficult enough grasping the meanings of symbols used by oneself and by one's culture, but it is even more hazardous assigning meanings to symbols used by people of other cultures.

It is helpful to distinguish, from an observer's point of view, *explicit* from *implicit* meanings of symbols. For Irish Catholic immigrants to England, the Friday abstinence had ceased generally to retain its original explicit meaning, that is, as a form of mortification. Implicitly, however, it had developed powerful meanings of identity. It linked immigrants to their cultural roots in Ireland and to 'a glorious tradition in Rome', as anthropologist Mary Douglas points out. The sudden removal of the abstinence requirement deeply distressed Irish immigrants. The English bishops had been completely unaware of the implicit meaning of the abstinence and its powerful role in giving immigrants a sense of identity and security in what they considered a hostile land.[11]

## Origins of symbols

Symbols, with their variety of meanings, are born because they respond to the subjective needs of people and their experience of life. For example, the colour yellow in the

Philippines today symbolizes the non-violent revolution against the corrupt Marcos dictatorship. Quite accidentally, people adopted yellow as the symbol of freedom; it became so powerful a symbol that Marcos at one point forbade all government employees to wear any yellow clothing to work during the election campaign period.

Since the emergence of symbols acceptable to people is a complex process, educators, politicians, and people in the mass media struggle to develop the art of symbol management for their particular aims.

---

*Example*:
When Paul VI died, his casket, in vivid contrast to tradition and to the baroque façade of St Peter's Basilica behind it, was made of very plain wood, according to the requirements of his will. The Pope wished to convey by this gesture that all people, no matter what rank or wealth they have in human society, are equal before God.

---

The process of symbol substitution or the change in the meanings of a symbol can take a very long time. People's grip on meanings is slow to be released. Jesus, *the* educator, knew that. At certain times, he followed the functional substitution approach, that is, he accepted existing symbols but aimed to purify them rather than abolish them entirely (Mt 5:17). It was an uphill battle, even in his efforts with his disciples and apostles. Witness the difficulties he had on the road to Emmaus with two of his disciples (Lk 24:13–25).

# Myths and mythologies[12]

Contrary to popular belief, myths are not fairy tales. Myths, along with symbols (Paul Ricoeur defines myth as a 'symbol developed into narrative form'), form the very heart of every culture. Without myths, we are unable to know what things are, what to do with them, or how to relate to them. The nature and role of myths, however, are very poorly understood. Hence, in this part of the chapter I will clarify:

- the nature and types of myths (and mythology, which is a network of interrelated myths);
- their function;
- how they change;
- and the importance of understanding how they can influence us.

## Myths reveal truths

A myth explains to people the origins of natural and social realities and the interrelationships that exist or should exist between people and their deities, and between a people and their universe. In other words, a myth is a story or tradition that claims to reveal, in an imaginative or symbolic way, a fundamental truth about the world and human life. This truth is regarded as authoritative by those who accept it.[13]

*Example*:
This is the creation mythology of the white section of the New Zealand society. The country was colonized by hardy, adaptable, democracy-seeking and creative people from Britain and Ireland. New Zealanders thrive on challenges and can do most things, especially if equipment or supplies are limited. This is how the present agricultural economy of world repute was built up. And these are the qualities most esteemed by New Zealanders today, finding perfection in such mythic heroes as Edmund Hillary, the first person to climb Mount Everest.

Thus, a sudden change in the mythic structure of a people is generally a catastrophic experience for them, since the mythic structure is, in the last analysis, the way people impose order on the world and hold back chaos. We see this more clearly by observing other cultures, or even our own history, than by looking at the present mythological structure of our own culture. Our myths are so much a part of our imaginative life that it is extremely difficult to recognize them, observe them objectively, and assess the degree of their influence on us.

In the example of my experience at the Tokyo subway station, I discovered in a dramatic way just how important my cultural mythology is to me. I had taken it completely for granted, until I found myself in a situation in which, for a brief moment, it was not influencing me. The sudden and unexpected finding of the small kiwi symbol returned me to my mythic roots. Notice that I did not sit down and say to myself: 'This is my New Zealand mythology. I must live it now!' No, once I had identified with my country through the kiwi symbol, the mythology of my culture returned to affect my behaviour, though with very little conscious effort on my part.

## Myths respond to needs

Mythologies, according to cultural anthropologist Joseph Campbell, are created in response to four needs:[14]

1. *A reason for existence*, i.e. a need to find some satisfying meaning for why things exist.

2. *A coherent cosmology*, i.e. the need to know where we fit in a comprehensible and, we hope, safe world.

3. *A social organization*, which together with supportive attitudes, allows us to work together in some degree of harmony and thus avoid chaos.

4. *An inspirational vision*, i.e. an overall view that inculcates a sense of pride, e.g. a spirit of nationalism.

---

*Example*:
In the creation mythology of the USA, the Great Seal of the nation (which is copied on one side of the one-dollar bill) reminds Americans that God, or some extraordinary destiny, calls them to participate in a new Exodus, a new journey, from the poverty and oppression of other nations, in order to join in the building of a new promised land. This myth gives meaning to the lives of Americans by fitting them into a coherent cosmology. The Constitution, and its supportive sentiments of equality, freedom, and respect for the rights of the individual, provide a system of social organization that guarantees a person's rights to be a part of this journey into the promised land. The fact that Americans have been called by God to participate in this work of building, while others struggle in abject poverty and oppression elsewhere, is a vision that instils within them a sense of pride. It gives them a reason for continuing to struggle, to succeed in life, no matter how enormous the obstacles, and to express that achievement through visible material symbols.

---

## Triple function clarified

Three clarifications need to be made:

*Firstly*, myths speak primarily—since they are made up of symbols—to the hearts and feelings of people, even though there is also a cognitive or intellectual dimension present. And, as we have said above, it is difficult to ponder objectively on what affects our hearts so deeply.

*Secondly*, myths reflect values in life but do not go into detail about how values are to be reconciled when they appear to be in opposition. For instance, American mythology does not tell us how the stress on individual rights is to be reconciled with the need to work for the common good. In the Gospel, Christ does not go into detail to tell us how we are to be prayerful people and, at the same time, be actively involved in struggling to build up a world of justice.

*Thirdly*, myths can contain, or have solid foundations in, historical realities. The purpose of myth and history differ, however; myth is concerned not so much with a succession of events as with the moral significance of these happenings. A myth is a 'religious' commentary on the beliefs and values of a culture.

Thus, Abraham Lincoln can be viewed historically or mythologically. As seen from the historical perspective, he is depicted as fitting into a definite time period, influencing and being influenced by events around him. If, however, he is evaluated as a person who exemplifies the virtues of zeal for the rights of the individual, honesty, inventiveness in the face of difficulties, and hard work, then we are measuring him by the foundation mythology of the nation. Likewise with Winston Churchill. From the mythological viewpoint, he exemplifies the greatest qualities of the 'best type of Englishman': stubbornly resourceful, patient, and gifted with dry humour in the presence of apparently overwhelming difficulties. Judged by the mythologies of some other cultures, e.g. Nazi Germany, both men would be considered weak, narrow-minded and ignorant.

## Theories of mythology

There are four identifiable theories about how myths develop. Briefly, the theories are:

*Historical*:
Myths are incomplete descriptions of historical happenings. This view has little support today.

*Psychological*:
Some claim (for example, Carl Jung) that primordial images of the collective unconscious or 'archetypes' are expressed in myths. This view, however, denies to cultures any formative role. For Freud, myths and dreams are the projections of frustrated desires that the conscious mind represses, so that they eventually surface in distorted imagery. But the source of myth for Freud is far too much dependent on the individual. The role of cultures is ignored. Myths are the product of both conscious *and* unconscious elements.[15]

*Functional*:
The major role of myths is to legitimize elements of social life. This view, strongly held by Bronislaw Malinowski, overstresses the cultural role in the evolution of mythology and neglects the common elements present in all myths.

*Structural*:
Myths, according to Claude Lévi-Strauss, logically and imaginatively resolve oppositional relationships, e.g. order/disorder, that the conscious mind will not face.[16]
   Lévi-Strauss over-emphasizes an unconscious element that can occur in myths; he underestimates the visible role of cultures in the evolution of myths.
   Victor Turner has a modified form of this approach. (See Chapter 4, pp. 74–77.) Life is a movement from a world of predictable roles and structures to experiences of 'antistructure', i.e. periods in which people relate simply as human beings. In periods of antistructure, people feel the need to retell myths in order to rediscover their purpose for existence; they then return to their structured world. In the evolution of myth, culture and the unconscious interact.[17]

Turner's view is strongly supported today by many anthropologists, though they continue to acknowledge the valid aspects of other views, particularly those of the functionalist school.

---

## Types of myths

The more important types of myths are the following:

## 1. Creation/identity and regeneration myths

Creation myths like to speak about *first causes*; in them, people express their primary understanding of mankind, the world, time and space. A perfect example of this is the creation story in the Book of Genesis. In highly symbolic, narrative language, we are told that God created the world, our first parents sinned and we are called to co-operate responsibly with God in continuing his creation. On a far less exalted level, there are the creation stories telling how nations were formed. For example, the white Australian culture was born in an atmosphere of violence, injustices and the harshness of a cruel landscape; the mythic creators of the culture are tough, individualistic, creative, and impatient with anything that smacks of pomposity and authoritarianism.

Whenever the creation myth is relived in ritual, it may be called a regeneration myth. The sacred time of the founding of the culture or nation breaks into the present, profane world through ritual, providing people with a renewed sense of identity and belonging. For example, the Exodus event, the creation myth of the Israelite people, is also a regenerative myth; whenever the Israelites feel lost they retell, and are energized or regenerated by, the founding story of the nation, and express it in ritual (see Psalm 78). At the bicentennial celebrations of 1988, to mark the foundation of contemporary Australia, people felt the need to re-enact ritually the landing of the first settlers.

If the reliving of the founding story is to be authentic, people are expected to undergo a deep interior and exterior change; they cannot be mere spectators.

## 2. Charter myths

These myths legitimize actions in the present or in the future. For example, people who are influenced by the Genesis myth of creation feel legitimized in their work of dominating nature. The American political system of checks and balances is legitimized in the Constitution myth.

## 3. Eschatological myths

These are myths about the end of an age or the end of time (e.g. 2 Pet 3:13). They speak about key issues of life, death and resurrection, future rewards and punishments, even an apocalyptic insight into the future age of peace and plenty. Often they tell of a former age of peace and contentment that was lost, but is to be restored if people act rightly. They are the driving force behind the way people live their morality and institute revolutionary movements. Communism offers its golden age of the classless society, one to be shared by those who battle against oppressors. The collective champion or culture hero in this myth is the proletariat which struggles against, and eventually overcomes, the bourgeoisie.

# 4. Dominant, supportive and directional myths

Generally within a mythology, one myth, e.g. a creation myth, will stand out over other myths. This is called a *dominant* myth. The other myths complement or support this dominant myth. Some myths are *directional* because they indicate how the foundational or creation myth is to be lived out. The written American Constitution, which established the political system, would be a directional myth.

## The role of heroes and heroines in myth

As narratives that help us feel at home with ourselves and our world, myths frequently recount incidents of exemplary individuals, whose manner of living shows how the mythical values of our culture are to be expressed. These heroes and heroines venture out into the unknown world, where they battle against evil and articulate the tensions we feel, e.g. the tension that exists between the individual and society. They offer various ways of resolving these tensions.

Such heroic individuals are an enormous comfort to us. People like George Washington and Abraham Lincoln for North Americans, Lord Nelson (of Battle of Trafalgar fame) and Winston Churchill for the English, the saints for believers, or founders of religious congregations for their respective members, show that the mythical values can be put into practice. These people also show that the forces of chaos and evil can be kept at bay or related to in a culturally acceptable way.

---

*Examples*:
In the Western film genre, as in *Shane* (1953) or *Cat Ballou* (1965), the hero or heroine is a strong, self-contained individual unknown to or not fully accepted by society, who has exceptional abilities that he or she uses to defend a powerless society successfully against the evil actions of the villain. The once-rejecting society finally accepts the saviour. Americans can identify with this type of person, otherwise the Westerns (or their updated equivalents) would not be so enduringly popular.

Suffering and violent death are a constant theme in Filipino films. The typical hero is a simple person, who is abused and humiliated, often sexually. The audience feels sorry for, and identifies with, the character. The attention is always on the victim. Tension builds up until the hero cannot stand it any longer. Extraordinary, bloody violence ensues, during which even the hero is sometimes killed. Some observers have claimed that this hero is a metaphor for the Filipino people themselves. Certainly, Filipinos can identify with the brutally murdered Ninoy Aquino, as they do with other assassinated saviours in the past, because such a person fits their image of the hero.[18] (See Chapter 4, pp. 75–77.)

---

People not of American or Filipino cultures would find these expressions of the mythological hero or heroine difficult to understand and, subsequently, hard to identify with. Each culture has a unique type of saviour to match its particular mythology.

## Myths can change: myth management

New myths are created and old ones are maintained, constantly revised, or lost completely because of a varied flow of forces, changing needs, and new ways of seeing things. The creation, revision, or disappearance of myths is termed *myth management*. Myth management occurs through such processes as myth extension, substitution, drift and revitalization. We will briefly examine each of these processes.

## 1. Myth extension

When people ransack the past to find legitimation for the present, there is myth extension. For example, British politicians compete with each other in claiming that their particular policies—not those of the opposing parties—rightly represent the 'true British traditions' of fairness and justice. The North American mythology is rooted in the belief that Americans are building the new promised land of peace, plenty and justice. This accounts for the constant references to 'the American Dream' by a wide variety of people. They seek to justify an equally disparate choice of actions, goods and promises. Writers, orators and politicians strain for eloquence and pour out effusions of lofty dreams. No one ever considers that there may not be a promised land ahead.

Sometimes revision or extension takes place if only the *meaning* of the specific myths, not the words themselves, is changed. The North American foundational myth—which includes the 'revelation' that 'all men are created equal', for example—is still vigorous, even though Americans have come to include blacks and all women in an originally very restrictive assertion. Although the meaning of the myth is much extended, the 'fact' of equality is still considered to be unchallenged. Notice that the community itself is involved in one way or another in revising or extending the myth's meanings or emphases.

## 2. Myth substitution

Myth substitution is a difficult and often painful process. Marxist Soviet leaders seek to manipulate their people, often under the threat of violence, by inventing new myths to legitimate their power and supremacy.

Sometimes a new myth becomes acceptable through a process of education, persuasion and example. Paul VI, in order to stress the servant role of the papacy, put aside the use of the regal tiara which had developed over centuries as a symbol of political, even worldly, power.

## 3. Myth drift

Drift occurs when myths change, degenerate or disappear without deliberate planning on the part of individuals or groups. Sometimes the dominant myth is distorted because a secondary myth assumes an exaggerated position. This has happened to the Genesis creation story. Extreme capitalism, with its emphasis on individualism, displaces the original stress in the myth on our responsibility to be co-creators with God in this world. Social consciousness is thus downplayed in what has become a distorted myth. Marxism, with its stress on the future Communist golden age, is a secularization and vulgarization of the same creation myth; for, remove God, and individual dignity is left unprotected.[19]

## 4. Myth revitalization

Myths can speak about how chaos became cosmos or an orderly world. When a people or culture is threatened with chaos, or experiences chaos, it feels the urge to rediscover the original creation myth (sometimes referred to today as 'its roots'), and to relive the creation story. In the reliving of the myth, people seek once more to achieve identity, courage and self-worth. This repeatedly happens to the Israelites. When they finally admit their chaos—their sinfulness, idolatry or injustices—they retell their creation story, that is, about the time when Yahweh made them into his chosen people (e.g. see Psalm 107).

Note the key factors in revitalization:

- a feeling of chaos/confusion;

- the emergence of cultural heroines or heroes, e.g. the Old Testament prophets, who are in touch with the culture's creation roots;

- and the willingness of people to participate in the reliving or reappropriation of the founding story.

The myth can be updated, distorted or purified in the process. In the following example from the mass media's efforts to update mythic heroes, new symbols, with which people in the contemporary world identify, are introduced.

---

*Example*:
In North America, the hero of the Western film has been updated through the *Rocky* and *Rambo* films of Sylvester Stallone. The vigorously individualistic, macho, physically strong, thoroughly self-contained and silent person, the 'truly American' hero, is centre stage once more, destroying villains with modern firepower, using helicopters in place of horses, restoring the morale of the American people, and prepared to return at any time when needed to uphold the American way of life. Notice, however, that in the light of the Gospel, and indeed of the creation story of America itself, this updated mythic hero is a moral distortion of what the hero *should* be, because of the senseless use of violence.

---

# Ritual

Since ritual will be considered in a later chapter in detail, it is sufficient here to repeat an earlier definition of it.

Ritual is the repeated, symbolic behaviour of people belonging to a particular culture; myth explains the meaning of this or that particular ritual. For example, the mythology of a nation can be understood by carefully watching and experiencing its rituals. No one who watches the British royal ceremonies—e.g. the royal weddings, the annual opening of Parliament—will miss the special emphasis the monarchy has in the nation's mythology. Nor would anyone who witnessed the relighting of the Liberty torch in New York harbour in July 1986 fail to feel that America's mythology is rooted in respect for freedom, equality and individual rights.

We discover what people consider important by the way they use rituals. Some people, for good or bad, are more sensitive to our need for rituals than others:

*Hitler*, supported by his ritual experts, ruthlessly manipulated and created public rituals to express his distorted mythology of Germanic racial superiority.

*Walt Disney*, on the other hand, recognized how rituals could be used positively in his films and parks. A stroll through the streets of Disneyland or Disney World offers visitors the chance to live out national and childhood myths through rituals. These streets—spotless, godly, and patriotic—are full of warmth and, sometimes, even cloying cosiness; they are places in which the outside world, when admitted, is scaled down to safer, softer dimensions. In Frontierland, one can feel and live out once more the mythic roots of the nation and one's childhood.

On his journeys, *John Paul II* testifies to his role as bishop *among* bishops by being visibly in close companionship with local bishops, e.g. at Mass.

# Reflection questions

## To the reader

1. Can you identify any incident in your life, e.g. sickness, a culture shock reaction, death of a dear friend, in which you experienced a feeling of chaos or a dramatic loss of meaning? How did you react to this incident?

   If you experienced personal chaos, do you think this has helped you appreciate the role of symbol, myth and ritual in your life?

2. As a result of the explanations in this chapter and your own experience, try to explain to someone what a symbol and a myth are.

## To a discussion group

1. What are the pivotal symbols in your culture? Do they clash with Gospel values?

2. Reflect on Psalm 107. What does it tell you about symbols and myths of the Israelites?

3. What key symbols did Jesus use in his own personal lifestyle to teach us about fundamental values of his message?

4. What are the power symbols in your parish? Do they clash with Gospel values? If they do clash, what can you do about the situation?

5. In the religious services in your parish, can you identify various kinds of myths?

# Suggested reading

Biallas, L. J., *Myths, Gods, Heroes, and Saviors* (Mystic, CT: Twenty-Third Publications, 1986).

Dillistone, F. W., *Power of Symbols in Religion and Culture* (New York: Crossroads, 1986).

Douglas, M., *Natural Symbols: Explorations in Cosmology* (New York: Pantheon Books, 1970).

Douglas, M., *Implicit Meanings: Essays in Anthropology* (London: Routledge & Kegan Paul, 1975).

Fawcett, T., *The Symbolic Language of Religion* (Minneapolis: Augsburg, 1971).

Kottak, C. P. (ed.), *Researching American Culture: A Guide for Student Anthropologists* (Ann Arbor: University of Michigan Press, 1982).

Morris, B., *Anthropological Studies of Religion: An Introductory Text* (Cambridge, UK: Cambridge University Press, 1987).

Turner, V., *The Ritual Process: Structure and Anti-Structure* (Ithaca, NY: Cornell University Press, 1977).

# 3 Understanding different cultures

Culture is shared meaning. To comprehend meaning, one must see the world as others see it, to comprehend experience in terms of others' frame of reference (James Peacock).[1]

## Introduction

There are thousands of different subcultures within the Western world, some shared by relatively small numbers of people, others by larger sections of the population. Newer nations, like the USA and Australia, have developed over the last two centuries through massive migrations from all parts of the world. Each migrant group has tended, sometimes for generations, to retain their own subcultural identity, some more vigorously than others.

Since the end of the Second World War, however, Western Europe has attracted to itself, especially through immigration from the Third World, a notable increase in subcultures. About 30 million people entered Western European countries as workers or workers' dependants in this period; though many returned to their countries of origin, many have remained. In Britain, over 3 million people were born in countries as diverse as Pakistan and Australia. Islam is Britain's fastest growing religion (the second major religion in France); in 1986, Muslims, for the first time, outnumbered Baptists and Methodists combined.

Hence, to speak of *the* one French culture, *the* one English or *the* American culture is too simplistic, if no reference is made to the traditional and migrant subcultures in these countries. Each subculture requires a different pastoral approach. In this chapter evangelizers are offered *four* instruments or models of cultures to help them to understand more objectively the complex world of cultures/subcultures.

An anthropological model is not a perfect representation of the real world. Rather, a model is an effort to construct, from the study of many cultures/subcultures, an *ideal* type, that is, the highlighting of the major behavioural emphases common to most of those studied. Unnecessary details are omitted. Because reality is so complex, no one model is normally sufficient to enable us to comprehend a particular culture/subculture.

# Models

## Folk/associational cultures

(This is a much adapted version of R. Redfield's folk/urban typology. Though anthropologically the model has its limitations, I find it an excellent introduction for multicultural audiences.)

Folk and associational culture types may be considered as polar extremes of a continuum. (See Table 3.1.) Between the polar extremes, there is room, in reality, for an unlimited variety of cultures, each embodying more or less of either of the extremes. For example, a culture that is strongly folk in its emphasis on the importance of group loyalty may at the same time be vigorously associational in its economic activities, e.g. in Japan.

| | Folk culture | Associational culture |
|---|---|---|
| 1. Self-image: | From social relationships | From one's own efforts |
| 2. Role of tradition: | Guide to present/future | No influence |
| 3. Language: | Concrete/dynamic/story-telling | Abstract/concise/technical |
| 4. Social organization/ relationships: | Personal<br>Group-oriented<br>Extended family<br>Credit/debt | Impersonal<br>Superficial<br>Nuclear family<br>Contractual |
| 5. Land: | Personal ties | Economic unit |
| 6. Time: | Person/event<br>Punctuality unimportant | Impersonal<br>Punctuality important |
| 7. Investment: | In social relationships | In future economic growth |
| 8. Religion: | Sacred–profane same<br>Fatalism<br>Sin: social | Sacred–profane divided<br>Science controls life<br>Sin: individual |
| 9. Social control: | Group loyalty before justice<br>Informal sanctions:<br>fear—gossip/<br>—supernatural/<br>—ostracism<br>tension release:<br>—flattery<br>—humour | Justice before relationships<br>Formal sanctions: law |
| 10. Sex status: | Male domination | Equality |

**Table 3.1**  Folk/associational typology

45

# 1. Origin of the individual's self-image

## Folk culture

The individual's identity cannot be separated from the context of his or her relationships; he or she has reciprocal obligations to a variety of people—e.g. relatives, friends, the owners/managers of the firm—and these relationships define who a person is. For example, a Japanese worker may see his or her identity as coming first from the obligations towards his or her family, then the firm of employment.[2] The individual's identity and self-image is derived from a set of relationships with other people. (See Figure 3.1.) Ask a Pakistani migrant in Britain who he is and he will begin to describe a whole range of relationships. When the evangelist Matthew wanted to define who Jesus is, he rightly started by listing a long genealogy (Mt 1:1–17). Many peoples of the world would understand Matthew's logic.

## Associational culture

Here the uniqueness of the individual is emphasized in defining the self, not the relationships of the individual with other people, e.g. relations, employers. The individual will be involved with other people, but not to the extent that his or her uniqueness or freedom of movement is interfered with. Within the USA, for example, individuals may feel the need for personal autonomy so pressing that they have trouble making and sustaining commitments to others, e.g. to family members, friends, jobs.[3]

# 2. Role of tradition

## Folk culture

What was done in the past is the guide to the present and the future.

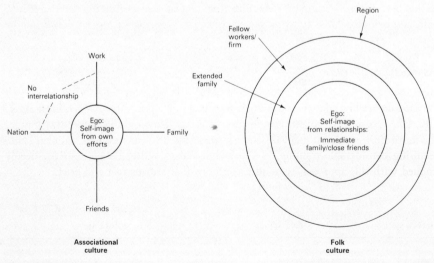

**Figure 3.1**  Sources of ego self-image

46

*Example:*
An Anglican priest, newly arrived in the Chatham Islands (part of New Zealand but with a subculture of its own)[4] from the mainland, told an islander to move the stall selling sweets at a parish fête from one part of the hall to the other. He was forthrightly told in reply: 'Never! We have always had the stall here and that is where it remains!' The stall remained where it was.

Older people are thought to know the traditions of the culture and so are treated with considerable respect. Young people have little or no influence.

## Associational culture

Here the stress is on the future. If a proposed improvement contradicts traditional ways of doing things, then the latter must give way. Hence, if this or that building, social relationship or form of government is an obstacle to change, then it is to be removed. As this culture is in rapid change, only young people are assumed to have the ability to keep up with new ideas, to create and invent. Older persons are marginalized (e.g. through early retirement) lest they obstruct the assumed creativity of younger people.

# 3. Style of language

## Folk culture

Language is concrete, dynamic, and filled with imagery. In the Psalms, for example, verbs are stressed rather than abstract nouns; the same point is repeated often in different words; dramatic references are made to nature, e.g. water, heavens.

Story-telling is a popular pastime, and a way of keeping alive the traditions of a people, e.g. among Fijians, in the South Pacific, each village has its own ballads about its history, for recitation on ceremonial or recreational occasions. Consequently, pastors when preaching must be concrete and give plenty of stories that enshrine the lessons.

## Associational culture

Here the language is concise, for people have little time for lengthy discussions or unnecessary reading. So, there are short-cuts or abbreviations, e.g. UNO, UNESCO, UK, USA. Since it is a culture that fosters abstract, technological know-how for more and more creative action, many different forms of scientific or technical language exist, requiring considerable training to understand and to write. People who are deeply imbued with this approach respond to sermons that are abstract and brief.

# 4. Social organization

## Folk culture

The emphasis is on group, rather than individual, rights. Various expressions articulate the importance of group harmony: cohesiveness, togetherness, interdependence.

---

---

Frequently, the extended family or kinship system (i.e. a network of relationships based on blood and marriage) is at the heart of group life in folk culture. In Asia, the South Pacific and Africa, extended family obligations often have priority over anything determined by governmental laws. Migrants to Western countries continue to use the system as a source of individual and family support.[5] Modified extended family systems can continue to exist for generations in the heart of the most urbanized societies, e.g. in the lower socio-economic sections of Boston[6] and London.[7]

Often, social relationships within and outside the extended family system are held together by a complex process of debt and credit. A sense of obligation is at the heart of the traditional Japanese social structure; once a person does something for another, there is a corresponding obligation on the part of the recipient at some later date to respond with some valued favour. The system, with local variations, is to be found in many parts of the world, e.g. the credit/debt relationship is at the heart of the Mafia organization within America.

---

---

## Associational culture

This model of culture has been termed 'associational' in contrast to 'folk' mainly because most social relationships tend to be impersonal, superficial, loose and based on formal, contractual agreements. The individual is seen as superior to the group and he or she will avoid, as far as possible, any long-term commitment to the group, lest freedom of action is curtailed. The creation mythology of America supports such an exaltation of the rights of the individual.

The nuclear family system (parents and children) characterizes this culture. It is an increasingly fragile system and its life-cycle is short, i.e. the legal obligations of parents to children and vice versa are limited to only a few years.

# 5. Relationship to land

## Folk culture

The Israelites, in their exile in Babylon, movingly summarized how people in a folk culture can be so intimately related to the land that their very identity is intertwined with it:

> Beside the streams of Babylon
> we sat and wept
> at the memory of Zion . . .
> How could we sing
> one of Yahweh's hymns
> in a pagan country? (Ps 137:1, 4)

So many Irish lyrics cherished by emigrants reflect this same type of relationship. Land and people are one. Destroy the land and the people's spirit dies. In New Zealand today, the Maori, the original settlers of that country, are struggling for the return of their confiscated lands, as are also the Aborigines in Australia, for their identity as a people is integrally connected with the land. Traditionally the Maori had an extremely strong affection for their ancestral soil. For the Maori, the lands on which the ancestors had lived, had fought on and were buried in were always an object of deepest sentiment: 'mine is the land, the land of my ancestors'.[9]

## Associational culture

In this culture, land is fundamentally an economic unit. It is assumed that if a particular section of land does not provide adequate profit, it must be sold. The transaction will be done without grief over the loss of the land.

# 6. The concept of time

## Folk culture

The past, present and the future are seen as one; time can be calculated according to any important event that may occur from time to time.

Punctuality is unimportant. Appointments can be made, but they are easily broken because of more important values, such as the need to fulfil obligations to relations or guests. For Maoris in New Zealand, 'Maori time' is a way of arranging time to give due priority to Maori, not white New Zealand, values. For example, the latter expect meals to be punctual and other duties are normally of secondary importance. However, at Maori gatherings meals will be delayed, even for hours if necessary, until all guests have been formally welcomed with due ceremony.

## Associational culture

The past, the present and the future are broken up into clearly distinct sections. Punctuality for appointments is considered to be a virtue of high quality, no matter what sacrifices are involved. To be late for appointments means that people lose 'valuable time' and that could cost them considerable amounts of money or personal inconvenience.[10]

# 7. The meaning of 'investment'

## Folk culture

Inevitably, capital investment is subjected to the requirements of social relationships. Visible generosity in the giving of gifts is both a sign of one's prestige and also a form of investment in the future. Sin is the failure to be generous in gift giving or in the sharing of one's wealth with others. If I am lavish with gifts to people, I am able to call on them later for services in repayment, when I most need them.

As regards prestige, migrants from places like Asia are prepared to go into tremendous financial debt just to guarantee a lavish wedding for their daughters. If one fails to be lavish, one 'loses face' with members of one's group. Indian peasant farmers in Fiji are known to liquidate three or four years' savings, perhaps mortgage two or three years' future savings, in order to guarantee a socially acceptable marriage ceremony for a daughter.

## Associational culture

Conspicuous display or consumption of goods occurs in this culture also, but generally there is far more emphasis on financial investment for economic profit than on investment for social results. There must be saving, the 'wise use of money', to reap the most financial profit from investment.

# 8. Religion

## Folk culture

Here the sacred and profane merge into one; the spirits which are generally very personalized, e.g. God, the saints, deceased members of one's family or clan, are intimately involved in one's daily life and are ready to help—or cause harm, if they are not treated correctly.

It is generally assumed that most serious illnesses or crises are due to antagonized ancestral spirits. For example, sacred customs may have been broken and so the spirits are angry and revengeful. Or sorcerers (that is, people who can use magic harmfully or aggressively) may be acting on behalf of enemies to hurt individuals. A Maori man was driving his car when it began to sway dangerously, and without any obvious reason, across the road. He decided that the car's swaying was due to 'Maori bullets of revengeful ancestors'. He stopped the car and attempted to kill himself by jumping over a cliff, because he thought death was inevitable.

Dreams are important as a way of knowing what the spirit world wishes of humans.

---

*Example*:
Liz, a young Maori woman, killed her adopted son. The spirit of her deceased husband, it was claimed in court, had repeatedly visited her in her dreams to demand retribution for her marrying his brother within weeks of his own death. After she killed the boy, the spirit never troubled her again.

---

Fate (i.e. the spirits) will control one's life, unless one is lucky and can discover how to 'manipulate' its forces.[11] In Melanesia, e.g. in Papua New Guinea, the people distinguish between purely secular skills and 'true knowledge'. Purely secular skills are things which, given time, anyone can discover in the course of ordinary experience. By 'true knowledge', however, the people mean the mastery of ritual, the correct performance of which ensures success in important economic, social and political action. It also guarantees good health or its restoration. 'True knowledge' is the ability to harness the power of the spirits to the activities of human beings.

It is important to remember this, as spirits and human beings live together in a purely physical world, in which there is no distinction between natural and supernatural. The power and actions of spirit-beings are as real and alive as the world we see.

There is nothing illusory or imaginary about them. So when people fall sick, the immediate reaction is to find out just what spirit is the cause of it, discover the right (often secret) ritual, and perform it accurately. Results are expected immediately; if they are not forthcoming, the people suspect that they have recited the rituals incorrectly, chosen the wrong rituals, or no ritual is powerful enough to counter the forces of fate. In Samoa a small child fell ill. The family met together and concluded that the spirit of the recently deceased mother-in-law of the father was the cause; the family pushed a pipe into the grave and poured boiling water down it. The child was also given medicine from the hospital and recovered. But his recovery was considered primarily to be the result of the 'correct' ritual action over the grave.

The key insight is this: there is no real division between the supernatural and the natural world. The world of the good or bad spirits is not considered to be remote. The spirits live on the earth with human beings, and they impinge on every aspect of human living. Indeed, they are considered to be an essential and functional part of it, ensuring success in all ventures and guaranteeing good health provided the correct rituals are used.

---

*Example*:
Maria is a migrant to England from southern Italy. Her child is sick and she feels that his sickness is due to God's punishment for a sin she committed several years back. She has a dream that all will be well, if only she can place a lighted candle each day for seven days before the statue of St Anthony in the parish church. She does this, but the child remains sick. She hears of a 'new revelation' of the Mother of God and is given a prayer in her honour. The child recovers and the lady is 'satisfied with Mary, as the new way to control a world of fate'. (See Chapter 6, pp. 108–111.)

---

## Associational culture

What is considered sacred is distinctly separated from the profane world of business and everyday life. I no longer feel that I am controlled by fate, as expressed through sickness and so forth, because science can control most things. Only those things that science cannot control are called evil, e.g. some forms of cancer, natural disasters, an uncontrolled nuclear arms race.

Contact with the sacred is seen as necessary, if at all, only to guarantee one's life in the world to come. Deities or saints are considered very abstract realities, not at all personalized. Sin is the failure to work for one's personal well-being, e.g. the failure to compete sufficiently against other individuals for material success. Sin can be avoided or overcome through natural techniques of self-improvement, e.g. through various kinds of psychological programmes, which help to re-establish one's damaged self-image and confidence.

# 9. Methods of social control

## Folk culture

The assumption is that harmony and unity must be maintained within the group at all costs, even if the objective norms of justice are broken in the process.

Since there is so much personal, face-to-face relationship and mutual interdependence in daily life within a folk society, few risk major deviations from traditional customs and loyalty to the group. Group members are taught from early childhood to fear all kinds of human or supernatural punishments if anyone dares to deviate.

Sociologist Chie Nakane, writing on the way Japanese individuals are controlled by the group, notes: 'The feeling that "I must do this because A and B also do it" or "they will laugh at me unless I do such-and-such" rules the life of the individual with greater force than any other consideration and thus has a deep effect on decision-making'.[12] The fear of being mocked or laughed at is a most powerful agent in enforcing conformity to the group's norms. Just reflect on the following examples from both Western and traditional societies.

---

*Examples:*
Anthropologist H. G. Oxley, in his study of egalitarian 'mateship' among white male Australians, found that informal sanctions, e.g. the fear of ridicule and ostracism, are powerful forces to guarantee conformity of behaviour.[13]

John is from a village on the island of Rotuma in the South Pacific. One day I overheard another Rotuman child say to him: 'If you do not do what we want you to do, then you are just a silly "biscuit planter", like your ancestors!' Last century, when the British traders landed on the island, they distributed ship's biscuits to the inhabitants. In John's village the people put them into the ground 'so that they could have trees with biscuits as fruit'. Hence when anyone from that village today is tempted not to conform to Rotuman group life, people from other villages will threaten to mock them with words like: 'What can you expect from "biscuit planters"?'

---

There is also the dreaded fear of supernatural reprisal, if norms are broken.

---

*Example:*
Two young men, one a white New Zealander and the other a Maori, were raiding a bank late at night. Suddenly the burglar alarm sounded and the two grabbed what money they could and fled out the back door to safety. This meant fleeing through a cemetery. The two were almost through to the other side, when the Maori stopped and refused to go any further. On recognizing he was in the cemetery, the Maori was suddenly gripped with fear of the spirits of the dead around him; if he continued, he felt they would punish him severely for the robbery. No amount of encouragement from his colleague would move him. So there he stood until the police arrested him.

---

There is also fear of ostracism, a punishment so well described in the Book of Genesis, after Cain had murdered his brother Abel. Exile from the group can mean the loss of one's identity as a person. And that is an horrendous punishment.

The Lord then said . . . 'You shall become a restless wanderer on the earth.'
Cain said to the Lord: 'My punishment is too great to bear' (Gen 4:10, 12, 13).

Various culturally acceptable ways of diffusing tension also act *indirectly* as methods to guarantee social order, e.g. consensus in decision-making, ritually controlled conflict, humour or clowning, flattery. In Japanese culture, there are strong pressures to obtain a consensus in decision-making, thus preventing dissident groups from feeling aggrieved if a decision were to be made against them.[14]

On occasions, conflict can be encouraged to emerge so that tension is not repressed to an explosive level. However, by common agreement, the conflict must not exceed ritually defined boundaries. In Britain, as anthropologist Max Gluckman points out, 'we fight periodical civil war on the hustings and in the ballot boxes'.[15] In the British Parliament, we speak of Her Majesty's Loyal Opposition, for their major task is to attack the government in power and thus release conflictual tensions, but the 'attack' cannot exceed certain clearly defined boundaries. Similarly, humour in word or cartoon can be a safety-valve to permit the release of conflictual tension; those in power are expected to take without complaint the attacks on their assumed arrogance and pomposity.

Some cultures, e.g. Samoan, cultivate the art of flattery. Potential rivals for power are publicly praised in the most flowery language for deeds they may never even have done. To attack such flattery publicly is to appear ungrateful, so they cannot allow their anger to erupt into conflict.

### Associational culture

Unlike the folk culture, the aim here is to preserve, at all costs, the objective norms of justice, even if, in the process, the group is broken apart. For example, people from folk-culture countries found it impossible to understand the 'ruthless, nationally divisive pursuit of justice' during the Watergate crisis in the USA. There are formal, clearly defined sanctions to which all are subject, no matter what their social or political position may be. Thus, drivers know that if they break the speed limit they must suffer the consequences, even if they are the Prime Minister or members of the royal family. The police and the courts are the guardians of the laws, and justice must be administered with objective honesty.

## 10. Sex status

### Folk culture

Women in folk culture are generally considered inferior to men. The three great religious–cultural traditions of Asia, Confucianism, Islam and Hinduism, consider women fundamentally inferior to men. Women are assumed to be too emotional, less than equal to males in decision-making ability and professional competence. Migrants from Asia inevitably bring with them to Western countries these same attitudes.

## Associational culture

In law, women are equal to men and the law protects women against sexual discrimination or harassment.

---

*Summary of model*:

1. The two culture types are polar extremes of a continuum. Between the polar extremes, there is room for an unlimited variety of cultures, each embodying more or less of either of the extremes. Thus, one could be thoroughly associational in one's investment policies and social interrelationships, but folk in one's religious attitudes and practices.

2. The folk-culture type is one in which behaviour is highly traditional, personal, frequently based on kinship ties, and controlled by informal pressures and due respect for 'supernatural sanctions'. Sin is a failure to fulfil one's social obligations.

3. The associational type is future-oriented, social relationships are impersonal, superficial and loose. Sin is the failure to be self-sufficient or to achieve one's personal ambitions.

---

# Grid and group cultures

Anthropologist Mary Douglas[16] has developed four types of culture, using to do so, two variables: *grid* and *group*. By *grid*, she means the the set of rules according to which people relate to one another. For example, there is a grid that regulates how crew members of an airplane should interact. In this case we speak of a *strong* grid, because the rules are very clear on how individual crew members must relate to the captain. They must obey or lose their jobs. The second variable is the *group*. This is a community's sense of identity in relationship with people beyond its boundaries. For example, the feeling of group identity of *this* particular plane's crew may be weak (though the grid remains strong), because individual members strongly wish to fly with different personnel.

Douglas takes the two variables and constructs four models of cultures:

# 1. Strong group and strong grid

In this culture the boundaries of the group, and how individuals are to relate to one another within the boundaries, are sharply defined. People are expected to fit into a bureaucratic, hierarchical system. Hence, the questioning of the system by anyone other than at the very top is discouraged. For example, prior to Vatican II, the Roman Catholic Church fitted this model rather well: non-Christians and Protestants threatened the boundaries and must be converted or avoided; the world had to adapt to the unchanging Church and rules of life and of ritual were very precisely structured. The unchanging ritual of worship reinforced tradition and the sense of belonging to the Church.

## 2. Strong group and weak grid

Here the sense of belonging to this group rather than to another is strongly felt; there is, however, a lack of clarity as to how individuals are to relate to one another. People will form together loose, social, egalitarian units to compete more effectively with one another. They are forever intensely suspicious of each other, for they fear that people are taking advantage of them. They blame others for problems they experience. Some may even feel that people who compete with them for positions in society are encouraging witchcraft (malevolent power that works through humans as an involuntary force), or sorcery (malevolent magic consciously aimed by humans against one another), to attack them.

Despite the internal tensions that lead to conflicts, people retain a strong sense of belonging to the group; they take very special care to prevent outsiders breaking through the group's boundaries or disrupting the common sense of belonging.

In the Chatham Islands subculture, people were very confused about how to relate to one another; sometimes they deliberately ignored or gossiped maliciously about fellow islanders they did not like. When things went wrong, they immediately blamed people in their midst who they imagined were out to harm them. However, the moment someone not from the Islands spoke ill of any one member, all became immediately united and defensive of their common sense of belonging.

## 3. Strong grid and weak group

People are strongly individualistic and competitive, but they have a very weak sense of belonging or of having obligations to the group. Individuals form alliances with one another to provide better opportunities for competitive successes. But such alliances are very fragile, since they are held together only for the self-interests of the individuals themselves. These alliances break apart once more profitable interrelationships appear. To sin is not to take advantage of this or that relationship, that will guarantee for me an economic, social or political advantage. Morality in this type might be termed 'Watergate', i.e. 'do everything to get ahead, without any concern for the common good'.

This culture is favourably disposed for the emergence of all kinds of prophetic or charismatic leaders, e.g. at the political, social and religious levels. The prophetic leader, at least until a more skilful leader arises, is able to manipulate individuals or segments of the population for the benefit of followers.

The political system of the USA is an example of this model. Party loyalties are very fragile. People are politically 'manipulated' to join this or that alliance, depending on what will most benefit them as representatives of the individual states or of particular pressure groups. Party loyalty is maintained if it serves the competitive self-interests of the politicians. A skilled President, e.g. a Johnson or a Reagan rather than a

Kennedy or a Carter, is able to get his policies through Congress by enticing sectional groups to agree—on condition they are able to benefit in the process.

## 4. Weak group and weak grid

In this culture type, people are thoroughly individualistic and drift, without any sense of belonging to a group. This is the 'meism' or self-fulfilment culture. I join this or that group only as long as it does not require me to follow any rules, or commit myself to the needs of the common good. The moment the group places pressure on me, I drift away.

This type of culture flourishes in times of social upheaval when people lose their sense of belonging, or when traditional rules of interacting with one another are destroyed or severely questioned. Thus, during the Expressive Cultural Revolution of the late 1960s, when every political, social and religious tradition was openly questioned or rejected, there developed various hippie and fragile commune movements. Sin would here be defined as any act by an individual which did not respond to the need for 'my self-fulfilment'.

## Culture of poverty

People are poor if they are unable to have access to what is generally considered to be a reasonable standard and quality of life. In Britain, about 4.8 million people are living *on* what is considered the poverty line, 2.8 million live *below* this level. In the USA, more than 33 million people—about one in every seven—are poor, by the government's official definition; one-fourth of all rural children now live in poverty. They have inadequate housing, food, medicine, and educational/employment opportunities.

The Culture of Poverty model[17] describes a type of poverty. It depicts a certain category of poor people: those who have lost all hope of getting out of their social and economic deprivation. Their poverty deprives them of involvement in educational and governmental structures which are the necessary avenues to get out of their suffering. Their feeling of hopelessness, or fatalism, becomes the very source of meaning and belonging in their lives; tragically, it is transferred from parents to children, who are thus taught to accept their poverty rather than to hope that they can develop skills to escape it. It is estimated that about 10–15 million Americans experience this culture model. (See Figure 3.2.)

## Consensus/conflict cultures

These two types of cultures are especially popular among social scientists. In recent years many Church workers who struggle to alleviate poverty have turned particularly to the conflict-culture type to help understand and remove the causes of oppression.

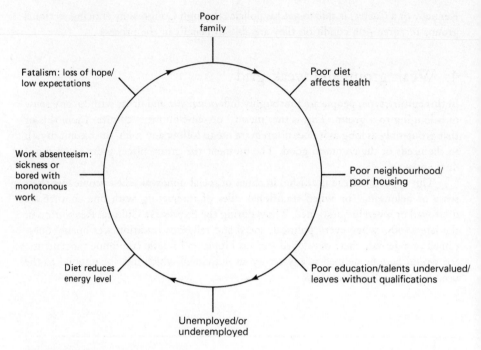

**Figure 3.2**  Culture of poverty cycle

# 1. Consensus culture

The assumption is that the culture is held together because people at all levels of the culture are committed to a common set of ideas and beliefs. Conflicts do exist, but there are traditional ways to resolve them, without fracturing the atmosphere of the overall cultural consensus and unity. In-depth change in the culture is slow, since people only hesitantly change their ideas and attitudes. They prefer a sense of order and predictability to the disorder and uncertainty that mark rapid swings in beliefs or attitudes.

# 2. Conflict culture

The most distinctive aspect of this culture type is the domination of individuals and groups by the more powerful. If there is order and peace, it is merely a façade, since people are being oppressed by the more powerful political and economic classes.

The powerless may accept an inferior economic, social and political position because those in power have been able to manipulate them through propaganda and education to accept their subservient position.

For change to occur of any quality, there must be socio-economic and political structural changes that will allow the less powerful to assume the necessary power to control their own lives. However, the powerful will not give up their position of domination, except through conflict.

The notion of power is crucial to the understanding of this model. Power is the ability to influence, a *resource* that may or may not be used. The following typology by Rollo

May will illustrate the various forms of power that are considered to be at the heart of this model:[18]

---

1. *Exploitative power*: the ability to coerce others by *force* to act.

2. *Manipulative power*: the ability to move people to act in certain ways for the *primary* advantage of the one who has the power.

3. *Competitive power*: the ability to interact with another for a scarce resource.

4. *Nutritive power*: the ability to *serve* others.

5. *Integrative power*: the ability to work *with* others.

---

In the first and second kinds of power, I use power in such a way that I do not respect the other person, who is the object of my actions. These are the two types of power, especially referred to in the conflict-culture model. In this model people have exploitative and manipulative power, but also they control the institutions or structures that perpetuate the use of this power. For example, the culture of white South Africa is conflictual; it is held together primarily through the use of exploitative and manipulative types of power. And these forms of power are exercised through those institutions or structures that are especially concerned with the blacks: education, justice, employment, housing, transport. Consensus exists in South African society to this extent, that the majority of whites *alone* accept this form of relating to the blacks.

Social scientists generally accept that every culture has qualities of both types: the characteristics of one type may be more evident at a particular time than those of the other. This conflict-culture type is particularly acceptable to those change agents who feel change is too slow; they claim that by fostering more tension and conflict the desired changes will occur.[19]

In his encyclical *Sollicitudo Rei Socialis* (1987) John Paul II uses the conflict model to explain why the rich become richer, and the poor poorer, in the world today.[20] So much of world poverty, in the final analysis, is a moral ill brought on by the sins and omissions of many people. Hence, the Pope speaks of *sinful* structures, that is, those structures of oppression that are the result of 'the concrete acts of individuals who introduce (them) . . ., consolidate them and make them difficult to remove. And so they grow stronger, spread, and become the source of other sins, and so influence people's behaviour.'[21]

## Social analysis

Social analysis is an action-oriented educational process which aims to help people become more *critically* aware of the ways in which they are responsible for the oppression of others, or are themselves oppressed by structures or institutions, e.g. governmental, legal, educational, business.[22] It is claimed that people are poor because others consciously or unconsciously use power exploitatively and manipulatively to oppress them. The culture-conflict model, understandably, is more acceptable to social analysts than the consensus-culture type.

The aim of the analysis is not just knowledge, but a commitment to work for structures in which all can exercise nutritive and integrative power. Inevitably, the information that emerges in social analysis is itself conflictual; people of goodwill are bound to feel annoyed when they discover the stark reality of how they or others are manipulated or oppressed. They recognize that structures must be changed, and this means threatening the security of those who benefit from the present structures of domination.

---

*Example*:
In New Zealand in 1986, the indigenous Maori people comprised some 7 per cent of the total New Zealand labour force, but they made up 20 per cent of all unemployed people. Of all Maori students leaving secondary school in 1984, about 65 per cent of males and 60 per cent of females had no formal qualifications; non-Maori percentages were: male 32 per cent and female 25 per cent. Though Maori form only 12 per cent of the population, 50 per cent of prison admissions are Maori.

Social analysis shows, however, that decisions are made *for* Maori people by non-Maori officials. The minority Maori subculture has not achieved justice in education and employment opportunities through consensus structures. These structures have been exploitative, in favour of the white culture. Tension and conflict are emerging, as more people realize this fact through social analysis.

---

# Reflection questions

## To the reader

1. What culture model do you find most helpful? Why?

2. Of the grid/group cultures, which one describes best the culture you live in?

3. Are you aware of any exploitative structures in the country in which you live? If so, who is suffering? Are you able to help other people become aware of what is happening?

## To a discussion group

1. What culture model best describes the culture of the country in which the group lives? Are there any points that you think should be added to the description of the model you have chosen?

2. What type(s) of power characterizes the relationships within the organizational structure of your parish?

3. How would you go about helping, in a practical way, the people you are evangelizing to grasp the culture model that best describes their way of life? What New Testament texts do you think would be most helpful for them to use, in measuring their culture according to the values of Jesus Christ?

# Suggested reading

Byron, W. (ed.), *The Causes of World Hunger* (New York: Paulist, 1982).

Douglas, M., *Purity and Danger: An Analysis of Concepts of Pollution and Taboo* (Harmondsworth, Middx: Penguin, 1970).

Douglas, M., *Cultural Bias* (London: Royal Anthropological Institute of UK and Ireland, 1978).

John Paul II, Encyclical Letter *Sollicitudo Rei Socialis* (1987).

Holland, J., and Henriot, P., *Social Analysis: Linking Faith and Justice* (Maryknoll, NY: Orbis, 1984).

Kavanaugh, J. F., *Following Christ in a Consumer Society: The Spirituality of Cultural Resistance* (Maryknoll, NY: Orbis, 1982).

Keesing, R. M., *Cultural Anthropology: A Contemporary Perspective* (New York: Holt, Rinehart & Winston, 1981), pp. 65–107.

Pascale, R. T., and Athos, A. G., *The Art of Japanese Management* (London: Allen Lane, 1982).

Report of the Archbishop of Canterbury's Commission on Urban Priority Areas, *Faith in the City: A Call for Action by Church and Nation* (London: Church House, 1985), pp. 169–355.

Roman Catholic Bishops' Conference, USA, 'Economic Justice for All: Catholic Social Teaching and the US Economy' in *Origins*, vol. 16, no. 3 (1986), pp. 33–74.

Shorter, A., *Jesus and the Witchdoctor: An Approach to Healing and Wholeness* (London: Geoffrey Chapman/Maryknoll, NY: Orbis, 1985).

Smalley, W. A. (ed.), *Readings in Missionary Anthropology* (Pasadena: William Carey, 1978).

Sobrino, J., *The True Church and the Poor* (Maryknoll, NY: Orbis, 1984).

# 4 Understanding culture change/chaos

I love chaos: it is the mysterious, unknown road. It is the poetic element in a dull and orderly world (Ben Shahn).[1]

## Introduction

Ben Shahn, an American artist, is right. Chaos destroys the predictable. It can, *if* we allow it to, challenge us to ask fundamental questions about life, about how to create new meanings, order, a sense of belonging, in the midst of a changing world.

Thus no significant change or cultural movement is made unless there is an experience of chaos, i.e. a loss of security, meaning and sense of order. There must be a death before there can be life, whether it be at the natural, human or the spiritual levels. Seeds die that there may be life. Thus Yahweh confronted the Israelite people through Jeremiah with the salvation truth—life out of death: 'This day I set you over nations and over kingdoms, to root up and to tear down, to destroy and to demolish, to build and to plant' (Jer 1:10). For there to be building and planting, there must first be destruction and demolition.

This chapter is about how:

- cultural change occurs or how new life can spring up out of cultural chaos, provided people do not deny its potential as a catalyst for growth;

- social movements in particular influence culture change.

However, just as culture is complex, so also is the process of culture change. Three models will be explained to help readers grasp what happens in culture change, how it begins, and what occurs when people try to resist it in various ways.

## Change and social movements

Culture change occurs when there are significant alterations in the meaning system of a culture, that is, in its symbols, myths and rituals. There are four major, identifiable ways in which the meaning system can change:

*Changes in technology*:
E.g. the invention of the motor car made it possible for people to extend their interests beyond one particular place.

*Changes in population*:
E.g. the ageing population in the Western world means that people must be more economically creative to support the increasing number of retired persons.

*Action by official planning agencies*:
·E.g. governments, church administrations all attempt to direct change according to their own respective values.

*Action through social movements*:
E.g. the civil rights or women's liberation movements.

---

While all four ways are important, a major concern of this chapter is to explain what happens when social movements seek to influence cultural change.

---

*Definition*:
Social movements are socially shared activities and beliefs, under the leadership of a dedicated person or group of individuals, that demand, or resist, change in some aspect of a culture.

---

# Qualities of social movements

Four emphases can generally be identified in social movements.

## a. Power emphasis

Commonly a social movement aims to obtain political power in order to change the system in its favour. It can do this either through reformist or revolutionary methods. If the former, then the social movement will use the ordinary legal or political processes sanctioned by the culture. If revolutionary methods, then non-legal action may be used to overthrow the *status quo*, e.g. the Palestine Liberation Organization.

## b. Value emphasis

A value is what an individual or a group considers desirable for society and which influences their choice of ways, means, and ends in action. Social movements can aim to persuade the society at large, through all kinds of education, that the values they stand for are important. For example, the ecological movement sponsors various mass-media campaigns to win people over to their cause.

## c. Personal emphasis

A social movement can concentrate its effort not on the wider society, but on improving the quality of commitment of its own members, e.g. various programmes for Christian believers: Gospel reflection programmes, charismatic renewal, Ignatian Spiritual Exercises.

## d. Resistance emphasis

There are movements to prevent change, e.g. the Old Believers, that is, people who refused to accept the reforms of the Patriarch Nikon within the Russian Church of the seventeenth century; the Lefebvre movement, as long as it remained within the Catholic Church, resisted changes initiated by Vatican Council II; the contemporary anti-abortion political pressure groups around the world. Those involved in the resistance movements believe that suggested changes are for various reasons inimical to the well-being of a particular society.

A movement can of course be using all four emphases at the same time. It can also change its approach. For instance, in several parts of the world, the anti-nuclear campaign stressed the importance of educating the public about the dangers of nuclear power or weapons. But in recent years groups have been organized to resist, through various kinds of passive and active protest rallies, the presence or introduction of nuclear power or weapons. In some countries, e.g. New Zealand, people have sought and obtained political power in order to enforce the nuclear-free policy.

# Models

The following are three models of what happens to cultures when they are being pressured to change, especially through various types of social movements. Remember, a model highlights only the key features in cultures or in culture change.

---

## *Culture change reaction model*

---

Six stages can be identified in this model (see Figure 4.1).[2] There is nothing deterministic about the process of people moving from one stage to the next. In fact, it is possible for people to become locked in on one phase and even to move back to previous stage(s). Recall the notion of an *anthropological model*: it is an *exaggeration* of certain features which tend to be present in reality.

## Stage 1: Cultural consensus

The cultural *status quo* is generally accepted by people.

## Stage 2: Initial unease/stress

A social movement threatens cultural consensus. Immediate reactions to the threat may be somewhat mixed: some may experience a touch of euphoria, for the social

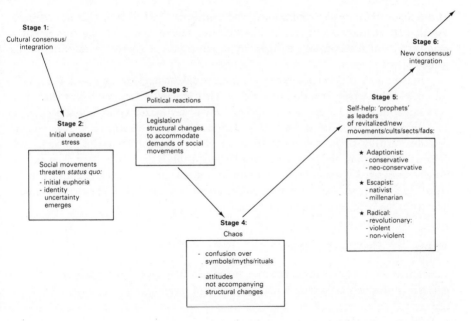

**Figure 4.1**  Culture change reaction model

movement involves them in an exciting new venture, a break from routine. Many, while accepting in theory the new movement's ideals, do not realize that these ideals will soon demand of them changes in their personal and social lives. Others experience an unease, even stress, which they are unable to explain fully, the feeling that the new movement is endangering their own cultural security.

## Stage 3:  Political reaction

The pressures from the social movement for change can no longer be ignored. The reaction is to accept its demands at the political level. This means adjustments are to be made by the receiving culture to accommodate through *legislation* only the movement's policies. Any attitudinal change or adjustment that the legislation requires is not thought to be necessary on the part of people whose culture is threatened by the social movement. On the other hand, people who are committed to the social movement may also react initially by assuming that once the legislation has been passed, no further commitment to the movement is necessary.

## Stage 4:  Chaos

People find themselves confused, in malaise, in chaos; they discover that their cultural identity is no longer intact. The social movement has undermined the very foundation of their own security and sense of belonging. No amount of legislation is able to provide the much-desired sense of unity and common purpose. With the old symbols, myths and rituals either gone or seriously undermined, the people's coherent world of meaning has disintegrated.

As regards members of the social movement, which acted as the original catalyst of the chaos, they are also disillusioned and confused. The legislation has not effected the desired attitudinal changes in the culture. Hence, some of the movement's members become vigorously militant in an effort to get people to conform to its values.

In the midst of the chaos, however, some people struggle to cope with the stressful situation by *denying* that the chaos exists. They ignore the fact that their culture has been undermined and that there is need for new or revitalized symbols if adjustments to a changing world are to be made. Various rituals of denial occur, e.g. people describe verbally or in document form an ideal world of successful cultural and personal integration, and then actually believe that this *is* the reality. Denial, which is usually considered as among the most primitive mechanisms of defence, consists in an effort 'to disavow the existence of an unpleasant or unwanted piece of external reality. The truth has become anxiety-provoking.'[3]

# Stage 5: Prophetic reaction

Individuals with creative talents choose one of several ways to lead people out of their cultural confusion or chaos to a renewed sense of meaning:

## 5.1 Nativistic/fundamentalist reaction

(See Chapter 7, pp. 124–127.) Leaders offer people a return to the old symbols, myths and rituals that existed before the confusion started, i.e. stage 1. This is escapist, because the leaders will not allow the culture they wish to resurrect to change in any way. The tendency is for the political or religious group to become a sect, that is, it claims to possess a monopoly of access to the truth or salvation; the 'evil world' must be avoided.

## 5.2 Conservative reaction

There is a return to the way of life before the chaos emerged, though not in an escapist nativistic way. The restored culture will be open to change but entirely on *its* terms; hence, there is to be no dialogue with the contemporary world.

## 5.3 Millenarian reaction

Leaders attract people because they promise dramatically rapid, 'miraculous' ways to achieve a new cultural identity. All kinds of fads emerge; as people become disillusioned with one, they turn to another. Millenarian movements may evolve into political or religious sects, e.g. Marxism is essentially a millenarian movement, as it assumes that when the proletarian revolution succeeds, all classes/divisions will be abolished.[4]

## 5.4 Neo-conservative reaction

Leaders offer people a way out of chaos through a new form of integrating the past with the world in change, even if it means accepting bold, new ideas through dialogue with all kinds of social movements, but the route chosen must not be at the cost of more chaos or confusion. This reaction differs from 5.2 above. Dialogue with the contemporary world is necessary, but every change must be slow, evolutionary and disciplined.

For example, during the Roosevelt administration in the 1930s, those who fostered some welfare services for the poor and involvement by government in the economy (the New Deal) felt that American life needed a greater sense of order and control, if the nation was to come through the Depression. But they were not radicals; the industrialist and corporate capitalism had to be kept intact.[5]

## 5.5 Radical reaction

Leaders reject the past entirely; they offer the people revolutionary means to move out of the chaos. Either they seek to invent new mythologies, or they significantly adapt the original ones to the realities of life in the world. Unlike the neo-conservatives, they aim to achieve their goals even if it means the further disruption of cultural order. For example, by comparison with the New Dealists in the USA, the Labour government in the UK in 1944 sought to establish a welfare-state system that aimed to change radically, if necessary, the social structure of the nation.

# Stage 6: Integration

A new or restored meaning system is achieved, and there is a consensus among the people that it is acceptable.

The following three case studies illustrate the relevance of this model:

# Case Study 1: Reinterpreting the creation myth of the USA

Over the last fifty years in the USA, the civil rights and the feminist movements have dramatically expanded their influence and effectiveness. They threatened, and then forced changes to, the creation mythology of the culture. The pattern of what happened can be better understood in the light of the culture change reaction model.

# Stage 1: Consensus to 1945±

The creation myth included the revelation that 'all men are created equal', but for the vast majority of white, male Americans, this did not include blacks (or to a lesser extent women, Jews and Catholics), who had to accept submissively an inferior human/social status. However, with Franklin D. Roosevelt's New Deal in the mid-1930s, which opened welfare services and government positions to blacks, black expectations rose, and more aggressive black leaders emerged. Consensus was being seriously threatened.

# Stage 2: Initial unease/stress to 1960±

In the early 1940s, only a tiny fraction of black Americans belonged to civil-rights organizations. With revitalized leadership, some of these agencies obtained in 1941 from the President, by threatening mass militancy, an Executive Order forbidding employment discrimination on the basis of race, creed and colour. It was only a beginning. The National Association for the Advancement of Colored People eventually succeeded in the mid-1950s in having the Supreme Court state that 'separate educational facilities are inherently unequal'. Reactions from the whites were immediate; the Ku Klux Klan and other resistance movements were revitalized.

## Stage 3: Political reaction, 1960–1968±

In this period, there developed the powerful, non-violent action for civil rights. Politicians grudgingly legislated for change. But, as this action only slowly weakened segregation in schools and social life, black militant movements emerged, e.g. the Black Power Movement, which became suspicious of the non-violent philosophy of Martin Luther King. The ghetto riots across the nation from 1965 to 1968 resulted, however, in louder demands from whites for the imposition of 'law and order'.

There were now two powerful political movements on collision course: on the one hand, the two-pronged struggle for civil rights—the one non-violent, the other increasingly militant—and on the other, the growing white conservative backlash movement. This potentially explosive atmosphere was further fuelled by the increasingly vocal protest against the USA's involvement in the Vietnam War, and, secondly, by groups demanding women's rights.

The movement for women's rights received considerable impetus, when an amendment was accepted to the Civil Rights Act of 1964, requesting the prohibition of sex discrimination in private employment. This was followed by a more aggressive and militant form of feminism, women's liberation, as a growing number of women, in imitation of a more militant black civil-rights movement, realized that the political action to achieve equality was far too slow. The white male-centred interpretation of the American creation mythology was under violent attack from both blacks and women's liberation movements.

## Stage 4: Chaos, 1968–72+

The year 1968 explosively introduced this stage of intense, cultural chaos, e.g. the assassinations of Martin Luther King and Robert Kennedy, the eruption of more black anger at the failure to obtain justice and employment, the seizure by students of university buildings, and the riots at the Chicago Democratic Convention.

Along with the above events, which would have been enough in themselves to shatter the confidence of a nation, there broke out within the Western world, but especially in the USA, what can be called the Revolution of Expressive Disorder or Chaos. It was essentially an attack on all human boundaries and taboos: political, intellectual, moral, sexual and social. It was an intense effort to enshrine the rights of the individual as supreme over all forms of bureaucracy and political manipulation.[6]

By the end of this period, people were exhausted by the chaos, and by the claims and counter-claims, that this or that movement truly articulated the heart of the nation's dream. Not surprisingly, the backlash against what was thought to be the forces of chaos was already happening. For example, in July 1968 the desecration of the flag was made a federal crime, and in November Richard Nixon was elected President, promising a return to 'law and order'; power was to be ceded to the forces of the status quo, chaos contained, boundaries restored.

# Stage 5: Prophetic reaction, 1972 and beyond

The most notable characteristic of this period, so far, is the emphasis on the rising power at all levels of society of cultural conservatism and patriotic nationalism. Nixon was supported by this power; Ronald Reagan was elected in 1980, enthusiastically assisted by such fundamentalist groups as the New Right, as inspired by Richard Viguerie,[7] and Jerry Falwell's Moral Majority. Social movements for civil rights have lost their drive, and at times they have been split by internal rival factions.

The following are observable reactions in more detail to the chaos of the late 1960s and early 1970s.

## Nativistic/fundamentalist reaction

Religious cults (or sects) of all kinds, e.g. the Unification Church, emerged, or old ones were revitalized. These cults offer a tightly structured meaning system to people dissatisfied with the amorphous values of the counterculture stage. And they often reinforce the capitalistic emphasis of American mythology, that is, there is nothing the individual cannot do if God is on her or his side! On the other hand, some cults, e.g. Hare Krishna, opt out of the capitalistic dream in favour of the other thrust of the American dream: the search for community untainted by this world's evils.

## Conservative reaction

This reaction, particularly evident in the post-Jimmy Carter years, has two emphases. On the one hand, there is a return to old capitalistic values of hard work, individual initiative and the assumption that the poor are as they are through their own fault. On the other hand, there is a quasi-imperialist, even simplistic, belief that the enemies of the American dream outside the nation must be kept at bay and punished, e.g. Communism in South America and Asia, the anti-nuclear protesters such as the New Zealand government.

For conservatives it is as though the movements for civil rights, from the 1930s through the 1960s, had not occurred. There is concern to be involved in the wider world, but primarily for the self-interest of the USA. The circumstances that led to the Irangate scandal aptly illustrate the philosophy of the conservative reaction: nothing is sinful provided it aims to preserve the American dream from contamination.

## Millenarian reaction

Enter the prophets of health fads, self-help programmes, natural therapies to offer instant, much-needed, personal meaning systems to people confused by the chaos.

## Neo-conservative reaction

The liberals who pressed for civil rights in the 1960s are overwhelmed by the bitterness and confusion of the chaos. They become neo-conservatives, that is, they desire change, but it must be slow and orderly. They are to be found at all levels of society today, e.g. Michael Novak in the area of theology.

## Radical reaction

Leaders who stress simple uncomplicated answers to the loss of cultural and personal meaning systems are the most acceptable in this period, e.g. political campaigners, religious television preachers. The swing towards privatized religion intensifies, with its emphasis on clearly stated personal meaning systems and its lack of concern for the needs of other people. Before the end of the 1970s, Senator George McGovern highlighted the change in emphasis: 'It is unfashionable now to worry about the poor and minorities and to defend the idea that they, too, deserve an opportunity'.[8]

## Stage 6: Integration

As yet, there are few signs of any significantly new, national move for civil rights for the poor of the USA. Not surprisingly, therefore, the increasing efforts by leaders within the mainline Churches to inspire concern for social justice at home and abroad received, and continue to receive, very little positive response. The pastoral letters of the Catholic Bishops on peace and the control of nuclear weapons, and on the evils of the capitalistic system, have obtained little support as prophetic statements aimed at integrating the Gospel with the needs of the world. These attempts to integrate the Gospel message with the social needs of the USA are radical, for they go against the popular, contemporary interpretations of the American dream.

## Case Study 2: Chaos/creativity in religious life

In the light of present trends, many religious congregations within the Roman Catholic Church will cease to exist within the next fifty years. The reasons for this have been discussed elsewhere,[9] but the following briefly explains to some degree what has happened to religious life since Vatican II in the mid-1960s.

## Stage 1: Consensus

For several centuries prior to Vatican II, the Catholic Church stressed its role as *the* unchanging symbol in an ever-changing world. The latter had to adapt to the Church, not vice versa. Religious life reflected this view. Thus, even active congregations were quasi-monastic in structure, dress, and relationships with the world (perfect examples of the strong group/strong grid culture model explained in Chapter 3). Moreover, at the heart of the creation story of religious life, there was the assumption that religious are a spiritual elite. It was thought that they alone in the Church are especially called to holiness. As stated by Pope Urban II in 1092, religious are the 'strong' ones: 'from the beginning the Church has always offered two types of life to her children: one to aid the insufficiency of the weak, the other to bring to perfection the goodness of the strong'.[10]

## Stage 2: Initial unease/stress, 1965–67±

Vatican II removed the false creation mythology that had given elitist identity to religious, by stating bluntly that *all* people are called to holiness, not just religious. Secondly, religious were reminded that, like the Church itself, they must adapt their lives to the pastoral needs of a rapidly changing world and find their identity primarily in their union with Christ.

Religious reacted to the second challenge with initial zest and euphoria. Customs and structures that belonged to a former era were quickly put aside. Many religious, while enjoying the changes, nonetheless began to feel ill at ease with the removal of the symbols that had given them a sense of order and predictability. Moreover, as the excitement of the changes died down, religious started to become aware that Vatican II had not substituted a new mythology, or reason to exist, for the one it had destroyed. If all people are called to holiness, then what reason is there for the religious to exist? Better to be a lay person in the world without the restrictions of religious life! Thus, the unease/stress began. A feeling of drifting emerged and has intensified ever since.. Religious, uncertain of their identity, withdrew in large numbers from their congregations and this added to the unease/stress of those who remained.[11]

## Stage 3: Political reaction, 1967–1970±

Religious sought to halt the sense of drifting without a clear identity by political action; that is, they attempted to define their identity through legislation at provincial and general chapters. They thought that structural changes and documents containing the vision of each congregation would somehow remove the feeling of malaise. It did not.

## Stage 4: Chaos, 1970–?

Religious have moved from confusion to chaos; there is the feeling of being benumbed, paralysed because, like the Israelites before them in the desert, there seems no way out of the crises that daily confront them, e.g. the failure to recruit new candidates, the closure of houses and apostolates, the lack of identity.

For some, the rituals of denial are popular escape routes from the chaos. The rituals take the form of feverish distracting activity in congregational meetings for the writing of yet more documents of identity; in some way or other, it is felt that the composing of new documents is the equivalent to a conversion to a new identity. Others are so disoriented that a sense of hopelessness about the future grips them. Others, however, are deeply concerned about the denial of reality within their religious congregations. They recognize the need for specially gifted people, that is, refounding persons, who can lead them into new creative relationships between the Gospel and the world around them. For these people the chaos is a positive experience.

## Stage 5: Prophetic reaction, 1972–?

In this stage religious do recognize the need for certain individuals to guide them out of the chaos. The following summarizes the various reactions of religious and, consequently, the types of leadership that they appreciate:

### Nativistic reaction

Leaders of the style of Archbishop Lefebvre emerge who claim that the unquestioning return to the symbols, myths and rituals of religious life before Vatican II will resolve the loss of meaning. Sect-like, these congregations withdraw from contact with the 'contaminating world'. Prayer is emphasized, but only the pre-Vatican II forms which stress personal/privatized holiness remote from the world's concerns.

## Conservative reaction

Leaders encourage the return to the pre-Vatican II traditions, but not withdrawal from the world. Souls are to be converted to the Lord, compassion shown to the poor, but the faith/justice apostolates are to be avoided as irrelevant and dangerous to one's vocation. New forms of prayer are allowed, e.g. as in the Charismatic movement, provided they do not lead to involvement in the social apostolate. Inculturation is considered a dangerous, 'leftist' insight.

## Millenarian reaction

(See Chapter 7, pp. 119ff.) All kinds of instant-success programmes are offered by leaders, e.g. encounter-group sessions, bodily relaxing techniques, immediate-union-with-God prayer sessions. Religious, unwilling to face the necessary faith/justice inner conversion, keep searching from one workshop to another for the 'right leader with the latest way to inner peace and firm sense of direction' for themselves personally.

## Neo-conservative reaction

Leaders, once avid supporters of change, but now frightened of the chaos and the extremes of attempted adaptation programmes, believe that only slow measured adaptation to the world will achieve new expressions of religious life. It is assumed that revitalization will be achieved by the *whole* community or congregation moving in response to agreed-to mission statements and strategic planning.

Creative religious, who believe that the chaos requires more radical linking between the Gospel and cultures than the whole group proposes, are marginalized, since they threaten the group's desired orderly approach to revitalization.

## Radical reactions

People attract other religious with a vision of radical, social-justice programmes; however, because they neglect the Christocentric faith in their vision, they conclude that religious life can never have a meaning. Others, truly prophets to their congregations, recognize that the only way out of the chaos is through radically new faith/justice programmes that link the Gospel message with the needs of the world today. They see that this demands within religious a deep union in Christ. They act accordingly and draw others with them.

It is too soon to say that leaders of this latter type are present in any significant way within religious congregations. Until they are present, there is little that can be said about how religious congregations will look in stage 6.

---

## *Culture revitalization model*

---

An historian of religion, Mircea Eliade, asserts that all traditional myths are cyclic: cultures regularly return to chaos as the preface to a rebirth.

Cultures, he says, have both sacred and profane times. Profane time refers to the daily round of eating, sleeping, doing business, giving birth, dying. In sacred times cultures ritually relive the times of their own origins; through ritual, a people returns to the times of chaos out of which its culture heroes originally created order, life. The escape into this sacred time connotes the return to immortality, the rescue from the world of meaninglessness.[12]

Modern nations, as well as tribal societies, may attempt to relive their primordial events and experience an escape into sacred time. It can be a dangerous journey. As Lance Morrow notes, 'Hitler's 1,000-year Reich, the tribe of furclad Übermenschen with Aryan fire in their eyes, lasted for twelve years. Hitler meant to inject his vulgar sacred time into profane time, but the sacred can never intrude for more than an instant. Any longer, and the results are monstrous.'[13] The following are three short case studies to further illustrate the insight.

## Case Study 1: The Exodus

In Egypt, the Jewish people suffer humiliations, political tyranny and material misery. Escaping from these oppressive conditions, the Israelites enter the desert under the leadership of Moses. This escape and this journey form their core religious experience, their creation story or myth; here they become a people under Yahweh. They experience both their own sinfulness and the forgiving presence of Yahweh.

Thus the Passover ritual becomes for them an annual revitalization experience, for the foundation of this ritual is the retelling of the Exodus event. In the ritual, they *revivify* their relationship with Yahweh and they are reminded that, for this relationship to be authentic, there must be a response to Yahweh in justice and love. The reliving is re-creative; it inspires the people to renewed action in the name of Yahweh, because they are again reassured of his protection.

## Case Study 2: The USA and the 1984 Olympic Games

The Games took place in Los Angeles after two decades of political turmoil and national and international humiliation in Vietnam, the chaos of the late 1960s, and Iran. The nation needed to express and reassure itself that at last a healing had taken place; once more values consensus existed. According to a writer in *Time*, the extravaganza of the opening and closing of the Games offered Americans the chance to relive ritually their founding mythology: 'The belief was reborn that Americans can do, well, anything'.[14]

## Case Study 3: Britain and the Falklands War

Without debating the rights and wrongs of this war, one thing is certain. The spirit of nationalism gripped the British people with a speed and tenacity, not seen since the Second World War.

Eliade's insight may well apply here. Britain had become 'great' in the past because it had learned to 'rule the waves' and establish history's largest empire through the help of the world's most powerful navy. However, since 1945, with its empire disbanded, it has been reduced to a second-rate power. The Falklands War offered the people the rare chance to return briefly to the sacred time of their creation out of chaos, when a giant navy made Britain *the* world power. The sight of the ships sailing south to do battle in the Falklands became a ritual of revitalization, giving the British a renewed sense of meaning and national pride.[15]

## Culture change as a journey model

Last year I boarded a plane full of people leaving San Francisco for Australia. Ignoring the passengers around me, I quickly settled into a good novel. Suddenly, the plane was hit by a severe storm. We were thrown about in the most frightening manner. Quite without any formal introductions, I and all around me started to speak to one another, quickly using first names. Faced with such a powerful force of nature, we all became conscious of our common fragile humanity.

This type of event is what anthropologist Victor Turner calls a *liminal* cultural experience.[16] Without liminal experiences, persons and cultures can lose their creativity; they become suffocated with the sheer weight of customs.

## Explanation of liminality

Life should be a process or journey (see Figure 4.2), whereby persons move regularly through two types of cultures: *societas* and *liminality* cultures. In the societas culture, we all know our statuses and roles in daily living; for example, everyone has a status of some kind: father, mother, doctor, nurse, teacher, and so forth. With each title there is an expected form of behaviour, or role, which gives us a much needed sense of security and predictability.

However, in the second culture, liminality, statuses and roles are totally unimportant. What is important is that we are *all* of the one category, e.g. human

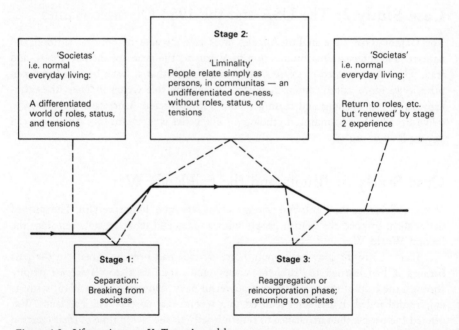

**Figure 4.2**  Life as a journey: V. Turner's model
(*Note*: Turner uses the term *liminality* for tribal societies, but *liminoid* for the post-industrial world. For the sake of simplicity, however, *liminality* is used of both types of society.)

74

persons or citizens of the same country, or brothers and sisters before the Lord. To experience values that are of critical importance in life, we enter from a world of statuses into a period of chaos or 'cultural nakedness'. The symbols that express this lack of social status/role differences are called *antistructure* symbols, e.g. the address at a religious ceremony—'sisters and brothers in the Lord'.

Liminality culture is of two kinds: spontaneous and normative or planned. When I boarded the plane in the above incident, I had clearly identifiable statuses and roles: that of a religious minister and an anthropologist. The moment the severe storm started, all the passengers became aware, out of a fear of death, of our oneness as human beings. At that moment, the culture of societas disappeared and an experience of spontaneous liminality took its place. The rich experience of common brotherhood/sisterhood is what is termed *communitas*.

A planned liminality culture, however, takes place when an event is so structured that it is expected people will experience a powerful common bond, provided they themselves are prepared not to obstruct the process. For example, religious services are structured to encourage the congregation to experience the communitas of their essential oneness as sinners begging forgiveness of the Lord. But, if participants are not open to conversion, there can be no authentic communitas.

We cannot remain permanently in liminality culture. Yet we need liminal experiences, for there we can be confronted with fundamental questions about, for example, the meaning of life, the purpose of society. Turner writes: 'Liminality here breaks, as it were, the cake of custom and enfranchises speculation'.[17] Ideally, every time we experience a liminality, we should be able to move out into societas with a richer insight into life and a commitment to give more of ourselves. My turbulent flight across the Pacific reinforced in me the belief that before God we are all equal; we desperately need his ongoing protection and his mercy.

There are always three stages in the liminality experience: the exit or separation from the world of 'ordinary living' (societas), the actual liminal experience itself, and the reaggregation into 'ordinary living' once more. Each stage may be short or long depending on the circumstances. As passengers of the plane, our exit from societas to liminality was frighteningly abrupt: namely, at the first unexpected attack of massive air turbulence.

# Case Study: The Filipino People Power Revolution

A writer in *The New York Times*, reflecting on the People Power Revolution of February 1986 in the Philippines, wrote: 'It was an historic wonder to see: shabby knaves who murdered and cheated their countrymen of the precious vote were swept aside by people who rose up in an act of self-determination inspired by the most basic human stuff—weeping, cheering, praying, singing and a sheer yearning for democracy'.[18] The impossible can happen through the power of people of all ages and statuses in society, if they believe that justice and dignity are their rights by birth.

However, the enthusiasm of those few days of revolution is being replaced by disillusionment about the slow pace of change. Corruption is returning. What went wrong with the revolution? The revolution was an experience of liminality in which the third stage, the reaggregation, has been poorly understood.

## Stage 1: Separation

This stage was extremely brief. In response to the call by Cardinal Sin, Archbishop of Manila, and fired by the Catholic Bishops' Conference's petition for a 'non-violent struggle for justice', thousands and thousands of unarmed people began on 22 February to mass outside the gates of the army camp to protect the rebelling troops.[19] The people's decision to go to the camp's gates, plus the actual leaving of their houses, constitutes the separation stage, that is, separation from the 'ordinary living' of societas (roles, oppression) (Figure 4.3).

## Stage 2: Liminality

The antistructure symbols are evident everywhere. People of all classes and statuses pray, talk and share food with complete strangers in a way that 'takes the form of a massive agape'.[20] There are also the symbols of the country's creation mythology (i.e. redemption through suffering and death), e.g. the crucifixes, the many pictures of the martyred hero, Ninoy Aquino. The people experience communitas when confronted with the real possibility of death.

## Stage 3: Reaggregation

Three years have passed since the liminality of the People Power Revolution. Some retain zeal for justice, some escape into a false spiritualism, others are disillusioned, and others return to corrupt ways. Overall, the reaggregation stage is failing.

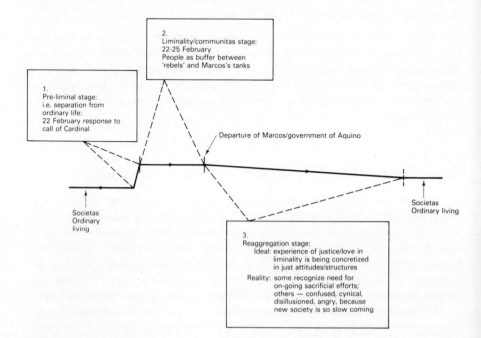

**Figure 4.3** The Philippines revolution: an initiation rite

*1. A cultural initiation rite*
A revolution, as occurred in the Philippines, should be an *initiation* rite for a nation's revitalized future.

As in all initiation rites, the third stage is the most lengthy and problematic. Mary Douglas, in her analysis of initiation rites, pinpoints the reason why this is so: 'It is consistent with the ideas about form and formlessness to treat initiands coming out of seclusion as though they were themselves charged with *power, hot, dangerous, requiring insulation and a time for cooling down*' [my italics].[21] Novices or initiands, as they leave the communitas of liminality, need time to discover how to integrate their experience of justice and love into a world of statuses, predictability and compromises. Since their communitas enthusiasm makes them 'hot and dangerous', they need guidance to be patient and committed. Otherwise, they can become cynical or disillusioned when confronted with obstacles to their zeal.

Following the revolution in the Philippines, however, the people were not trained for the necessary long and patient struggle together to give flesh to their revolutionary communitas experience of justice. It demands of millions of people an ongoing personal and communal conversion. Now, enthusiasm is turning to cynicism, despair, violence, and escape from the world into an unreal spirituality.

Jesus himself shows that it is not sufficient to have a liminal experience of conversion. That conversion must be carried over into real life, otherwise there is a dangerous vacuum in a person's life: '[The unclean spirit] says, "I will go back where I came from", and returns to find the dwelling unoccupied, though swept and tidied now. Off it goes again to bring back with it this time seven spirits more evil than itself. They move in and settle there. Thus the last state of that man becomes worse than the first' (Mt 12:43–45).

*2. Modification of creation mythology*
The People Power Revolution, however, did modify the mythology of violence and death: 'The yoke of oppression was thrown off by a single-minded use of non-violent means, a deliberate eschewing of the killing kind of violence as the last recourse to the establishment of justice'.[22] Having tasted justice through non-violence, they now know they can make it happen again.

# Reflection questions

## To the reader

1. What in this chapter do you find particularly helpful? When can you use the insight in your evangelizing work?

2. What model do you find particularly helpful in understanding better what has happened in the Roman Catholic Church since Vatican II? In the mainline Churches since 1965? Why?

# To a discussion group

1. Does the chapter give you any guidelines to help you if you are planning to introduce changes in your parish or in any particular organization?

2. In what ways should faith, hope and charity influence a leader who seeks to stimulate people to move out of cultural chaos?

# Suggested reading

Arbuckle, G. A., *Strategies for Growth in Religious Life* (New York: Alba House, 1987), pp. 3–22, 185–201.

Arbuckle, G. A., *Out of Chaos: Refounding Religious Congregations* (New York: Paulist/London: Geoffrey Chapman, 1988).

Barkun, M., *Disaster and the Millennium* (Syracuse, NY: Syracuse University Press, 1986), pp. 166–211.

Bellah, R. and A., *Habits of the Heart: Individualism and Commitment in American Life* (New York: Harper & Row, 1986), pp. 219–271.

Clecak, P., *America's Quest for the Ideal Self: Dissent and Fulfillment in the 60s and 70s* (New York: Oxford University Press, 1983).

Dickstein, M., *Gates of Eden: American Culture in the Sixties* (New York: Basic Books, 1977), pp. 248–277.

Felknor, L. (ed.), *The Crisis in Religious Vocations: An Inside View* (New York: Paulist, 1989).

Hornsby-Smith, M. P., *Roman Catholics in England: Studies in Social Structure since the Second World War* (Cambridge, UK: Cambridge University Press, 1988).

Turner, V. and E., *Image and Pilgrimage in Christian Culture: Anthropological Perspectives* (Oxford, UK: Basil Blackwell, 1978), pp. 1–39.

Vago, S., *Social Change* (New York: Holt, Rinehart & Winston, 1980), pp. 8–249.

# PART 2
## Inculturation: pastoral issues

# 5 The parish community: calling to inculturation

For where two or three meet in my name, I shall be there with them (Mt 18:20).

We are still dominated by the false view that the ministry of the Church is confined to bishops, priests and deacons. The whole pilgrim people of God share in ministry, and clergy and laity must be trained for this shared ministry (Anglican comment).[1]

## Introduction

Long before Vatican II, I asked my father what he thought our parish should be. He replied: 'Our parish should be a community in which we learn to relate to the Father, the Son and the Holy Spirit, in faith, hope and love, to one another and to the world in love and justice'. He was right. The parish should be a community in and through which we as individuals, families and groups discover how to live out, or inculturate, the Gospel message. The parish should aim to be a realization in miniature of the mystery of the wider communities: the local and universal Churches.

In this chapter we will:

- identify the different historical/theological ways in which the parish has been understood;
- explain the Gospel vision of what the parish should be;
- explain some of the difficulties that Christians experience today in trying to give flesh to this vision.

## The parish community: models

The parish is called a community. However, the word 'community' has different meanings, which have affected, over time, the ways in which we understand the nature and role of the parish. By clarifying the notion of community, we are better able to grasp the different historical/theological models of the parish.

*Firstly*, community can refer to a geographical place that has clearly marked administrative boundaries, e.g. a village, a city, a state.

*Secondly*, community can connote a set of social relationships to be found within a geographical place, e.g. citizens of this or that particular state. However, in this definition, nothing is said about the *quality* of the relationships, e.g. whether citizens relate positively or negatively to one another.

*Thirdly*, community is defined as a type of relationship giving people a sense of common identity, or a feeling of belonging together in some way or other. In this definition, there is no reference to locality because the sense of belonging together may exist between geographically dispersed individuals.

This approach to community, what can be called the 'we-sentiment', may be better termed *communion* to stress the sense of meaningful identity and shared experience. This non-territorial approach is increasingly popular, because advances in communication allow people to develop a sense of communion, even though they may live geographically great distances apart. The lack of physical presence to one another requires on the part of people, however, a very deliberate and sustained effort to develop and maintain a common sense of belonging and vision.

*Fourthly*, community can be defined as having both a territorial quality *and* a sense of common belonging.

Sociologist B.E. Mercer thus defines community as 'a functionally related aggregate of people who live in a particular, geographical locality at a particular time, share a common culture, are arranged in a social structure, and exhibit an awareness of their uniqueness and separate identity as a group'.[2]

These clarifications about the meaning of community help in defining the various models of the parish community.

---

## A. Traditional models

---

## 1. The administrative/territorial model

Prior to Vatican II, the Roman Catholic parish was commonly understood to be the primary, territorial unit of a wider, ecclesiastical organization, namely the diocese. The primary emphasis in this model is on community as locality.

## 2. Communal/rural territory model

Here, the parish boundaries are co-terminous with families who interact frequently, since they live and work in the same confined geographical area. Such a type characterized pre-industrial Western societies and may still be found within the same societies in some rural areas.

# 3. The 'service station' territory model

The parish community is an administrative unit covering a clearly defined geographical site, where, especially, urban-based individuals are able to satisfy their *personal* spiritual needs, e.g. baptismal, marriage and burial rites. Parishioners do not know one another. They have no wish to work with other parishioners to build the kingdom of love and justice in this world. Sociologist J. Fichter notes that the parishioners' communal 'social' bond with the priests and other parishioners is here 'analogous to that which an automobile owner has with the gas-station manager and with the latter's other customers'.[3]

# 4. The hierarchical/power structure model

According to this model, only the officially appointed or ordained members of a diocese or parish have ministerial power; parishioners must listen and obey without question if they are to achieve individual salvation. Theologian W. Burrows comments:

> The post-Reformation view—both Protestant and Catholic—of the church, as a community mainly concerned with individual salvation and the sacred, enshrines the official ministers in a privileged and central position. . . . The ordained minister is the primary vehicle (of Christ's salvific action), and the shape of the church is built around it.[4]

# 5. Ghetto–protective model

In the post-Reformation period, the parish, with its many diverse spiritual, educational and social services, was seen by Roman Catholics as a bulwark against what were thought to be the dangers of Protestantism. The Church was seen as the perfect, self-sufficient society with nothing to learn from other denominations and religions. So also the parish.

# 6. The ethnic–immigrant/personal model

The ethnic or immigrant parish, especially within the USA, aimed to provide an additional service for Catholic migrants: the sense of ethnic belonging in the midst of a vast, and strange, dominant culture. Ethnicity or one's language, not territory, defined the parish to which one belonged. The territorial parish, however, remained the ideal, the ethnic parish the temporary exception.[5]

---

## B. Vatican II parish community model

---

# 1. People of God/community of communities model

> The continuing validity of the parish depends upon regarding the Church as a community, and forming the local unit as a group with a fourfold purpose. It must be a community of worship, charity, apostolate, and witness.[6]

With Vatican II, the emphasis in defining the parish moves away from territory, or hierarchical/administrative structures, to people and the quality of relationships that should exist between them for the common good. This emphasis approximates in many ways to that articulated among some Protestant groups in the *early* post-Reformation period: a collaborative interaction between all ministers and people. In other words, in defining the notion of Church and parish, the third definition of community takes precedence: the sense of belonging and of working together, the sharing of different gifts by priests and laity, for a common cause.

This form of the parish may be termed 'the People of God' model. Let's look first at what is meant by 'the People of God'.

## a. The Church as the People of God

In choosing the phrase 'People of God' to describe the Church, the Council[7] was repeating a powerful, scriptural metaphor, which emphasizes the community dimension (understood as 'communion') of the Church rather than its institutional/hierarchical/geographical aspects. In the Church there are peoples of all nations, who have accepted faith in the crucified Christ, and they are one in the true People of God, the 'Israel according to the Spirit'. It is of this new People of God that we read:

> But you are a chosen race, a royal priesthood, a consecrated nation, a people set apart to sing the praises of God who called you out of the darkness into his wonderful light. Once you were not a people at all and now you are the People of God; once you were outside the mercy and now you have been given mercy (1 Pet 2:9f.)

As applied to the Church, the metaphor connotes:

- we are freely chosen and summoned by God in Christ;

- this requires of us a free response in faith;

- we are called to proclaim the mercy/salvation of the Lord to one another and to the whole world;

- all, priests and laity, are called to this task without distinction: 'There is a variety of gifts, but always the same Spirit; there are all sorts of service to be done, but always to the same Lord; working in all sorts of different ways in different people' (1 Cor 12:4–6);

- we are pilgrim people, detached from this world, yet committed to struggle ceaselessly within it to build the kingdom of love and justice, a sign of the 'new heavens and new earth, the place where righteousness will be at home' (2 Pet 3:13).

## b. The parish as the People of God

This restored appreciation of the Church as the People of God deeply affects the way in which the parish, one community within the local and universal Churches, should be defined. As the new Code of Canon Law puts it, the parish is to be a 'definite community of the Christian faithful which is established on a stable basis within a particular Church' (Can. 515). Instead of being a *geographical* locality, *where*, as was once emphasized, the parish becomes a *people* (pastors and other faithful) *who* together reflect on the Gospels/Church teaching and their implications for daily life;

experience community, that is, a oneness of heart and mind based on faith, hope and love in Christ;

show effective concern for one another through acts of charity and justice;

celebrate their unity and their dependence on the Lord through worship, especially in the Eucharist;

go out beyond themselves to proclaim the Gospel message of love and justice to a world that does not know Christ (see Figure 5.1).

No longer is 'territory' an integral requirement of parish. The overriding guideline in pastoral care and in the establishment of pastoral structures is to be: how people can best be aided to live out the Gospel life. Hence, while a parish normally will have clear geographical boundaries, when it is judged pastorally useful, as the new Code of Canon Law notes, 'personal parishes are to be established based upon rite, language, the nationality of the Christian faithful within some territory or even upon some other determining factor' (Can. 518).

# Mission, evangelization, ministry

## Mission

The *mission* of the Church, and therefore of every parish, is to continue the work of evangelization initiated by Christ. It is the struggle to build God's kingdom of justice and love in this world, a struggle that will reach its perfection, however, only in the fullness of the world to come.

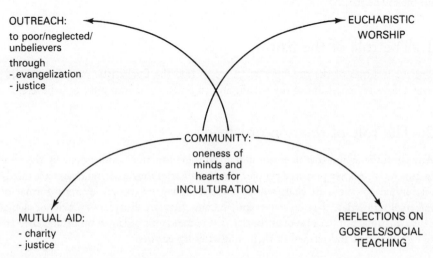

**Figure 5.1**  Qualities of the People of God parish community

# Evangelization and ministry

We evangelize through *ministry*. Ministry is any service presented in charity for the building up of God's kingdom, in the name of the Lord Jesus. So ministry, in this sense, is not restricted to ordained people, as the hierarchical/power structure model of Church and parish would have it.

Ministry, as we have defined it, is clearly evident in the early Church; the disciples find they have insufficient time for prayer and for the 'service of the world', because they are burdened with the task of distributing food to the poor (Acts 6:4). So others are encouraged to come forward for this ministry. The gathering of money for 'all the needs of the saints' is seen as a 'holy service' (2 Cor 9:12) or ministry. St Paul speaks of the ministries of healing, assisting and administering, which do not demand priestly ordination as a precondition (1 Cor 12:28). Provided the action is done for building the Church and in the name of the Lord Jesus, it is a ministry (Mk 8:35; 10:29).

One can distinguish, therefore, two broad categories of ministries: formal and informal:

> The *formal* are those ministries officially established by the universal Church or the local church, e.g. ordained priesthood and diaconate, Eucharistic ministers. All kinds of ministries can be formally approved of, if the particular authorities consider them to be especially significant for the building up of the Church. For example, a local Church might consider it important to introduce formally the ministry of the catechist, in order to highlight the critical role of catechetical instruction for the growth of the Church. Pope Paul VI uses ministry in this sense when he writes: 'It is certain that, side-by-side with the ordained ministries . . . the Church recognizes the place of non-ordained ministries which are able to offer a particular service to the Church'.[8]

> The *informal* ministries are all those apostolic actions that are directed to the building of Christ's kingdom within the Church and world, e.g. instructing people in the Good News, action for justice, parenthood. This is ministry in the broad sense that is often referred to in the New Testament.

The following summarizes some of the important consequences of the People of God model of the parish:

## 1. The role of the pastor

The main duties of the ordained priest are to lead the Eucharistic prayer, to preside over the sacramental life of the parish, and to unify the community of believers.

## 2. The role of the non-ordained

Any apostolic action that does not pertain to these functions can be done by the non-ordained, adequately prepared people. These ministries they undertake can be formally established by those in charge of a diocese. When lay people exercise formal or informal ministries, they do so *primarily* because they are disciples of Christ or agents of his mission, not because of authority that comes from ordained ministers; they are to be supported and unified in their ministries by pastors.

## 3. Collaborative action

Because a parish is a community of the baptized with different gifts, but with a common goal of evangelization, parishioners have the right to be involved in decision-making in all matters that do not relate to the strictly sacramental, e.g. liturgical and financial planning.

## 4. Formation for collaborative action

Efforts at power-sharing and collaborative action with the laity, on the part of ordained parish ministers, are insufficient, if they are not preceded and accompanied by a theological educational process and appropriate attitudinal changes.

---

*Example*:
Joe is a pastor. He has been running a parish discussion group about the need for a People of God parish model. At first it was very well attended by enthusiastic parishioners, but then very quickly the numbers dropped off. It became evident that Joe was intellectually converted to the model, but attitudinally he was not prepared to change. The parishioners felt this and so lost interest.

---

## 5. The particular ministry of the laity

The aspect of ministerial service that is unique to the lay state is that of being the Church-in-the-world, that is, inculturating the faith in the marketplace.[9]

# Building the People of God: parish communities

Overall, the shift from pre-Vatican II models of parish to the People of God parish model, while not without its tensions, has been generally positive. Within the USA, for example, it is said that 'if a major purpose of Vatican II was to reinstate the sense that all Christians . . . are responsible for corporate life in the local parish, then Vatican II is succeeding'.[10] Various agencies or movements are promoting the People of God parish model; even though a priest or a religious may act as an initial catalyst in their formation, many nevertheless remain fundamentally lay movements. We now look at some of these movements.

# 1. Basic Christian Communities

Basic Christian Communities (BCCs)—which sometimes are also called 'Basic Ecclesial Communities', 'House Churches', 'Intentional Christian Communities', 'Grassroot Churches', 'Churches from Below'—started to evolve in the late 1950s in Brazil, quickly spreading to other parts of South and Central America, the Philippines and, to a much lesser degree, parts of the First World. In Brazil, it is estimated that these communities number about 150,000.

A BCC is a group of individuals or families that know, care for and share with one another, worship together and seek to centre their life, relationships and activities on Christ. Their radical newness within the Church is stressed by Leonardo Boff. He claims that 'theologically they represent a new, ecclesiological experience, a renaissance of the very church itself, and hence an action of the Spirit on the horizon of the matters urgent for our time'.[11] They have evolved for the following reasons:

---

a. a growing awareness of the inadequacies of the traditional hierarchical/power parish model, as the number of priests decline; without priests, there can be no worship;

b. the discovery that the Gospel calls people to worship together, even when priests are not available;

c. the growing awareness by the people at the grassroots that they are economically, politically and culturally oppressed, and that together they can do something about it;

d. the recognition that small-scale, natural communities, e.g. based on family ties, geographical proximity, already exist and they can be used as foundations for inculturation: Gospel reflection, worship, mutual service and action for social justice.

---

It is possible to see three stages in the development of most BCCs as People of God movements:

- people meet to reflect on the Gospels and to pray;

- communities of mutual aid emerge, as people discover the Gospel imperative of charity;

- social/economic/political movements develop as people discover, on the one hand, their Gospel-based social-justice rights, and on the other, that they have the power within themselves, if united, to seek/demand structural changes for justice.

The initiative to begin BCCs often comes from bishops, priests or religious. However, once these lay-centred communities become self-moving, they inevitably,

|  | Traditional parish (hierarchical/power model) | BCC |
|---|---|---|
| 1. Structure: | hierarchical<br>strong | democratic<br>weak |
| 2. Doctrine: | very important<br>tradition-based | not important<br>Gospel-based |
| 3. Conducted by: | clerics | laity: male and female |
| 4. Social origins: | middle and upper classes:<br>supporters of social/economic/<br>political *status quo* | the poor becoming aware of rights<br>and obligations |
| 5. Sacraments: | instruments of individual salvation | signs of Gospel love/social justice |
| 6. Religious values: | stress individual piety | stress common action |
| 7. Centre of Church: | Rome | the poor |

**Table 5.1** Models of the parish in tension

especially at stage three above, begin to criticize traditional, ecclesiastical structures according to Gospel values. Hence, 'this "new birth" of the Church generally involves the bishop and priest in an identity crisis: the master becomes the disciple of his own disciples'.[12] Table 5.1 summarizes why tensions between BCCs and traditional parish structures are inevitable.

In the First World, BCCs have been slow to emerge; conditions that fostered the emergence of BCCs in the Third World are rarely present in the First World because:

- people have yet to become aware of the fact that the number of priests available to lead worship is declining rapidly: the number of priests in the USA will drop from the current 53,000 to fewer than 20,000 by the year 2007.[13] The projections for several large dioceses in Australia show that, by the mid-1990s, the number of active diocesan clergy in parishes will be a third to a half fewer than in 1976;[14]

- unlike the Third World, the mass of population is concentrated in the cities where natural, small-scale communities rarely exist;

- people who experience poverty may turn to existing agencies—e.g. trade unions, existing political parties—in order to achieve justice;

- cultures, e.g. as in the USA, that emphasize individualism rather than mutuality are not conducive to the emergence of vigorous community life based on sharing and service, a point well made by Robert Bellah and his associates in *Habits of the Heart*.[15] People may prefer to foster loosely binding support groups, which allow them to withdraw easily from co-operative ventures that interfere with their freedom.

Where BCCs *have* emerged in the First World, they tend to have the following qualities:

members feel the loneliness of urban living and the consequent need for community support;

dissatisfaction with the lack of quality liturgical/prayer/Gospel-theological educational services provided by the traditional parish structures;[16]

often the communities are pushed to the margins of existing parish life, because they are considered theologically and pastorally threatening by pastors and/or other parishioners;

at times, communities may be criticized for being elitist, i.e. for claiming that they alone have the 'right way to salvation';

in some instances, e.g. among poor Hispanics in the USA and the disadvantaged in southern Italy, there is an awareness that Gospel justice can and must be achieved through community action;

they are vigorously non-clerical; the equality of sexes is stressed;

at times they are openly ecumenical.

## 2. The Neo-Catechumenate communities

These communities, initiated in Spain in the late 1960s, are established as ways through which individuals and families are able to rediscover the power and obligations of their baptismal vows. The founder, Kiko Argüello, developed a theological–catechetical synthesis to help people rediscover the liberating qualities of their baptism. Consequently, hundreds of Neo-Catechumenate communities, possessing many of the qualities of BCCs, have developed around the world; many have been established in large city parishes in need of revitalization.[17]

## 3. Revitalization through credit union

In the mid-1970s in a parish within a particularly economically depressed part of the USA, 15–20 per cent of the male population had been without permanent employment, sometimes for ten years. Morale was intensely low. The employed feared loss of work; the unemployed felt unwanted by society, their sense of self-respect destroyed by having to be dependent on government handouts, on short periods of temporary employment and/or on the wage cheques of their wives. The parish itself was liturgically and apostolically lifeless.

When a new pastor was appointed, he spent several months just visiting and listening to people. He then called a public meeting and explained what credit union is, its philosophy and how it could be formed. No one responded. They were suspicious of yet another project initiated by 'another do-good pastor that would be bound to fail like every other one in the past'. The pastor waited. One day three men decided to look more closely at his proposal. They discovered that a credit union is a group of people, united by a common bond, who save their money together and make loans to each other for provident and productive purposes at low interest rates. It is run by members exclusively for the benefit of members. The three men recognized that, if the parish was to develop a union, members had to:

- reflect regularly on the Gospels to discover what true faith co-operation means;

- educate themselves about the philosophy and rules of credit unions.

Over a period of time, a parish credit union developed and, through it, the parish changed from a traditional model of dependency on the priest alone to a People of God community. These are some comments from members of the credit union:

- Our credit union is like Jesus Christ. It teaches me how to be compassionate. The more I save, the more I can help other people in need because credit union makes loans to them. They and I no longer are deformed through handouts. We can act for ourselves.

- The biggest gift of the credit union to me is the return of my dignity. I obtain loans on the basis of my character. No one had ever trusted me before this.

The morale of the parishioners rose rapidly; people learnt, through their own efforts, what Gospel communion and ministry means. The pastor, however, acted as a sensitive catalyst in the change process only because he knew, and believed in, the People of God model. He held back at the right time to allow people to emerge and minister to one another; he recognized that the credit union belonged to the people and not to himself.

## 4. RENEW: A programme for parish renewal

A parish-based spiritual renewal process was initiated in the Archdiocese of Newark, in the USA, in 1978; subsequently, this process has been adopted by many dioceses around the world. RENEW has three goals:

- to foster witness to the Gospel message;

- to form vibrant faith communities by calling parishioners to conversion;

- to promote shared responsibility for action towards social justice.

In brief, RENEW aims to develop parishes according to the People of God model described above. Effectiveness of the process depends, among other things, on the acceptance of two key assumptions: integral conversion (i.e. personal and apostolic) is a gradual process and, to help facilitate this conversion, there must first be a thorough leadership preparation within parishes. Leadership training usually lasts about a year before an entire parish is invited to become part of the two-and-half-year renewal process. At the heart of the RENEW process are small faith-sharing groups of ten to twelve people, who meet weekly to reflect on the Word of God, and on how to apply it in their lives and the world around them.

*Example*:
The New Zealand Catholic Bishops' Conference adopted RENEW in 1983. The faith-sharing groups became equivalently BCCs because:

a. people experienced a new way of being Church through a life of shared faith, vibrant love and firm hope;

b. people began to experience in a new way the person of Jesus, as discovered in the Scriptures;

c. women and men discovered qualities of leadership that allowed them to minister in ways they had previously not thought possible, or theologically correct;

d. people found, often for the first time, how to share their faith on an ecumenical level.[18]

# 5. Ecumenical ventures

*Examples*:
*Jesus Fraternity*
This community of Catholics, Lutherans and other Christian denominations was formed in Germany in 1969. Members are single or married and live according to the spirit and practice of the three traditional vows. There is a strong emphasis on prayer and missionary activity that aims to provide retreat centres to help outsiders discover how to pray.

*The Chemin Neuf Community*
Founded in France in 1973, the community aims to show that evangelization involves integrating professional, social and prayer life. The community is ecumenical, and contains single or married persons; strong emphasis is placed on prayer in common, regular spiritual guidance and biblical studies.[19]

# Tensions in revitalization

It is said that the American Catholic parish 'is no longer a haven from the secular world and Protestant bigotry. It is a vehicle for both experiencing the faith, and for motivating Catholics to relate to the broader community and to shape it according to Gospel values.'[20] In other words, according to this optimistic view, there has been, since Vatican II, a highly successful shift in attitudes and structures from the hierarchical/power model of the parish to the People of God model. To what extent this is true of this or that parish in any particlar country of the First World can only be answered by the parishioners themselves.

However, it is certain that the attitudinal and structural revolution in parish life continues to cause all kinds of tensions, some of which are listed below.

## Co-responsibility in decision-making: difficulties

## 1. Theological/pastoral pluralism

In a survey of theological orientations among Roman Catholic priests and religious in New Zealand, it was found that overall only 43.7 per cent felt quite at ease with the post-Vatican II theology of inculturation. Inevitably, therefore, this lack of consensus on inculturation makes it impossible to achieve an overall, consistent, pastoral approach to evangelization in dioceses. A pastor who strongly supports inculturation, and thus the People of God parish model, may have, as his successor, a pastor who rejects or merely tolerates such an approach.[21] The New Zealand pattern is also commonly found in other parts of the world.

As regards power-sharing, there can be considerable tension between pastor and people because expectations, or perceptions of what is happening, can differ widely. In New Zealand, for example, 40 per cent of pastors were very reluctant to share any significant power with their parish councils. In the USA, almost all pastors in a 36-parish sample believed that their parish council did planning, but one-third of their staff, and approximately half of the volunteer leaders, claimed that council planning was in fact not being done.[22]

This theological pluralism and hesitancy to share power on the part of pastors helps us to understand why small groups that deliberately bypass traditional parish structures emerge: people become weary of trying to change the theological and structural *status quo*.

## 2. Discrimination against women

Despite their competence and high involvement in parish affairs, women are excluded at top levels of decision-making within the Roman Catholic Church. The issue of clericalism and male dominance (or sometimes outright oppression) in Church affairs is only now beginning to be addressed in the USA. The first draft of the Bishops' pastoral letter on women in the Church states: 'We intend . . . to ensure that women are empowered to take part in positions of authority and leadership in church life in a wide range of situations and ministries'.[23] The same resolve is yet to be found in most other First World Churches. The ordination of women in some sections of the Anglican Communion is helping to challenge the Roman Catholic Church to research more deeply some of its assumptions about priesthood. There is growing dissatisfaction with the arguments traditionally advanced against the ordination of women.[24]

## 3. Elitism and parish involvement

There are complaints that some forms of BCCs are claiming to be 'the way' to salvation, and that people who are not members are made to feel they are second-class parishioners. This elitism is disruptive and makes overall planning for unity impossible.[25]

---

*Outreach: inculturation problems*

---

## 1. Efforts to impose/resist inculturation

Inculturation takes place in and through community decision-making and action. It cannot be something pre-packaged and then imposed on people from above, either by pastors or by parish committees. Liturgical changes have at times been imposed on people without adequate catechesis or consultation. However, there are also examples of pastors, in particular, who have refused to call parishioners to inculturation, e.g. by denying people a chance to deepen their participation in liturgies, by preaching in ways that ignore the call to be involved in social justice.

## 2. Middle-class 'take-over'/alienation of the poor

Sociologist Antony Archer argues that within the English Roman Catholic Church, the reforms of Vatican II favoured the middle class.[26] For over a century, the Church had provided for countless poor migrants (especially from Ireland) and working-class people a style of folk or devotional Catholicism that satisfied not only religious needs, but also the human need to belong within a country dominated by the powerful and wealthy. Vatican II reforms were interpreted and introduced by middle-class people according to their needs. Hence, *in* came a highly rational liturgy, *out* went devotional Catholicism. Out went, for working-class people, one important reason to feel that they were still understood by, and wanted in, the Church. I believe a similar pattern is to be found in other First World Churches.[27]

---

*Example*:
The Church of England acknowledges the danger of being over-identified with the middle class: 'a clergy drawn mainly from one section (in the case of

England, the middle class) is likely to have serious difficulties in communicating with members of other social groups'.[28]

# 3. Privatization of spirituality

It is claimed that 'on the one hand, the American Catholic laity appear more active in their parishes than the laity of any other country in the world, but that on the other hand, this religious energy appears more disconnected from public life than in any other nation in the world'.[29] American Catholics, according to this criticism, are not inculturating their faith; they have capitulated to the secular values within their national culture, values of self-centred individualism and privatism in morality.

Some claim that the Charismatic movement has overemphasized a personal, vertical relationship to God, to the neglect of action in favour of justice in this world.[30]

# 4. Neglect of minority cultures and the culturally deprived

'It is my conviction, and that of many others, that the Catholic Church, now a middle-class institution, has not yet discovered an effective method of ministering to the poor. Difference of social class, much more than difference of culture, is the fundamental problem.'[31]

The People of God parish model demands that parishioners respond to the cultural diversity and needs of peoples—within the parish boundaries—different from themselves. Most First World Churches and parishes have only hesitatingly, if at all, begun to recognize the need to relate the Gospel to a multicultural or migrant world.

*Examples*:
In the Church of England it is claimed that 'members of minority, ethnic groups . . . feel . . . ignored and relegated to the peripheries of church life. Many black Christians . . . have felt "frozen out" of the Church . . . by patrician attitudes.'[32]

It is asserted that 'the Australian Church has failed to enlist the participation of a large proportion of the Catholic migrants who have arrived in the last 35 years'.[33]

Diverse ethnic groups have been expected to fit into existing parishes, with little or no recognition of their diverse cultural or liturgical needs.[34]

In New Zealand, Roman Catholic and Protestant parishes have been extremely slow to recognize the cultural needs/rights of the indigenous minority, the Maori. In a national survey of Catholic Maori pastoral needs, it was found that a very small percentage—possibly as low as 1–2 per cent overall—would attend Sunday Mass regularly, compared with approximately 30–40 per cent of members of the dominant, white, Catholic majority. And of this percentage, only a fraction of Catholic Maoris would attend Sunday liturgy in parish churches, where the vast majority of parishioners are of non-Maori descent.

Here are some of the reasons given by the Maori for this refusal to attend:

'European liturgies are "too cold", that is, without colour and movement.'

'I used to go to the parish church . . . but I just could not keep at it. I would enter the church, walk up the aisle, but I would feel that everybody was looking at me. I would look down to see if my dress was right. It just looked and felt so poor. Then my hair felt bad. It was no good. I just cannot stop worrying during Mass about my dress and hair. How can I pray when I have such funny feelings!'

'At the parish church on Sunday, there is no Mass in the Maori language. We have to have the Maori Mass to relate to. We need our identity, our Maoriness to keep us alive. The Maori Mass means a lot to us. Even if you do not understand the language, somehow it gives you a feeling of belonging. It makes you feel good, gives the feeling of being accepted by others and by God.'[35]

In the United States: 'Ten years ago, we were saying comfortably that 85 per cent of the Hispanics . . . were Catholics. Today, we can at best say that 75 per cent of them are Catholics. The Hispanic is not leaving the Catholic Church freely; he/she is still being chased out by pastors and parishes who do not want them around . . . . In many instances, the US Catholic Church is still insisting more on conversion from the Hispanic culture into the US Anglo-Saxon-Protestant-based culture than on conversion to Christ within the Hispanic culture itself.'[36]

---

## 5. Poverty of liturgical/theological/spirituality services

Authentic liturgical reforms or adaptations require sensitivity to theology and to the cultural anthropology of ritual. In the enthusiasm to adopt liturgical changes, pastors and liturgical committees have not always had this sensitivity. Hence, in the USA, it has been found that 'important elements of the Mass structure are sometimes omitted or distorted . . . . Often . . . liturgy results in poor or inappropriate selection of prayers, readings, and, especially, music.'[37] In many parts of the world there is a lack of well-prepared courses in theology and associated disciplines for adults. The process of inculturation will remain hesitant as long as these facilities remain undeveloped.

# Reflection questions

## To the reader

1. Why is the People of God model to be fostered in parishes today?

2. What gifts of ministry do you have? Are you using these gifts in the service of others?

3. Are women being oppressed by structures and attitudes existing in your parish? If so, what can you do to help remove this oppression?

## To a discussion group

1. Of the models explained above, which one best describes your parish?

2. Can you find any texts in the New Testament that you could use to explain to others what is meant by the People of God parish model?

3. As a discussion group, how would you go about becoming a Basic Christian Community within your parish?


# Suggested reading

Boff, L., *Ecclesiogenesis: The Base Communities Reinvent the Church* (Maryknoll, NY: Orbis, 1986).

Brennan, P.J., *The Evangelizing Parish: Theologies and Strategies for Renewal* (Allen, TX: Tabor, 1987).

Clarebaut, D.C., *Urban Ministry* (Grand Rapids, MI: Zondervan, 1983).

Gremillion, J., and Castelli, J., *The Emerging Parish: The Notre Dame Study of Catholic Life since Vatican II* (San Francisco: Harper & Row, 1987).

Lee, B.J., and Cowan, M.A., *Dangerous Memories: House Churches and our American Story* (Kansas City, KS: Sheed & Ward, 1986).

Lovell, G., and Widdicombe, C., *Churches and Communities: An Approach to Development in the Local Church* (London: Search Press, 1978).

Macquarrie, J., *Theology, Church and Ministry* (London: SCM Press, 1986).

Power, D.N., *Gifts that Differ: Lay Ministries Established and Unestablished* (New York: Pueblo, 1985).

Rademacher, W.J., *The Practical Guide for Parish Councils* (Mystic, CT: Twenty-Third Publications, 1979).

Sofield, L., and Hermann, B., *Developing the Parish as a Community of Service* (Boston: Jesuit Educational Center for Human Development, 1984).

Tiller, J., *A Strategy for the Church's Ministry* (London: CIO, 1983).

# 6 Inculturation and ritual

The unexpected tires us: it also takes us longer to understand and enjoy than the expected (C. S. Lewis).[1]

Worship . . . must emerge out of and reflect local cultures (Report of the Archbishop of Canterbury's Commission on Urban Priority Areas).[2]

## Introduction

In general, ritual is poorly understood. When I asked a group of clerics how to define ritual, the majority said that it was synonymous with rules about how to celebrate the sacraments. Some thought it was the equivalent of formality or something superficial, empty, phoney, meaningless, unnecessarily repetitive, a boring ceremony to be suffered through from time to time.

Paradoxically, however, ritual is among the most basic, frequent, and important of human actions. In fact, without ritual, we cannot remain human. We would be totally unable to communicate with one another. Recall my brief definition of ritual in Chapter 2: through ritual action, we attempt to give flesh to the values and goals expressed in myths. And myths, remember, are stories or traditions that claim to enshrine fundamental truths about the world and human life. If we do not grasp what ritual means and how it is to be used, we may well obstruct or hinder our efforts to communicate the liberating truths of the good news. In this chapter, therefore, we must:

- clarify the meaning and types of rituals;

- use these clarifications to understand better the pastoral role of worship/sacraments;

- understand the cultural aspects of the rituals of popular religiosity.

## Defining ritual

Ritual is the stylized or repetitive symbolic use of bodily movement and gesture within a social context, to express and articulate meaning.[3] Ritual action occurs within a *social context*, where there is possible or real tension/conflict in social relations, and efforts are undertaken to *resolve* or *hide* it. For example, according to Western custom, when people resolve, or hide, a tension/conflict between them, they shake hands; it is a gesture of set form (stylized) that outwardly at least conveys the meaning that peace has been restored.

Let's look at this crucial dimension of tension/conflict more closely:

- Daily life is filled with ambiguity; it has its inevitable tensions, potential or actual conflicts, no matter how perfect a situation may initially appear. For example, I have a very close friend, but there is always the fear that some unforeseen event will threaten to break the friendship. So I feel the need to express in action—to reaffirm—my solidarity with him from time to time in some way or other, such as in offering a gift or writing a letter to mark a birthday. The ritual strengthens my friendship, but the possibility of tension/conflict will always remain; hence, ritual must be regularly repeated if its primary goal is to be realized.

- Not surprisingly, therefore, all cultures have rituals surrounding the dramatic, even fear-creating, experiences of birth, marriage and death. On these occasions, not just individuals are involved, but whole social groups are affected, so tension/conflict must be resolved or hidden to avoid disruption of social relationships.

- Similarly, my relationship with God is always fragile. Through sin, I could lose my friendship with him, so I pray to him, expressing my oneness with him in Christ and my desire to be always united with him. Others have the same fear, so we join together in a common act of worship or ritual.

Ritual, therefore, aims to express solidarity or oneness despite tensions in relationships. Hence, in ritual the aim is to express unity while, at the same time, being aware that the tensions of daily life always threaten that unity. W. H. Auden articulates the emphasis on oneness in ritual in this way:

> Only in rites
> can we renounce our oddities
> and be truly entired.[4]

# Qualities of ritual

## 1. Ritual as a dynamic tripartite process

Ritual is a dynamic process, the movement from one state or role to another, e.g. from child to adult, outsider to insider, single to married, conflict to reconciliation, sin to grace, death to life, uncertain to certain identity, profane to sacred. As is explained in Chapter 4, anthropologist Victor Turner focuses attention on the *tripartite* psychosocial phases commonly found in this dynamic process, namely, the separation, liminal and reaggregation stages.

We saw that there are two types of liminality: spontaneous and normative. For example, survivors from a sinking ship experience spontaneous liminality; status diversity is totally unimportant to these people as they face the very real possibility of death together, and this experience gives rise to a fellowship or communitas. Normative liminality exists when people deliberately attempt to establish a liminal situation that ideally should lead to a communitas experience. The sacraments are examples of normative liminality; they remind us that before God, no matter what our social status may be, we are all sinners in need of redemption.

## 2. 'Antistructural' symbols of liminality

The liminal stage is marked by the type of symbols used, and the formative role of mythology.

- The symbols of liminality are 'antistructural', that is, they connote a status for the participants that is unhierarchical and undifferentiated when compared with normal life. The survivors in the lifeboat instinctively recognize the irrelevancy of titles when faced with possible death—the universal, liminal leveller.

- In the liminal stage, participants are reduced symbolically to the state of *chaos*. For example, trainees for an elite Marine corps may be forced to live in what is for them spartan, chaotic conditions, stripped of all symbols of individuality, e.g. any variety in hair styles. Part of the aim of stripping away the familiar is to render participants more open to the influence of creative forces, as represented by creation or regeneration myths, which have little chance consciously to affect people in the ordinary, structured and busy routine of daily life.

- Often, the root metaphor in the mythology is death/resurrection. If participants interiorize, or are converted to, the mythology, they feel the urge, when they pass out of liminality, to *re-create* the world according to their experience of the mythology. The *status quo*, in which key societal values are compromised, will no longer be tolerated.

*Examples*:
If in the Ignatian Spiritual Exercises, the retreatant is to be open to inner conversion and to a creative apostolic response to this *re*-turning to the Lord, then the mystery or mythology of Christ's life, death and resurrection must be *re*-lived. The retreatant must become one with Christ in a communitas experience. The external silence, the complete withdrawal from ordinary duties and the demanding regime of meditations, are antistructural symbols established to evoke liminality and communitas with the Lord by an uninterrupted journey through the paschal mystery.

The North American Presidential nominating conventions are normative, liminal, ritual experiences. Each party platform claims to represent the only authentic interpreters and agents of the nation's creation mythology. The extraordinary hoop-la—the balloons, music, the hats, banners—are all antistructure symbols aiming to evoke liminality/communitas, hiding for the moment sectional differences.

## 3. From liminality to reaggregation

The liminal state is inherently unstable; people cannot live with chaos—that is, without the clarity of roles and statuses of daily life—for too long. They cannot maintain a state of being continuously 'inspired' through a communitas experience. Hence, the third stage of ritual is the reaggregation (post-liminal) process, whereby people move back into ordinary life and predictable structures. It can happen, though, that people become locked in the liminal stage, unable to return to ordinary living.

For example, the grief process, in all of its forms, is a ritual. Once an individual has heard of a significant personal loss, the separation stage begins, his or her world of meaning is affected; there is a feeling of chaos and so the symptoms of grief begin: anger, lack of interest in one's appearance and in what is happening to others. Slowly, the person in the stage of liminality becomes able to reflect on life and its purpose in the light of secular or religious mythology; he or she begins to look outward, as influenced by the mythology of death/resurrection, and gradually passes into the reaggregation stage.

If, however, people refuse or are unable to separate themselves from the deceased, they fall victim to chronic introversion, depression or despair, and they become dangerous to themselves and a cause of deep concern to others. If the ritual process is to be effective, people must pass through *all* three phases.

## 4. Varying lengths of the stages

The three stages of the ritual process are not all of the same length; in fact, their length will differ according to the type of ritual being experienced.

Thus, as we saw in Chapter 4, even though the liminal stage is critically important in initiation rites—e.g. a religious novitiate, baptism/confirmation/Eucharist—the reaggregation stage should be as long as, if not longer than, the liminal phase. For example, the newly baptized adult needs a period of adjusting to the world 'out there', lest his or her initial enthusiasm for the Lord's message be suffocated through contact with an unwelcoming and imperfect world.

Marriage is a *rite of passage* whereby an unrelated man and woman leave their families of origin and begin their own family of procreation. One major reason why marriages in the Western world are so often in crisis within a relatively short period after the marriage ceremony is that the ritual of marriage is inadequately understood. The following explains why this is so:

- In Western cultures, the ideology of romantic love is dominant: a woman and a man meet, fall in love, become engaged and rather quickly marry. The engagement is generally rushed. It is a euphoric time for the couple in which they busily plan financing for a house and prepare for the wedding ceremony (which is thought to be the only ritual required). Marriage is essentially a legal contract between two people, formally entered into at the ceremony. Following the ceremony, nothing more than romantic love is popularly thought to be necessary for the marriage to be successful.

  The liminal stage is the honeymoon—a very short period in which the couple is expected to experience such 'intense bliss' that no future tension or trial can ever destroy it! Little or no emphasis is given to the reaggregation stage; once the short ceremony is over, the couple are expected to survive on their own internal psychological, spiritual and financial resources. The duties of the families of the couple are *extremely* limited, e.g. the parents of the bride are generally expected to finance the wedding celebrations.

- In tribal societies in general, however, the marriage is not one brief legal act, but a lengthy process. Marriage is generally seen as an alliance between the kin groups of both parties in which the couple concerned is merely the most obvious link. In arranged marriages, for example among Muslims and Hindus, the union is organized by parents and relatives. It is primarily a relationship between families rather than between individuals. This does not deny the possibility of love. Young people marry and then fall in love.

  In these marriages, the ritual is not confined to a single act, but is a process spread over many months, even years. The liminality stage is lengthy, for here parents, relatives and the couple take time to 'become used to the idea' of the family alliance. At various stages in the process, gifts are given or exchanged; these symbolize to all concerned that the process is taking place satisfactorily. At some point in the process, the marriage is considered finalized, e.g. it might be symbolized by the birth of the first child. When the couple finally live together, there are rites of incorporation in which the wife in particular is taught how to be part of the extended family of the husband.

  The tribal marriage is not the ideal marriage type. However, it does illustrate how critically important are the three stages of ritual in the development of all human relations. When Western marriages ignore this process and overemphasize romantic love and marriage as a single legal act, it is inevitable that so many marriages rapidly fall into crisis. The actual engagement should formally mark the ritual beginning of the separation of the couple from their families of origin.

  The engagement period should be the liminal stage, not the honeymoon. During the engagement period, the couple should not only have the time to get to know one another well; they must also undergo instruction with the help of the wider community on the theory, and the practical details, of building a family and of living together (e.g. marriage as a sacrament, the psychology of intimacy, how to budget). After the actual marriage ceremony, the reaggregation stage begins. Here the couple must learn to adjust to one another as spouses–parents, and to society as a whole. They cannot do this alone and the community again must be involved in providing, over months or even years, acceptable guides/confidants.

# 5. Ritual and non-verbal symbols

Ritual is fundamentally traditional, i.e. it emerges out of the familiar world in response to our needs for security, identity and belonging, summed up in the word *meaning*. It is rooted in our experience; otherwise, it cannot touch our needs.

At the same time, rituals in response to people's need for meaning go beyond the frontiers of the visible or rational. Mere rationality, as articulated in words, is inadequate to express the whole range of human needs and, especially, the creative experiences that occur in liminality. Symbols (and thus rituals) that speak primarily to the heart or the imagination are expressed less by words than by predictable or stylized actions, stillness, silences and pauses.

---

*Examples*:
As my father lay dying, words became utterly inadequate and empty. I and other members of my family spontaneously used traditional, ritual gestures of *touch* and *silence* to express our grief and our union with him. We held his hands in silence, our hearts pushed to the very frontiers of existence where ultimate meanings of life and death are to be found in Christ's death and resurrection. The liminality of those minutes gripped us.

Every time I visit the Vietnam War Veterans' Memorial, Washington, DC, I cease to be just an onlooker. The atmosphere impels me to become a pilgrim. Surely, many of the 15 million people who have descended the gently sloping path to the V-shaped granite wall have been similarly transformed. Individuals fall on their knees on seeing the names of deceased friends or relatives on the black granite; others stand in silence, with heads bowed. Some reverently place mementos at the base of the wall—boots, a glass of whiskey, photos. Some just rub their fingers over the names of the deceased. These are cultural, ritual gestures that express what words cannot achieve.

---

People who are insensitive to the lessons of experiences of this kind assume that words alone can be used to articulate ritual. When the ritual appears not to grip people, they add yet more words, more and more explanations of the ritual, so that, as one complaining friend said in desperation, 'the explanations are longer than the Mass itself'. Little wonder that ritual can become increasingly wearisome and irrelevant to human needs. People then move elsewhere to discover rituals that relate to their need for space, for non-verbal, ecstatic or emotional expressions of oneness.

Some assume that ritual needs to be *constantly* changed in order 'to make it relevant'. Again, there is a failure to grasp the liberating power of structure in the ritual process. Repetition, provided it is not synonymous with mediocrity or shoddy action, can liberate people from worrying what to say or do. They are free to feel beyond the visible, to allow their imaginations to move beyond their surroundings, to contemplate and to listen. When my father lay dying, the gestures of touch freed us from distracting worries about how to express our grief. So also with the gestures of pilgrims at the Vietnam Memorial.

# Rituals are diverse

Ritual is the means through which we search for, establish, and preserve or celebrate symbolic order and unity for ourselves and for society. Wherever social interaction exists or is desired, then space will be given to ritual; not that people are necessarily conscious that the ritual process is occurring. Rituals aim to make the mythic values of a society concrete and experiential; they act out these values in social relations. And rituals are as diverse and numerous as social relations. The following are *some* key categories.

## Secular/religious

A ritual is religious if it relates people to the supernatural world or to what people consider to be the *ultimate* source of meaning in their lives. Secular rituals relate people to the ordinary things of daily living, e.g. work, eating. However, it is difficult at times to distinguish a religious from an apparently secular ritual. Key national values, as articulated in North America's founding mythology or its many aberrations, may be for people the source of their ultimate meaning in life, their god. Hence, for example, the pursuit of capitalism or of individual freedom becomes a ritual in itself.

## 'Models for'/'models of'

In 'model for' rituals, the function is to impose, reaffirm, and strengthen value consensus or conformity to the *status quo*, as desired by leaders of a particular society. The liminality phase of ritual, in which divisions within groups can be confronted openly and honestly, is barely evident or even permitted to be present, lest people discover their inner power to question freely the world around them. The reaggregation phase is dominant, when people are strongly expected to assent to the existing political or hierarchical power structure. Such is the case with the great Russian civil rituals, for example, the May Day parades in Moscow's Red Square.[5]

'Model of' rituals exist where there is already a strong value consensus within a group or nation; the consensus does not have to be imposed, but reaffirmed or strengthened and expressed through rituals, e.g. the cult rituals that surround the American flag, asserting nationally held values; or the Pope offering Mass, together with all the bishops of a particular country, to symbolize collegiality.

## Rituals of denial/scapegoating

Rituals either resolve the gap between the ideal and real world, or they *disguise* it by ignoring or denying that it exists.

Thus people can commonly produce self-congratulatory documents at conferences and refuse to recognize that the statements conflict with reality. These conferences and the written statements are rituals of denial; painful truths will not be confronted, but people hope that the rituals, in some 'magical' way, will remove the gap between the ideal and reality. For example, at a general chapter of a dying religious congregation, the superior general presented a very realistic assessment of the institute. Within one day, the report was being totally ignored and delegates proceeded to formulate documents that assumed the institute was numerically flourishing. Most left the general chapter proclaiming that, as one said, 'this was the best chapter; the spirit was marvellous and we accomplished much'![6]

The first two stages of the tripartite ritual process—namely, the separation and liminality—are ignored or deliberately abbreviated in rituals of denial. Why is this so? Simply because if these two stages are genuinely accepted, the realities of life must be faced up to. There must be an acceptance of death.

When people are unsure of what their collective values or identity are, they may initiate 'witch hunts' in order to discover 'deviants', who they feel are undermining consensus in society. The identification of these people and the charges they level against them are ritual ways of restating and reaffirming their collective values. The 'heretics' or 'deviants' become ritual scapegoats. This explains why there are periodic Marxist/political show trials, academic/political/religious purges, and even, at times, American Congressional investigations or Royal Commissions in some British Commonwealth countries.

A similar type of ritual process occurs when prophetic people threaten, or question, the political/academic/religious attitudinal or structural *status quo*. The prophets are felt to pollute the accepted system of belief or customs; they are ritually 'dirty', 'dangerous'. The subtle or open condemnation and marginalization of the prophets ritually assert the solidarity of the threatened group.

Prophets are liminal or antistructure people; that is, by their lifestyle, actions and words they confront the structured world of status, wealth, power manipulation and violence. They are without the power the world applauds. Their powerlessness gives them the freedom to challenge the world they disdain, for they depend on no one. Among such people are Gandhi; Old Testament prophets; saints such as St Benedict, St Francis, and St Ignatius; but, above all, Christ himself.[7]

# Rituals of death/grief

Rites of passage are rituals that mark the progress of an individual between relatively fixed and stable, culturally or religiously recognized states of rank, status, office, calling or profession. Each rite of passage means that there is an experience of death as the old status is put aside.

The prophet Jeremiah was deeply pained by the fact that the Israelites failed to recognize that key symbols of their social structure were disappearing or about to be destroyed: the temple, Jerusalem, the kingship (Jer 4:19, 20, 22). In our terminology, the Israelites disdained to accept the stages of separation and liminality; they ignored the need to let go of a dying world and to enter into a revitalized relationship with Yahweh and with one another.

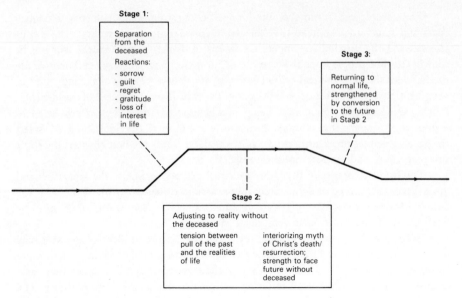

**Figure 6.1**   Ritual of death/grief

Jeremiah, however, did grieve. He expressed deep sorrow at the passing of the old symbols, and he agonized (the liminal stage) over what lay ahead. Finally, he trusts Yahweh who will be his strength in his own journey of life. (Figure 6.1 outlines what the grief ritual should be.)

Western society is no different from the world of Jeremiah. It is systematically removing death from our consciousness—a form of planned obsolescence. Anthropologist Geoffrey Gorer speaks of the 'pornography' of death, in that death is not to be mentioned publicly. It is to be dealt with as an object of private fantasy only. Rituals of death/grief are turned into rituals of denial. Death is a puzzle to people who are uncertain about the existence of an after-life; the way to avoid being troubled by uncertainty is to deny death and whatever is related to it.[8]

An entire industry has developed to remove the reality of death from relatives and friends; the 'loved one' is facially restored to 'robust good health' by morticians and is laid out for viewing in the 'slumber room'. All public grief must be discouraged. This is the denial of one of the most basic needs of the human person: the need to acknowledge death, to grieve the loss of the familiar and to struggle to relate anew to a world without the departed.

---

*Examples*:
My father's body was received into the church accompanied by New Zealand Maori women wailing in a stylized manner. The wailing is an invitation to people precisely to express sorrow. At the graveside a Maori elder spoke directly to the deceased and formally requested his spirit to rest: 'Go friend, to your mother and father. Farewell! Go to the belly of the land!' This was a reminder to all that the formal stage of separation had ended; they must now enter the liminality stage and learn from the death to face the future.

104

For many years, there was an official and public refusal in the USA to admit the tragic mistakes and failure of the Vietnam war, as well as the bravery and suffering of thousands of soldiers. Last summer, I found a poorly written notice in the centre of a New England village: 'Please understand that we are not asking for a parade, a monument or pity. But we do ask you to remember in your own way the 58129 Americans who died at the war in Vietnam. . . . We as individuals and as a nation learned something of human value for having been in S.E. Asia. The sacrifice we maintain was not futile.'

This is a poignant plea for the right to mourn publicly, the right to grieve and to learn from the lessons of defeat. The building of the national Memorial has provided a chance for people to mourn. As one commentator put it: 'We left so much in Vietnam . . . so many men and women . . . without a funeral to give focus to the grief and the emotions, without the ritual of saying goodbye. The Wall changed that; it is about the dead, but not for them. It is for the living. The Wall . . . lets us say goodbye.'[9]

## Civil rituals

Civil religion is the religious or quasi-religious consideration for various civic values and traditions in this or that particular nation. The rise of nationalism in the nineteenth and twentieth centuries gave a new and vigorous impetus to civil religions. The following become important: national creation mythologies, festivals or rituals that honour national unity, historical achievements and individuals ('national civic saints') who exemplify national virtues.

In Britain, the civil religion is expressed in rituals such as the annual opening of Parliament by the Queen. The civil religion and its rituals are vividly evident in the USA. For example, Presidential inaugurations are often expressed in religious phrasing, referring in broad terms to God and to the challenges that the nation faces as a modern Israel being led out of Egypt. Annual festivals such as Thanksgiving Day and Memorial Day aim to integrate families into the civil religion, or to unify the people according to its values.

When established religion weakens its hold on a country, civil religion and its rituals may tend to take stronger root in the lives of people. However, in the West, with the possible exception of the USA, nationalism has weakened after the excesses of the 1939–45 World War, thus lessening the importance for the moment of civil religions and rituals. On the other hand, civil religion and rituals are avidly encouraged in Eastern-bloc and dictator-controlled nations in an effort to achieve and guarantee mass loyalty to the regimes.[10]

## Rituals of reversal/rebellion

In many cultures there are examples of rituals of status reversal. For example, it was customary in a particular Zulu tribe for the king's subjects to challenge his authority annually, over a three-day period. The king was verbally abused and ridiculed, called to explain his decisions and behaviour over the past year and, finally, threatened. For the rest of the year, it was assumed that the king would ridicule the people and demand that they be accountable to him. In some traditional societies women are expected to take on for a short period, e.g. a few days, the roles of men. This happens also in many Western cultures, e.g. in Australasia, the men are expected to barbecue the meat at outside picnics, although traditionally men keep well away from the kitchen, for inside cooking is the duty of women. In many Western universities, students are allowed each year—e.g. for a few days prior to graduation day—publicly to attack with considerable freedom, licence or mockery the civil, ecclesiastical and university authorities. If they, or anyone else, did this at any other time, they would normally be arrested for being public nuisances or disturbing public order.

These rituals highlight the basic ambiguity within society: authority and roles are important for order, but at the same time they restrict freedom. The rituals temporarily articulate and resolve the ambiguity or tension. Anthropologist Max Gluckman argues that these rituals of rebellion and licence function as a mechanism of psychological/cultural catharsis. They ultimately reinforce the social order: ritual rebellions against the king, or against the cultural dominance of the male in Western cultures, release tensions and therefore strengthen the Zulu institution of kingship and the male position of superiority within the traditional Western household. He claims that the rituals represent and discharge real social tensions connected with hierarchical relations and, as a symbolic protest, they reduce the possibility of real conflict.[11]

# Inculturating the liturgy

The above analysis of ritual will assure the reader that:

- ritual is a complex process;

- it is a response to the basic need for people to communicate with one another and with a world beyond the visible (in whatever way this is understood);

- established rituals are not lightly to be interfered with.

Hence, the following are some of the significant conclusions about ritual that evangelizers must bear in mind in preparing public worship or the celebration of the sacraments:

- we communicate through symbols, myths and rituals; they speak primarily to the heart/imagination;

- non-verbal symbols/ritual, e.g. silence, are generally more powerful in conveying meanings than the verbal;

- rituals express in action an underlying mythology; ritual specialists wishing to adjust the rituals to changing circumstances must be thoroughly aware of the mythologies, otherwise the adapted rituals will not be authentic;

- ritual is a tripartite process; the length of each stage depends on the nature of the ritual;

- rituals are repetitive; people feel at peace with the predictable; changes in ritual must be made with caution and in co-operation with the people themselves;

- rituals should 'speak for themselves', that is, they should require a minimum of explanation;

- rituals must be thoroughly prepared; mediocre or shoddy presentations do not inspire the imagination.

I believe that in the Roman Catholic Church we generally moved too fast in initiating *much-needed* liturgical changes after Vatican II. Even now, the above guidelines are often ignored. To be more precise:

- We confuse symbols with signs, thus thinking that a symbol could be changed with speed and replaced by another; signs *point to* things and speak directly to the intellect, the rational or logical part of our life. Symbols *are* the objects represented. A symbol opens us to another order of reality that is beyond the immediately perceptible; only the heart or the imagination can grasp the inexpressible. What the heart holds to can be changed only slowly.

- Because we fail to grasp the fact that the most powerful symbolism is the non-verbal, our liturgies are often too wordy. We want to explain the meanings of everything, forgetting that faith and the heart alone can ultimately reach out to the inexpressible, or that words are often the least powerful symbols for communication.

- For inculturation to occur in the liturgy, we need not just an awareness of people's symbols, but a sound grasp of the theological mythology that must underline the ritual. As Ladislas Orsy puts it: 'Liturgical laws are not like ordinary disciplinary laws. . . . Their purpose is to help the community to perceive the presence of a mystery and help lead the members to adoration.'[12] God is both immanent and transcendent; in reaction to past abuses, we overdo the emphasis on the former, neglecting the fact that the human person has an insatiable desire for mystery to be expressed in appropriate symbols.

- Changes were often imposed from above on people; inculturation requires their involvement at all stages. Sociologist David Martin reflects on the tension between diverse liturgical goals of the person in the pews and the cleric: 'the average layman . . . his feeling for liturgy is habit tinged by affection. It is based on associations: people known, things remembered. The clergyman wants something more than association: he wants community.'[13]

The promulgation of the Rite of Christian Initiation of Adults (RCIA) in the early 1970s, following the restoration of the catechumenate in the Roman Catholic Church, highlights the importance of appreciating the tripartite process of ritual. The initiation rite is seen as a journey of some considerable length, for conversion is a slow process that requires the free response to God's grace, under the inspiration and assistance of the ecclesial community. The three stages of ritual are evident in the rite, the second and third being especially lengthy, as befits an initiation rite (see Figure 6.2).

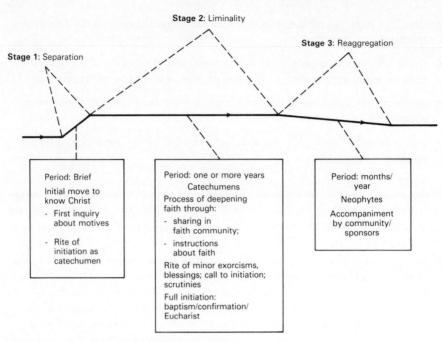

**Figure 6.2** Rite of Christian Initiation of Adults (RCIA)

# Popular religiosity: reflections

> At its core the religiosity of the people is a storehouse of values that offers the answers of Christian wisdom to the great questions of life. . . . It creatively combines the divine and the human, Christ and Mary, spirit and body, communion and institution . . . intelligence and emotion. . . . Due to lack of attention on the part of pastoral agents . . . the religion of the people shows signs of erosion and distortion.[14]

One evening an elderly Irish friend said to me: 'I must rise before the sun and go to the parish church. I will walk around the mission cross seven times, reciting a decade of the rosary on each circuit, making sure that I finish before the sun rises. Then I know that Mary our Mother will hear my petition for good health.' I was not long ordained and his words baffled me: 'How could this man, who had seemed so holy and charitable, be so superstitious?'

This incident brought me into contact with what is generally called *popular religiosity*. I know now that the application of the term 'superstitious' to my friend's ritual was elitist, pastorally simplistic and arrogant. Popular religiosity, through which the faith of millions of people is expressed around the world, is far more complex and positive than I had realized, as the above Puebla extract indicates.

## Defining popular religiosity

The expression refers to beliefs and practices, relating to supernatural or super-empirical beings or powers, existing *independently* of, or not officially sanctioned by, those in authority of formal religions. It is called *popular* because it is thought that this form of religion belongs to the *masses* or the working class only, as opposed to the middle class or the educated elite.

These descriptions, however, are too restrictive. Go back to Chapter 2 and read again the analysis of folk/associational culture types. Notice that in a folk culture, religion is integral to everything that people do; so much so that religion is not a *way of looking at life*, but a *way of life*.

People in a folk culture are concerned with the immediate, concrete need. They express their relationship to one another and to the deity and spirits through concrete symbols; feeling or imagination is dominant, not rationality or intellectual analysis. They recognize the need for all kinds of mediators, e.g. saints, as agents to intercede for them in a world that is seen as always working against them.

One final clarification: individuals can be highly analytical in their social and business life, but at the same time devoted to popular religiosity. The ritual action of my Irish friend now makes a lot more sense; he was expressing in his own cultural way his deep trust in the supernatural.

Reflect on the following.

---

*Examples*:
The revised Holy Week liturgy was introduced into one Filipino parish church, and the pastor removed all opportunities for the parishioners to express their own colourful popular religiosity. It was dull, and thoroughly verbal. After the first year, participation dropped off dramatically, because the people had decided to develop their own liturgies, well away from the church, in their Basic Christian Communities or on the streets outside.

On one occasion a Filipino pastor told the people: 'Vatican II decreed that we should pray only to Christ and not to all the saints'. Therefore, he told them, the statues would be removed and destroyed the following day. That night his sleep was disrupted. Hundreds of people had broken into the sacristy to pray in tears before the statues, to bid them farewell in a spirit of reverential faith.

---

## Pastoral reflections

## 1. Cultural gap in expressing faith

The gap between my Irish friend's way of looking at religion and my own was basically cultural. I had been trained to look at life, not imaginatively but rationally, to make clear distinctions between the past, present and the future. From this cultural perspective, I viewed at least unconsciously the cultures of other people as inferior. I failed to appreciate that the Irish religious culture had developed over centuries; it had given meaning and protection to millions of people in the face of sustained oppression. It continues to do so, when people like myself who exude an arrogant sense of cultural and faith superiority confront them.

One major reason why Hispanics in the USA today find it extremely difficult to fit in with existing parish structures is because middle-class, white Americans no longer consider popular religiosity a legitimate way to the Lord. As the Notre Dame Study on Catholic life in the USA records: 'many Catholics today regard these devotions . . . as outmoded relics from the Church's past'.[15] Most Hispanics do not agree.[16] They will never feel welcome until host parishes recognize that, for millions of people, popular religiosity is a legitimate way of life and contact with the supernatural.

In New Zealand many Maori Catholics complain that they feel ill at ease in the churches of middle-class white people, and comment on the latter's liturgies: they are 'so cold', 'no one sings', 'you give the sign of peace, get a cool handshake in reply, but no one greets you after Mass; they all run for their cars', 'we feel oppressed in the presence of such people with power'.[17]

---

## 2. Pastorally experience popular religiosity

One way to develop a better understanding of popular religiosity is for devotees of the latter to invite others to join them 'on their home ground'. Invariably, middle-class parishioners are moved by the feeling of hospitality and the warmth of celebration. The hosts feel self-confident in their familiar setting.[18]

## 3. Cultural conversion is never-ending

No human or particular cultural way to the supernatural is ever perfect. People who are at ease with rather rationally organized liturgies need reminding that the imaginative side of their lives must also be cultivated for the Lord. People of popular religiosity require their analytical or critical powers to develop more, drawing strength from their faith to challenge injustices and secularism through example and action.

In both cases, however, there must be extraordinary sensitivity on the part of pastors and evangelizers—no pushing, no condemnations. It requires understanding, encouragement and the provision of well worked-out pastoral instructional programmes on the requirements of Gospel-centred prayer and faith/justice-oriented action. Conversion is a never-ending process of purification for all of us.

---

Pastor Jeff is invited to bless a gravestone erected in memory of a New Zealand Maori elder by his family. The blessing is to take place at a special ceremony of unveiling the gravestone (*kohatu*) one year after the elder's death. Jeff, however, knows that the people fear that, if the blessing is not done, the spirit of the deceased may cause them harm. They have not grasped the fact that Jesus has risen and his gift is that of love, not fear. He is concerned that his presence at the graveside will symbolize his acceptance of the people's belief in the power of spirits to haunt the living. What should he do?

Jeff decides to bless the grave, but he uses the opportunity to speak with the family beforehand about the Christian symbolism of death and the saving power of Christ. At the graveside he also explains the nature of the blessing. To receive the grace of the Lord for oneself and for the deceased one, we should be open to ongoing conversion, not out of a servile fear of a punishing master, but in response to an all-loving Saviour.

Jeff's approach is quite correct. He reacts according to the pastoral principle of functional substitution, as explained in Chapter 1. He realizes that it will take a long time for his catechetical method to have a deep impact on the people's understanding of what Christian death means.

---

# Reflection questions

## To the reader

1. Does the definition of ritual surprise you? If so, why?

2. Can you describe an experience of non-verbal ritual that deeply affected you personally?

3. It is said that rituals of denial occur frequently in human communication. Why do you think this is so?

## To a discussion group

1. What are the qualities of good parish liturgy? Are they being realized in your parish liturgies?

2. Why are non-verbal symbols generally more effective in communication than verbal?

3. Are there any groups in your parish that are especially noted for popular religiosity? Can you suggest ways in which the parish can better appreciate the qualities of their worship?

# Suggested reading

Bocock, R., *Ritual in Industrial Society: A Sociological Analysis of Ritualism in Modern England* (London: George Allen & Unwin, 1974).

Browning, R.L., and Reed, R.A., *The Sacraments in Religious Education and Liturgy* (Birmingham, AL: Religious Education Press, 1985).

Collins, M., *Worship Renewal to Practice* (Washington, DC: Pastoral Press, 1987).

Collins, P.W., *More than Meets the Eye: Ritual and Parish Liturgy* (New York: Paulist, 1983).

Fourez, G., *Sacraments and Passages: Celebrating the Tensions of Modern Life* (Notre Dame, IN: Ave Maria Press, 1983).

Greinacher, N., and Mette, N. (eds), *Popular Religion* (Edinburgh: T. & T. Clark, 1986).

Gremillion, J., and Castelli, J., *The Emerging Parish: The Notre Dame Study of Catholic Life since Vatican II* (San Francisco: Harper & Row, 1987), pp. 77–98, 119–160.

Schreiter, R. J., *Constructing Local Theologies* (London: SCM Press, 1985), pp. 122–158.

Turner, V., 'Passages, Margins, and Poverty: Religious Symbols of Communitas' in *Worship*, vol. 46, nos 7 and 8 (1972), pp. 390–412, 482–494.

Upton, J., *Journey into Mystery: A Companion to the RCIA* (New York: Paulist, 1986).

Worgul, G. S., *From Magic to Metaphor: A Validation of the Christian Sacraments* (New York: Paulist, 1980).

# 7 Sects, 'the cults' and inculturation

America's religious establishments are flourishing on the fringes but languishing in the mainline (Wade C. Roof).[1]

Some of the small sects are amongst the very few religious institutions in Britain today that are still increasing (Robin Gill).[2]

Fundamentalism is on the march in Israel as elsewhere (Geoffrey Wigoder).[3]

## Introduction

Over the last twenty years, the mainline Protestant, Roman Catholic and Jewish institutions have lost considerable support around the world. However, evangelical, conservative and fundamentalist sects/cults or movements, advocating traditional morality and lifestyles, are spreading with considerable speed. For example, fundamentalist missionaries from the USA 'are winning 400 converts every hour in Latin America'.[4]

On the other hand, all kinds of often non-Christian or quasi-religious, therapy-oriented movements have sprung up. Terms such as 'sects', 'the cults', or 'new religious movements' are now used freely, and generally pejoratively, of these new phenomena. These movements are often the objects of considerable anger, either by parents whose children have opted for the cults, or by leaders of mainline Churches, who see their flock being proselytized by highly committed missionaries of the new movements. At times, anti-cult activity has led to governmental investigations, criminal charges and public harassment.

However, despite the often bitter feelings and controversy surrounding these new religious movements, there is much that evangelizers of the mainline Churches have to learn from them. They should especially look at why young people are attracted to the movements in the first place. Often, these alternative religions arise simply because the traditional Churches have failed to nourish the spiritual and human needs of people. Hence, in this chapter, I attempt:

* to clarify the meaning and origins of these movements;

- to suggest ways in which evangelizers may learn from these movements and react to them pastorally and positively.

I suggest that readers first re-read Chapter 4, giving particular attention to the Culture Change Reaction Model.

# Clarifying terms

An understanding of new religious movements, e.g. sects/cults, is difficult for two reasons. Firstly, because the movements are generally of fairly recent origin, it is difficult to find sufficient research material on them to make confident objective conclusions. Secondly, social scientists frequently complicate matters by applying a diversity of meanings to words like 'religion', 'secularization', 'sects' and 'cults'. The following working definitions, however, would have general acceptance:

## 1. Religion

Religion is a body of beliefs/rituals that ultimately give meaning to life. What is meant by *ultimately*, however, is interpreted in one of two ways:

a. substantively, i.e. the *ultimate* means that religion is oriented to supernatural beings; or

b. functionally, i.e. every society has some set of common values that answer questions for people about the ultimate meaning of life, e.g. it could be capitalistic values for some, Marxist values for others.

If the functional approach to religion is used, it is possible to agree, for example, with sociologist Robert Bellah, that the Western cultural revolution of the 1960s was really a religious crisis. People struggled anew for *meaning* in their lives. Many found this meaning in new religious movements that had little or nothing to do with Christianity or other traditional religions. Both approaches to religion are used in the following text.

## 2. Secularization

The definition of *secularization* differs according to one's particular way of defining religion. If it is substantive, then secularization is the process in which the ways people think and behave are less influenced by religious teaching, symbols and institutions that are based on supernatural values.

114

For example, in most European Protestant nations, and to a lesser degree in the industrialized sections of Roman Catholic Europe, church membership has markedly dropped off; religious institutions are less prominent; their personnel have less status and authority, and supernatural beliefs have become less generally accepted. In North America, while there has been growth in church membership, many churches have become more secular to the extent that they provide more social facilities for integrating their adherents into the community, stressing the psychological comforts of religious belief, e.g. peace of mind, health and adjustment. The more challenging dimensions of Christianity, e.g. sin, the cross, mortification, the apostolate of social justice, tend to be played down.

*Secularism* is the 'view of life that limits itself not to the material in exclusion of the spiritual, but to the human here and now in exclusion of one's relation to God here and hereafter. It is the practical exclusion of God from human thinking and living.'[5]

If the functional approach to religion is preferred, secularization connotes changes in the way religion is expressed. For example, religion in today's industrial nations is increasingly being presented in less institutional, more individualistic, less theistic forms, in which the ultimate meanings about life are sought in such activities as self-help or therapy programmes or fads. Religion, according to the functional approach, will never disappear, as people will always be searching for ultimate meanings.

---

## 3. Sects/cults

---

Sects/cults can be looked at from traditional or contemporary perspectives. Both approaches are helpful and complement each other.

## 1. Traditional meanings

### Sect
A sect is a form of religious grouping:

- it is established in protest against, and usually separating from, another religious group;
- its formation represents support of beliefs, ritual practices, and moral standards, most commonly believed by sect members to be a return to earlier and purer forms of the particular religion;
- the membership is limited and earned by individual performance;
- it accepts, at least in theory, democratic government by all believers;
- total loyalty is demanded of the adherents to the group, which may deal harshly with errant members;
- it is hostile or indifferent to the secular society and to the state.[6]

Sects can be distinguished by their view of salvation, e.g.:

## a. Conversionist sects

They seek to change the world by transforming individuals through evangelism, e.g. fundamentalist groups like The Salvation Army, Pentecostal movements.

## b. Revolutionist sects

They are particularly pessimistic about the world, which they believe can be transformed only by a dramatic supernatural intervention, e.g. Jehovah's Witnesses.

## c. Introversionist sects

Rejecting the world as evil, they withdraw from it in order to protect their purity and foster holiness. For example, the Amana Society is one of the oldest and largest communal sects in the USA; founded in Germany in 1714, in reaction to what it considered to be the rigid dogmatism and ritual formalism of the Lutheran Church, the community migrated in 1817. The sect believes that God relates directly with people through inspiration and revelation. Authentic Christian living demands simplicity, and this requires that the sect isolate itself from the world. The Amish communities are possibly better-known examples of this type of sect.

## d. Gnostic sects

Claiming to have a special body of esoteric teaching, they, e.g. Christian Scientists, try to apply this knowledge in everyday life, especially for the attainment of material success, health and self-realization. They do not withdraw from the world.[7]

## e. Manipulationist sects

They accept the world's values, but they offer a superior or esoteric way for attaining them. For example, the Church of Scientology was founded in 1955 and aims to increase the self-knowledge of its adherents through a system called Dianetics. It is claimed that special counselling assists followers to remove pain and negativity (engrams) of the past.[8]

## f. Millenarian sects

These sects expect the imminent and miraculous transformation of this world by supernatural means. Most are also messianic. That is, salvation is to be directed by a human agent of the divine, and a sect's adherents must commit themselves totally to this person.

These sects, e.g. the early Mormons, often show an activist or aggressive response to their rejection of the world, assuming that revolt must accompany the overthrow of the existing order; Ayatollah Khomeini's conservative Muslim crusade is a contemporary example. The Rastafarian movement, a mixture of African and Christian concepts, drawing support from dispossessed blacks yearning for a sense of self-pride and identity, is possibly the fastest-growing millenarian sect of the 1970s and 1980s. Its followers dream of a black messiah who will lead them back to Africa and a fullness of identity. It first appeared among the poor in Jamaica in the early 1930s, and has spread among black people to Britain, parts of Europe, Australasia and North America.

Cargo Cults is the name given to millenarian movements of Melanesia (and parts of Polynesia), in the South Pacific. Like all millenarian sects, these movements flourish during periods of social/political disruption. It is claimed that specified ritual actions and bizarre practices will suddenly bring their adherents material goods, and a better, even paradisaical, life. They have their messianic leaders, who often encourage their followers to destroy their food crops and then sit and wait for aircraft (sometimes to be piloted by ancestors) to land on primitive airstrips. The aircraft will be loaded with the goods of the Western world.

---

*Examples*:

In 1962, a group of North American surveyors erected three cement survey-markers on a peak of Mount Turu in Papua New Guinea. A movement developed in which the leaders claimed that, if the markers were destroyed, 300 American 707 jet aircraft would land on the mountain top and disgorge money and manufactured goods. This would usher in a period of peace, flourishing gardens and political independence.

Thomas Merton, in 1968, the year he died, felt that many in the Roman Catholic Church had adopted a 'Cargo Cult' approach to renewal. He taped his fascinating reflections after reading a study on Cargo Cults in Papua New Guinea: 'Common to all Cargo-type movements . . . is the need to abruptly repudiate everything old. . . . Either you accept the whole works, the whole Cargo message, or else you perish with the repudiated past. You are destroyed as irrelevant and obsolete. . . . I think it would be really useful for us to take stock . . . of the possibility that we, too (in the Church), are involved in the tidal wave of Cargo mentality.'[9]

---

Millenarianism is an integral part of Western history. The Jewish religion centres on the hope of a future golden age and, of course, Christianity has reinforced this expectation with its teaching about Christ's second coming. The Christian hope of the age of perfect justice and love has over the centuries undergone many aberrations, especially in times of profound social or political disorientation. Marx and Lenin evolved the most powerful such aberration in recent centuries, with their emphasis on the golden age of the classless society.

I think the above comment by Thomas Merton about Cargoism within the Roman Catholic Church is valid. With tremendous speed, after Vatican II, we did destroy with too little discrimination symbols of the past, expecting that a golden age of renewed Catholicism would emerge. We had too little concern for inner conversion. The contemporary enthusiasm for this or that latest 'revelation' of the Mother of God, in which the imminent destruction of the world is 'foretold', or the 'sins of Vatican II' are denounced, surely reflect this ever-present tendency for people to run after millenarian dreams. In 1968, I found a millenarian movement within an extended family of middle-income Maori Catholics in New Zealand; they had been dispossessed of their lands and cultural roots. The movement's followers had for many years dreamed of a religio-political messiah, who would emerge from their midst. Through his leadership they would have their lands restored to them and they would achieve a revitalized cultural identity. Just prior to my contact with this movement, the longed-for messiah—a young schoolboy—had just been identified, through a complex process of 'discernment', by the leaders of the movement.

## Cults

The term *cult* is used in many different ways, usually with the connotations of small size, a search for a conversion experience, lack of an organizational structure, and the presence of a charismatic leader.[10]

In contrast to a *sect*, a cult tends to be a more spontaneous and open movement, lacking specific membership requirements, offering particular concrete benefits to its adherents, rather than the comprehensive world-views and conceptions of salvation typical of religious sects. Thus there are political cults, e.g. a group of people attached to a particular charismatic leader, religious cults, e.g. followers of an Indian guru, and self-improvement or therapy cults. A more recent example of a self-improvement cult is the New Agers. Followers emphasize the importance of material wealth/physical health, and the ways to achieve these through self-improvement exercises; followers must achieve mastery over deeply held negative thoughts.

## 2. Contemporary meanings

The controversial new religious movements (many of which were inspired by non-Western, or non-traditional Western, religious ideas or leaders) that proliferated in the 1970s were labelled by journalists and others pejoratively as 'the cults', confusing the above distinctions between sect and cult. 'The cults' are more accurately sects in the traditional sense described above, because of their elitism, and for example, their vigorous efforts to make and retain converts.

'The cults' diverge from the traditional notion of sect in their emphasis on *deviance*, that is, they often draw their inspiration from *outside* the dominant traditions of the culture, e.g. Krishna Consciousness depends on Indian religious thinking; and they hold to highly unconventional ideas of religion, politics, economics. The traditional idea of a sect, on the other hand, assumes that it is a schismatic variant of a dominant religious tradition.

Most of the contemporary cults are *millenarian* in emphasis; they assume the present order will come suddenly to an end and their members alone will be saved. Not all, however, show a quality of aggressiveness or violence. Yet, because they condemn the present social order, they inevitably alienate other people and at times cause vigorous controversy.[11]

## 4. New religious movements

In recent years, because of the emotional connotations of the words 'cult' or 'sect', new more neutral terms have been introduced to describe these contemporary movements: 'new religious movements', 'new religious groups', 'alternative religions'.[12]

# Origins of new religious movements

(See also Chapter 4, pp. 64–72.) Cults and sects are an integral part of human history. Ronald Knox, reflecting on Church history, speaks of the periodic 'excess of charity over unity', that is, cliques or elites of Christian men and women who in bursts of enthusiasm seek to live a less worldly life than their neighbours under the guidance of the Holy Spirit; they move apart from other believers, but they in turn compromise with the world and new groups emerge under rival prophets.[13] Invariably, some secular or religious catastrophe sparks off such movements; people feel lost and yearn for meaning and direction.

In the following section, we describe the major catalyst, namely, the Revolution of Expressive Disorder of the 1960s, that sparked off the emergence of an unprecedented number and variety of new religious movements, both outside and within the Christian tradition.

## The Revolution of Expressive Disorder: 1967–1972±

> The sixties are over, but they remain the watershed of our recent cultural history; they continue to affect the ambiance of our lives in innumerable ways (Morris Dickstein).[14]

From about 1967 through to the early 1970s, the entire Western world experienced a dramatic, and highly intense, transformation in its cultural values and behaviour patterns. This extraordinary upheaval, called the Revolution of Expressive Disorder, started as a form of cultural revolution among a small group of committed radicals, and climaxed by changing some of the most profound· habits and assumptions of Western society. Especially through the actions of white middle-class youth, everything was affected: politics, arts, education, religion. What was considered shocking in 1967 is so taken for granted today as to be unnoticed.[15] Gerald Howard considers the period as 'a spirited, wildly inventive era—a decade of great social and political upheaval when ideas and customs collided in every corner'.[16]

Sociologist Bernice Martin points out that the most common characteristic of the revolutionary liminality was the symbolism of 'antistructure', 'anti-order', 'anti-predictability'. The gaudy dress, the long hairstyles, and the new beat music of pop stars like the Beatles, or the art forms of painters like Andy Warhol, are apt symbols of this cultural upheaval. It was essentially an attack on boundaries, limits, certainties, taboos, roles, systems, style, predictabilities, form, ritual. For example, extravagant, unconventional sexuality and the dramatic increase in the use of drugs like pot and LSD were seen not just as ways to satisfy individual desires, but as means to attack traditional taboos or moral boundaries.

Inevitably, as Robert Bellah notes, there was a massive erosion of the legitimacy of traditional institutions: business, government, education, the Churches, the family.[17] These institutions were seen to have compromised with values like freedom, self-expression, the dignity of the human person; the continuous and competitive pursuit of money, or the involvement in foreign wars, e.g. in Vietnam, also conflicted with these values.

Overall, the revolution was an attempt to make ambiguity and uncertainty not a mere passing feature of life, but a total way of living in itself. Yet the revolution had a major paradox. On the one hand, there was the earnest effort to develop structureless individualism with its burning zeal for immediate self-fulfilment, liberation from all restraints on freedom. But on the other hand, there was also the push towards the collectivity, in which the individual became smothered by the collectivity itself, e.g. through commune-style living, uniformity in antistructure clothing or hairstyles. We will now see that these two opposing emphases were eventually expressed in two different types of sects/cults.

## Religious reactions to the Expressive Disorder Revolution

The poet W. H. Auden was right when he wrote:

> The Road of Excess
> leads more often than not to
> the Slough of Despond.[18]

People cannot live in liminal ambiguity, uncertainty, cultural malaise or normlessness for too long. If they attempt to do so, they fall into despondency or despair. People at heart yearn for meaning, order, structure or predictability in life. Revolutionary movements can succeed only if they very quickly provide new structures of order, to allow people to 'settle down with some semblance of social and psychic safety'.[19]

The Revolution of Expressive Disorder was no exception. The revolution's influence in developing order, or meaning, through religious beliefs and practices can be seen over the last twenty years at three levels (see Figure 7.1):

- in the early emergence of 'the cults';

- in the struggles within the mainline Churches to cope with the impact of the cultural upheaval;

- in the development, in the 1970s/1980s, of conservative and fundamentalist religious movements.

## 1. The emergence of 'the cults': 1967–1975±

The revolution-disoriented young, mostly from fairly prosperous middle-class families, rejoined the structures of society and accepted its competitive values, or/and they enrolled in new or revitalized religious cults/sects or in conservative Evangelical non-mainline Christian Churches. Contrary to popular belief, the overall number who joined the cults/sects was relatively small, whereas the conservative Evangelical groups received large numbers, e.g. the Assemblies of God, the Pentecostal Holiness Church.[20]

Many mainline Churches had suffered during the revolution a widespread malaise, resulting from a loss of institutional vitality and direction; they were

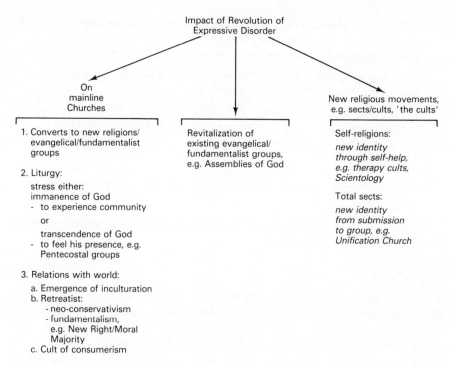

Figure 7.1   Impact of Revolution of Expressive Disorder

thoroughly ill-prepared to respond to the spiritual and ideological upheavals of the time. Significant numbers of young people felt that these traditional Churches had so compromised with secular values, or had become so bureaucratic and unfeeling, that they were unable any longer to provide the desired havens of understanding and meaning.

Older people, even while still retaining weakened membership in mainline Churches, or while joining Evangelical movements, sometimes turned to interests like astrology to provide meaning in their lives. Astrology placed the meaning of life into a large universal overview; personal meaning and universal meaning could now fit neatly into one system of thought.

In brief, what has been the appeal of these new religious movements (including the Evangelical conservative Churches) for young and adult people over the last twenty years? People who were caught up in a world of confusion had certain deep human needs. The movements claimed to offer ways to respond to those aspirations. The needs were:

a. *For an experiential religion.* Religion is not presented as something heavily theological, but as something to be experienced here and now. As one Pentecostal said: 'I *feel* God's love now. I know he is speaking to me.'

b. *For an intimacy in community life.* The emphasis is on experiencing a sense of sharing and belonging in small-group activity.

121

c. *For a clarity of meaning and direction in life.* Religion is presented simply, clearly, with a minimum of theological language and distinctions, e.g. 'this is what happiness is and this is the way to achieve it; this is sinful and that is not'.

d. *For therapeutic services.* Many groups provide ways to help people adjust, e.g. from a drug culture; adherents feel safe and supported.

e. *For a chance to assert independence.* Particularly in the case of the cults, the first act of teenage assertion of adult independence may be to join a cult. It can be a way for teenagers to tell parents that they are henceforward going to make decisions for themselves.[21]

---

Two major types of new religious movements emerged: the 'self-religions' and the 'total sects' or 'world-rejecting sects'.[22]

## Self-religions

These stress exclusively the mental, spiritual and physical perfection of the individual. They aim to offer the individual therapeutic, supposedly scientifically based, services to achieve a new self-directing, personal identity, so that he/she is not dependent on any external structure or groups for security in the midst of a highly competitive and changing world. Thus, there developed all kinds of self-help texts and programmes, e.g. encounter and rebirthing groups.[23]

This emphasis on self-discipline, as the way to subjective self-assurance and well-being, is also to be found in movements like Hare Krishna,[24] Zen and Ananda Marga, who drew many recruits from casualties of the revolution's drug culture. They provided a quasi-family atmosphere to support the individual in pursuit of personal integration through self-discipline.

---

*Example*:
Alice, aged 30, from a middle-class family in London, tells this story: 'Ten years ago I got into drugs badly. My parents, and police, told me to "pull myself together". I did not know how. No one wanted to help me from the local Anglican parish. One day, I saw a Hare Krishna group; they seemed happy and invited me to be with them. After months of more misery, I did. What peace! With comradeship, demands for self-discipline, I managed to break my drug habit. I did not worry about what they believed, but what they offered me by way of friendship and discipline. Later I came back to being an Anglican and I find Christ now in my faith as never before. I also "pushed" the parish into offering help to druggies like I was.'

---

## Total sects, or world-rejecting sects

Here, the emphasis on individual identity and self-direction gives way to the dominance of the group; the individual's sense of belonging and identity will come, not so much from internal self-discipline, but from submission to the demands of the group.

Hence, in the Unification Church (Moonies), some of the Jesus People and the Children of God, there is an explicit hierarchy of command, firm control and a radical restriction of both personal privacy and choice. For example, Moonies have mass-arranged marriage ceremonies in which hundreds or thousands of members are wedded simultaneously, often to individuals they have never met before. While these marriages are not intended necessarily to be flesh and blood relationships, nonetheless, the ceremonies indicate the type of control members must allow the Church to have over their lives.[25] Some of these anti-world cults, e.g. Moonies, demand of their followers an absolute obedience to their leader/group. In fact, many movements require the renunciation of their family ties to be a test of the sincerity of their submission to the group.

---

*Example*:
Alan, a New Zealander, aged 29, tells his story: 'I left New Zealand six years ago a desperate person, struggling for meaning in my life, in a mess with drugs. I arrived at Los Angeles airport, my first visit to the USA. I stood there not knowing where to go. Two young people came up to me, spoke kindly and offered me accommodation. They were Moonies, but I did not know this immediately. I went with them, enjoyed the rigid regime of the house, the sense of purpose in the community. I found there meaning and a belonging that my Catholic education had not given me. Sure, I did not want to see my family any more. After all, what had they done for me when I most needed them!'

---

# 2. Mainline Churches: reactions to the Revolution of Expressive Disorder

Though all mainline Churches were deeply influenced by the revolution, the Roman Catholic Church was especially affected. Vatican II challenged Catholics to break out of their ghetto culture in order apostolically to confront the world. They were simply not prepared for this confrontation, most certainly not for the Revolution of Expressive Disorder. The effects of the combined impact of the council and revolution were traumatic for many Roman Catholics. Their meaning system, which had been a coherent and well-integrated world-view of a ghetto Church, collapsed with remarkable suddenness. Avery Dulles could therefore write in 1981 that the Roman Catholic Church 'seems, for the first time in centuries, to be an uncertain trumpet'.[26]

Here are a few reactions to the revolution within mainline Churches:

## Liturgical reactions

The revolution helped to emphasize the importance in liturgy of feeling or emotion, and the need to adapt to different pastoral situations. However, not infrequently under the direction of unprofessional liturgists, all kinds of disrupting excesses occurred, e.g. it was thought that the liturgy, in order to be relevant, must be constantly changing, or more and more explanations must be given of the liturgies. Some people thought that feeling and prayer are the same. Hence, if they did not feel they were praying, there was no prayer. On occasions, in an effort to build parish communities, liturgical organizers overlooked the ultimate purpose of prayer: God is to be worshipped!

Bernice Martin, reflecting on the insensitive interpretations of Vatican II, and on the Anglican Lambeth 1958 Conference documents, comments that 'it is taking a long time for the clergy to notice how badly it has all backfired, leaving the Churches banal and cliquey and driving the transcendent, the ecstatic and the daemonic to lodge in the "lunatic fringe" '.[27] Instead of attracting the victims of the revolution seeking a sense of personal order and meaning, these Churches further alienated them.

## Various conservative reactions: 1970s

A backlash within the mainline Churches was not particularly evident in the 1970s, except in such relatively small groups like the Lefebvre movement that demanded the return of the pre-Vatican II Church. A revitalized Pentecostal movement, however, found its way into all the mainline Churches and, from some points of view, it can be considered a conservative effort to obtain religious identity in the midst of growing cultural and liturgical confusion. Many followers of the movement hoped that Pentecostalism would provide a new source of divine authority, to replace the crumbling of the old authority structures of the Church and its rituals. They expected a direct personal experience of the divinity.

Catholic Pentecostalism (or the Charismatic movement) is criticized, and at times correctly, for its over-dependence on subjective feelings, unprofessional scriptural interpretations of religious experiences, the male dominance of its organization, and the encouragement it gives to its followers to avoid the social justice apostolate whenever it over-stresses the purely spiritual.[28]

# 3. Fundamentalism and the New Right: 1970s/1980s

Fundamentalism, in its more restrictive sense, is a 'modern version of Christianity that stresses biblical literalism, premillennialism and absolute moral rules'. More generally, however, fundamentalism 'is a historically recurring tendency within the Judeo-Christian–Muslim religious traditions',[29] that periodically happens as a search for meaning in the midst of rapid culture change; fundamentalists are anti-intellectual and thoroughly intolerant of people who differ from them. At times, as is the case of the followers of Ayatollah Khomeini, violence is used to impose what they consider to be orthodoxy.[30]

The following explains the popularity of fundamentalism today, especially in the USA; particular emphasis is given to its Protestant religious and political expressions. Later, there will be brief comments on the ways in which fundamentalism is emerging within the Roman Catholic Church.

## a. Fundamentalism/evangelicalism

The traditional image of Protestant evangelicals and fundamentalists—that they are older, poorer, worse educated, and more likely to be female—still has some truth to it. But these faiths are increasingly attracting converts, e.g. in the USA, among members of the upwardly mobile lower middle class.

It is difficult to assess accurately the numerical strength of the two interconnected faiths—fundamentalism and evangelicalism; a recent Gallup poll in the USA concluded that one out of every three American adults considers himself/herself to be an

Evangelical. A common quality for Evangelicals is that they have all had some kind of direct spiritual experience; thus they speak of being 'born again'.[31] They vigorously affirm what they consider to be traditional lifestyles and values, the virtues of self-help and hard work. In the past, they have long considered religion to be a private affair, though they have cared deeply about the need for governments to control gambling, alcoholic intemperance and pornography.

Part of their appeal is that they offer, like all sects, decisive, authoritarian answers to contemporary issues, a quality of particular value to people utterly confused by the cult of uncertainties of the counterculture of the 1960s. Theirs is a world of God/Satan, Christ/AntiChrist, Christian/'secular humanists'.[32] The counterculture excesses—e.g. its support of pornography, abortion, opting out of the competitive capitalistic world, increased aid to the poor, anti-war programmes—were seen as signs of the fast-moving, satanic 'secular humanism'.

## b. Political fundamentalism: the New Right

The New Right is an ideological *political* movement, with its distinctive set of values and clear-cut answers to contemporary social and economic challenges. It has developed considerable support by being able, through its leaders, to go beyond traditional party lines and speak directly to voters. In the USA, the founding figures were people like William F. Buckley, Jr, and Barry Goldwater; Ronald Reagan became a highly effective communicator of the movement's beliefs.

Tremendous support for the movement has come not just from the rising lower urban middle class, but also from rural, small-town, and religiously fundamentalist citizens who have lost their cultural and economic power. They see the breakdown in morality, and the growing government support for welfare services, as ways of undermining the nation's local and international strength. For them, it is patriotic to support a *laissez-faire* market capitalism and decreasing aid to the poor. In other words, the New Right movement is an attempt to revitalize and reinforce the creation mythology of the American nation, along markedly conservative lines.[33]

Britain also has its New Right; simply expressed, the aim of Thatcherite conservatism, as seen by Anglican theologian John Atherton, is to destroy the ethos of a welfare state and replace it with a structure that encourages the revitalized Victorian virtues of self-help and enterprise.[34]

## c. The Moral Majority—the New Religious Right

Traditionally fundamentalists, as noted above, were seen 'as anti-political soul-savers who waited for the second coming of Christ, wanted to live decent lives and be left alone except when they would convert others'.[35]

This changed dramatically in 1979, when Evangelical fundamentalist Jerry Falwell recognized that, 'In spite of everything we are going to turn the nation back to God . . . the national crisis [is] growing quickly out of hand'.[36] Organized political action was now seen as the only way to achieve the traditional aims of evangelicals and fundamentalists. Thus, Falwell formed the Moral Majority, dominated by Protestant fundamentalists, but drawing together sympathetic Protestants of all kinds, Jews and Roman Catholics. Its platform was sharply focused: pro-life, pro-traditional family/morality, pro-American, pro-national defence and pro-Israel.

The New Right movement, now supported by the Moral Majority, benefited from religious legitimation; the revitalized conservative 'ideology is pronounced identical with the will of God for America'.[37] Reagan received explicit and militant support from the movement in the Presidential elections of 1980.

## d. Neo-conservatism

This movement differs from the various forms of conservative reaction already described in several ways. It is composed of a wide variety of intellectuals, and social scientists in particular, who would have been categorized in the counterculture days as the 'moderate left–"liberals" '.

Their radicalism has waned, as they contemplate contemporary socio-economic trends. Neo-conservatives join with the New Right in demanding a revitalized moral and work discipline, but the former claim that their concern arises from a thorough grasp of contemporary research, not from *a priori* fundamentalist/Evangelical beliefs about what society should be like; secondly, neo-conservatives are not nostalgic about an agrarian past, or the virtues of the rugged individualism of the frontiersman and cowboy.[38] And, unlike the New Right's followers, they support in principle a moderate form of the welfare state, but they insist that, for socio-economic reasons, it must not be extended at present.

Over recent years, the World Council of Churches, the Anglican and the Roman Catholic Churches have all pointed to the structures of sin that oppress millions of the poor, both in the economically underdeveloped and richer nations, e.g. the 1985 Report of the Archbishop of Canterbury's Commission on Urban Priority Areas (*Faith in the City: A Call for Action by Church and Nation*), the 1986 US Catholic Bishops' Pastoral Letter on the US Economy, and the 1987 encyclical letter of John Paul II, *Sollicitudo Rei Socialis*. Liberal capitalism and Marxist collectivism are criticized for their oppressive structures. The Churches call for a more rationally planned economy, better distribution of wealth, and participative structures that allow the poor to be involved in local and national decision-making.

Neo-conservatives, e.g. Peter Berger,[39] Richard Neuhaus and Michael Novak in the USA and Edward Norman in England, criticize these documents for containing, they assert, a swing towards, or acceptance of, leftist/Marxist thinking. Theologically, neo-conservatives assert, the emphasis is on the horizontal to the detriment of the divine transcendence. These critics believe that the present capitalist system must be defended as the only authentic method to protect the freedom of people.[40]

Neo-conservatives have a very narrow view of what the Gospel means and, consequently, of what evangelization should be about; liberal capitalism, not just Marxism, can be a source of oppression for countless millions, a point vigorously emphasized by John Paul II in his encyclical, *Sollicitudo Rei Socialis* (e.g. see para. 20).

## e. Roman Catholic fundamentalism: 1980s

Fundamentalist reactions, within the Church, to the confusions caused by the impact of the upheavals of the Revolution of Expressive Disorder and Vatican II, have become especially powerful and vociferous since the early 1980s. Catholic fundamentalism, particularly in the USA, is marked by:[41]

---

a concern, with Protestant fundamentalists, for the dangers of 'secular humanism', that is, the *assumed* undermining of the religious heritage of the nation through the conspiracy of liberals, media, government and leftists in theology and ecclesiastical administrations;

an elitist assumption, as in all sects, that fundamentalists have a kind of supernatural authority and right to pursue and condemn ruthlessly those who disagree with them, e.g. bishops;

a highly selective approach to what they think pertains to the Church's teaching, e.g. statements on ecclesiastical authority, private sexuality or incidental issues are obsessively highlighted, but the papal or episcopal statements on social questions are ignored, or considered matters for debate only;

concern for accidentals, not the substance of issues—e.g. the Lefebvre sect emphasizes Latin for the Mass, failing to see that this does not pertain to authentic tradition;

the vehemence and intolerance with which they attack co-religionists, who are striving to relate the Gospel/tradition to the world around them; this is a most tragic and dangerous quality, for so much energy is wasted in the attack and defence that should be directed outwards in the cause of the Good News;

nostalgia for a pre-Vatican II golden age, when it is assumed 'that the Church was then a powerful force in the world, with one universally accepted liturgy, undivided by misguided devotees of inculturation'.

---

# Pastoral reflections

If the Church does not reinterpret the religion of the Latin American people, the resultant vacuum will be occupied by sects, secularized political forms of messianism, consumptionism and its consequences of nausea and indifference, or pagan pansexualism (Puebla Document).[42]

1. It is hard to avoid strong emotions when discussing contemporary sects/cults, e.g. there are charges of brainwashing and sexual excesses, the dramatic breaking-off of relations with parents, the tragedy of 900 people of the People's Temple sect dying in 1978 in Jonestown, Guyana, under the direction of a messianic leader.

However, it is critically important to get behind the true and false accusations, in order to learn from the causes of these movements. People are caught in the state of personal and cultural confusion. They are not finding in the mainline Churches the sense of identity, a vibrant spirituality, the belonging and care, that they have a Gospel right to expect. Hence, as the Puebla Document quoted above notes, people turn else-where, e.g. to sects, consumerism, to fill a spiritual vacuum bereft of meaning.

The following comment summarizes some of the main reasons why the sects/cults are attractive, and the challenge they pose to mainline Churches:

Cults operate as surrogate extended families and, moreover, provide novel therapeutic and spiritual mystiques which confer meaning on social processes. . . . In so doing . . . they exploit the weaknesses of existing institutions (churches, nuclear families, psychiatry) and perhaps pose a threat to these institutions.[43]

2. Concern for the rise of sects/cults must not, however, weaken the commitment of the Churches to inculturation, that is, the faith/justice apostolate. Christianity is called to transform society, not only to attend to the souls of individuals. If Christians do not accept this transforming challenge, then they will themselves become a sect. They will be a frightened, inward-looking group of people, as the apostles were before Pentecost. They will flee from constructive, Gospel-demanded confrontation with culture, fearful lest they lose their own sense of security or that the Church will cease to exist. The words of rebuke, addressed by Christ to Peter, apply here also: 'Get behind me, Satan! Because the way you think is not God's way but man's' (Mk 8:33).

3. On a practical level, this means:

- fostering Basic Christian Communities, adapted to the local conditions, in which people can experience, with a sense of meaning and belonging, that *they* are the Church;

- devising adult catechetical programmes that include the contemporary social teaching of the Church;

- challenging people, through example and preaching, to be open to the gifts of faith and courage; without these gifts of the Lord, Christians will readily escape into themselves and form protective, elitist sects in order to guard themselves from 'the evils of the world';

- in relating personally to sect/cult members
  —avoid hostile, heated arguments; membership of these movements is not a question of logic, but generally of a sincere need for meaning and belonging; expressions of anger and vigorous disagreement will only affirm people in the rightness of their belief;
  —be an example of Christian patience and peace; the best witness to the truth of your beliefs will be your own inner peace built of faith and concern for justice;
  —do not rely on yourself alone, but pray for God's help.

4. Many young people, who left the mainline Churches during and after the Revolution of Expressive Disorder, did so because they felt these Churches had become spiritually desiccated. Prayer had become too formal, too wordy, too horizontal, lacking a meditative/contemplative base.

Let's face it. The tragedy is that mainline Christianity has a rich heritage of mysticism and contemplative prayer; yet, we have denied this heritage to people for centuries, wrongly believing it was a gift only for 'elite' people, like religious. Yet, *all* are called to sanctity and so to the highest forms of prayer.[44]

In recent years, some efforts have been made to revitalize our contemplative heritage and make it available to all. Much more has yet to be done.

5. Within the Roman Catholic Church today, there are new lay or lay/clerical movements developing, e.g. Comunione e Liberazione, Opus Dei, Neo-Catechumenate communities, Focolare. These movements are being rightly or wrongly criticized for having fundamentalist qualities. In a spirit of openness, these movements should evaluate themselves and, if necessary, discard fundamentalism and rediscover the heart of Gospel life.[45]

# Reflection questions

## To the reader

1. In the chapter, what do you find particularly helpful? Why?

2. If you belong to any parish organization, is it open to the views of non-members? Is it interested in injustices that people suffer in your local area?

## To a discussion group

1. If there are any sects/cults in your local area, what do you know of them, e.g. their recruitment methods, authority structures?

2. Invite a member, or former member, of a sect/cult to talk to you about why they joined. Do their comments fit the explanations given above?

3. Do you detect sect-like groups in your own parish community? If a group is open to dialogue, arrange a meeting so that you might share your mutual concerns and pray together.

4. What is contemplative prayer? What practical steps could you take in your parish to help people develop a spirit of prayer?

# Suggested reading

Appel, W., *Cults in America: Programmed for Paradise* (New York: Holt, Rinehart & Winston, 1983).

Beckford, J.A., *The Trumpet of Prophecy: A Sociological Study of Jehovah's Witnesses* (Oxford: Basil Blackwell, 1975).

Beckford, J.A., *Cult Controversies: The Societal Response to the New Religious Movements* (London: Tavistock, 1985).

Bromley, D.G., and Hammond, P.E., *The Future of New Religious Movements* (Macon, GA: Mercer, 1987).

Caplan, L. (ed.), *Studies in Religious Fundamentalism* (Albany, NY: State University of New York Press, 1987).

Cohn, Norman, *The Pursuit of the Millennium: Revolutionary Millenarians and Mystical Anarchists of the Middle Ages* (New York: Oxford University Press, 1974).

Douglas, M. *et al.*, *Religion and America: Spirituality in a Secular Age* (Boston: Beacon Press, 1982).

Holland, C.L., *The Religious Dimension in Hispanic Los Angeles: A Protestant Case Study* (Pasadena: William Carey, 1974).

Marsden, G. (ed.), *Evangelicalism and Modern America* (Grand Rapids, MI: W.B. Eerdmans, 1984).

Martin, B., *A Sociology of Contemporary Cultural Change* (Oxford: Basil Blackwell, 1981).

Melton, J.G., and Moore, R.L., *The Cult Experience: Responding to the New Religious Pluralism* (New York: Pilgrim Press, 1982).

Wilson, B., *Magic and the Millennium* (London: Heinemann, 1973).

Wilson, B., *Religion in Sociological Perspective* (New York: Oxford University Press, 1982), pp. 89–179.

# 8 Inculturation and youth subculture

Rock 'n' roll was very simple music. All that mattered was the noise it made, its drive, its aggression, its newness . . . The lyrics were . . . one step away from gibberish . . . [It] was a kind of teen code, . . . that would make rock entirely incomprehensible to adults (Nik Cohn).[1]

## Introduction

Youth subculture (or 'youth culture', as it is sometimes called) is an entirely new phenomenon in the Western world and, more recently, in Japan. (I use the word 'youth', not the less pejorative 'young adult', in reference to culture or subculture, because it contains certain important connotations in social-science literature.) It came into existence from about the mid-1950s onwards. Young people became noted for various protest and resistance movements against the adult society (including the mainline Churches) that they considered alien to them, uncaring and hypocritical. The Churches are still struggling both to understand this new phenomenon and how to respond with the message of Christ.

In this chapter we will:

- explain how youth subculture developed;

- describe its different types, and how it is encouraged to continue through a variety of socio-economic forces;

- describe how youth subculture could be a Christian initiation rite into the world and the faith community;

- suggest some pastoral responses to the needs of contemporary youth.

# Origins of youth subculture

## Youth subculture: meaning

Recall a key conclusion from Chapter 1: symbols, myths and rituals form distinctive cultures; they give meaning to people's lives.

A subculture contains some of the qualities of the dominant culture, but also contains distinctive symbols, myths and rituals that people in the subculture cherish, because they give particular meaning and identity to their lives. In every subculture there is always an element, sometimes strongly evident, of protest against the dominant culture of which it is part. The more people of the subculture feel threatened by the dominant group, the stronger and more vivid will its symbols of protest or resistance be. Take the example of the Roman Catholic Church in the USA prior to Vatican II. It was the best organized and the most powerful of the nation's subcultures. The more Catholics felt threatened by prejudice or bigotry against them, the more they developed their own symbols of identity, e.g. their school system, the ethnic parishes.

Youth subcultures are especially rich in distinctive symbols: dress, hair styles, music, rituals of protest or resistance to being absorbed into the adult world. For example, rock music became for the youth culture a highly popular art form, because it gives at the same time both the symbols of individual possibility and doubt as well as 'the symbols of collective security and comfort'.[2]

It is completely impossible to grasp the power of a youth subculture, if one is not prepared to enter as far as one can into the inner meanings of its symbols. A difficult, but an essential, task!

## Defining youth subculture

Simply stated, youth subculture is a way of life

- which emerges because of the lengthening period of time between childhood and adulthood;

- it is marked by uncertainty as to identity,

- because the young are told no longer to be 'childish' in their ways,

- but equally they are given no status in the adult world;

- thus, because they are without status, prestige and privileges of either children or adults, many young people feel lost and annoyed by the experience, and establish their own status systems, marked by distinctive *symbols* of fashion, music, boy/girl relationships and rebelliousness against adult authority;

- they become morally and intellectually dependent not on their parents, as was once the case, but on one another;

- for many young people, youth subculture is a period of great personal turmoil as they struggle to develop a new identity;

- for others, while they accept many of the lifestyle symbols of their peer group, they nonetheless work towards integration into the adult society in an uncritical and conforming way;

- others are unable to achieve integration, or entry into the adult world, because its symbols/rituals are denied them, e.g. through unemployment, the lack of educational opportunities.

There is no one youth subculture; rather, 'youth subculture' is an umbrella expression that covers a variety of styles, e.g. there are identifiable 'middle-class', 'working-class' and 'black' youth subcultures. They all tend to have some symbols in common, e.g. commitment to particular forms of music, but they also differ in various ways from one another.

## Origins of youth subculture

The Western world from the 1950s has become increasingly unable to provide young people with a clear-cut age that tells them when they should cease to be children and move to the stage of adulthood. Consequently, the youth subculture has emerged, and its existence continues to be reinforced, mainly for the following reasons:

## 1. Changes in age structures

Statistically the youth group—that is, people in an age bracket between children and adults—noticeably developed only in this century as a result of improvements in medicine and health. In the USA, between 1790 and 1840 society consisted only of children and young people, the median age being 16; in 1950 the median age had jumped to 30.8. By 1976, the 10–19 and the 45–64 age brackets were almost the same in numbers, each being around 22 per cent of the population.[3]

## 2. Intergenerational tensions

As young people move from childhood, they feel the urge to act independently of adults, especially of their parents. The tension is natural and occurs in all cultures. However, in the Western world there was an additional reason for this tension occurring: by the 1960s young people were attaining sexual maturity three to five years earlier than in 1900, because of the overall improvements in health.

## 3. Increased spending ability

Youth during the period of high employment in the 1950s and 1960s were able to earn high wages or receive increased pocket money. Lacking family commitments, they had considerable independence and opportunities for leisure activities.

## 4. Consumer industry

The commercial industry, sensitive to the increased spending power of youth, and the leisure time available to them, moved quickly to develop a response to fashion, entertainment and other consumer needs of youth. From 1955 to 1970, while expenditure on total personal consumption in the USA rose by 150 per cent, spending on recorded music increased fivefold—and roughly 75 per cent of all recorded music sold today, in monetary terms, is rock or other 'pop' music.[4]

The goods and services produced further helped to identify a separate youth subculture in society. And the consumer industry has a powerful self-interest reason to maintain and foster the self-conscious identity of youth subcultures.

## 5. Power of the mass media

With the evolution of television in particular, role models in the form of pop artists, e.g. Pat Boone, Elvis Presley, the Beatles, were able to have an immediate and universal impact on the youth world.

## 6. Extended education

As the educational requirements for skilled work continued to rise, so also did the time necessary to acquire the qualifications increase. Students were further delayed from having to assume the duties of adulthood.

## 7. Protest movements against injustices[5]

From the 1950s onwards, especially during the Revolution of Expressive Disorder in the 1960s, protest movements against all kinds of assumed or real injustices, e.g. unemployment, war, nuclear armaments, impersonalism of government and church institutions, became associated with youth. The adult world had been saying that there must be no more world wars, yet nuclear armaments, the war in Vietnam, were being not only sanctioned, but hypocritically encouraged according to the views of young people. These movements helped to draw people's attention to the fact that a new subculture was emerging in society.

- Within Britain (see Figure 8.1), the forms of protest depended on the type of class one belonged to:

    Middle-class youth opted to protest against nuclear armaments, the 'imperialism of the West'; since little came of these protest movements, the hippy movement, which rejected all structures in favour of 'freedom and love', emerged.

    Working-class groups, however, reacted to their increasing marginalization in society—their loss of roots, unemployment. The Teds saw in the black immigrant section of Britain the cause of their alienation and failure to get

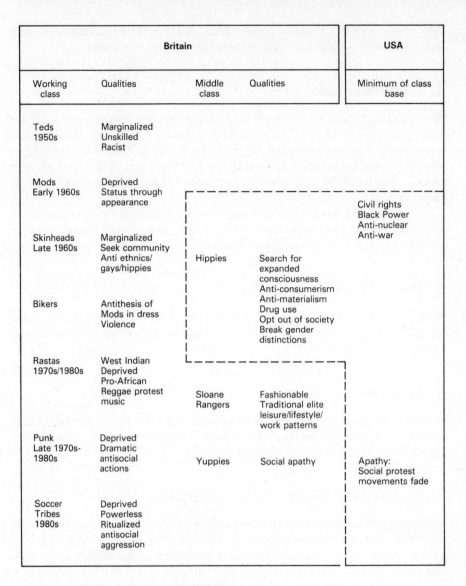

| | Britain | | | | USA |
|---|---|---|---|---|---|
| Working class | Qualities | | Middle class | Qualities | Minimum of class base |
| Teds 1950s | Marginalized Unskilled Racist | | | | |
| Mods Early 1960s | Deprived Status through appearance | | | | Civil rights Black Power Anti-nuclear Anti-war |
| Skinheads Late 1960s | Marginalized Seek community Anti ethnics/ gays/hippies | | Hippies | Search for expanded consciousness Anti-consumerism Anti-materialism Drug use Opt out of society Break gender distinctions | |
| Bikers | Antithesis of Mods in dress Violence | | | | |
| Rastas 1970s/1980s | West Indian Deprived Pro-African Reggae protest music | | Sloane Rangers | Fashionable Traditional elite leisure/lifestyle/ work patterns | |
| Punk Late 1970s- 1980s | Deprived Dramatic antisocial actions | | Yuppies | Social apathy | Apathy: Social protest movements fade |
| Soccer Tribes 1980s | Deprived Powerless Ritualized antisocial aggression | | | | |

**Figure 8.1** Youth subcultures: protest/resistance movements

ahead in society. Subsequent groups, e.g. Mods, Skinheads, Rastas, Bikers, also felt that the only way they could achieve a sense of belonging was to be different from the rest of the world around them. They were prepared to do this, even if this meant, as was the case with the Skinheads, Bikers, and Soccer Tribes, violent action against the dominant society. Unemployment has become a common experience of these protest groups. In Britain in the mid-1980s, the unemployment rate for youth is very high. The worst affected are blacks and working-class people.

- In the USA, where the class structure is less rigidly defined, the protest movements tended to transcend class lines, e.g. in civil rights, anti-war, Black Power movements.

# 8. Youth seen as scapegoats for evil

In times of rapid change and social chaos, people become confused. As Stanley Cohen says, people experience 'moral panic'. They yearn to discover who are the 'causes' of this disorientation and loss of acceptable moral values. Movements such as the Teds, Skinheads or Soccer Tribes in Britain, which are expressions of deviant youth subculture, are presented by the mass media as the 'folk devils', the evil ones who undermine accepted moral values in society. They are visible reminders of what morally we must not be.[6] Thus, the highlighting of real or imagined deviant youth behaviour is an example of the ritual of scapegoating referred to in Chapter 6 (pp. 102–103).

---

## Symbols, heroes and rituals of youth subculture

---

The most powerful symbols in any culture tend to revolve around sex, violence and romanticism. As regards the youth subculture, there are two added areas that evoke powerful symbols: authority and control.

In summary, the underlying story or mythology in youth subculture is basically that of 'antistructure', that is, 'anti-normal', 'anti-authority', 'anti-boundaries', 'anti-control', 'anti-adult'. A brief review of dominant symbols and rituals of youth subculture illustrates what is meant.

## 1. Types of music

Music, in any culture, is a powerful expression of the values of the culture and, at the same time, is itself a carrier of these values from one generation to the next. This is dramatically true of youth subculture, because so much of the music is anti-society. Most lyrics are incomprehensible to the adult world, but adult society says that music must be comprehensible, the words must make sense, the sounds controlled. 'Well', says the youth world, 'our music will be the opposite', that is, meaningless to the adult world.[7] And as rock music developed, so did its anti-establishment quality; today it can glorify sex, drugs and violence.

The origins of the music of the youth subculture again illustrate its anti-normal or anti-predictable quality. Black rhythm and blues material in the USA had been identified with racial oppression and life in the ghettos. It was not for whites.

Yet by the mid-1950s Pat Boone, the white American singer, was attracting an enormous teenage response, because he was using some aspects of black rhythm and blues material. Young people found in his risky, though somewhat bland, use of anti-white music a way to articulate their own anti-adult feelings.[8]

Elvis Presley, from a working-class background, drew on black musical traditions with far more skill and blatant sexual aggressiveness. Older people saw in this music, with its loud, rhythmic, sexual connotations, the values of rebellion against tradition and against themselves. The fact is, however, that Elvis, the one who reoriented rock music, also changed the character of Western culture. The Expressive Revolution would not have happened in the same way or to the same degree without rock music. We now live in a world that Elvis Presley helped dramatically to mould.

But the Beatles went further than Elvis in their anti-adult, anti-institutional music and lifestyle. For example, in the lyric of the song 'Getting Better' of 1967, there is an attack on the rigidity of school structures: '. . . The teachers that taught me weren't cool—You're holding me down, turning me round—Filling me up with your rules.' With their Liverpool working-class backgrounds, and their creative musical professionalism, they were well equipped to articulate anti-class sentiments in highly expressive rituals.

Reggae music among West Indian youth has its roots in a Jamaican society of poverty, slavery and colonization. Today this music offers black, unemployed West Indian youth in Britain the chance both to criticize a society that is racist and lacking in equality of opportunity, and to speak about their ultimate return in triumph to Africa.[9]

Finally, the world of pop music offered its devotees immediacy of satisfaction. People had to feel an immediate sense of belonging, in contrast to the restraints and self-sacrifices demanded by the adult society. Whatever could not be *felt*, could not be real.

## 2. Dress symbols

Words and music were important symbols, but far more effective was the dress and action image presented by the professional, mythological heroes of the youth culture. People like Bob Dylan and the Beatles brilliantly learned how to turn their lives into performances. Hence, when John Lennon attacked the Church or expressed the 'supremacy' of the Beatles over Jesus Christ, or when Dylan carried a lightbulb wherever he went, thousands of adoring peer-conscious fans did the same. When the Beatles in 1964 first arrived in the USA, the most powerful reason for their enormous impact on young people was not their extraordinary ability with guitars, nor their clever lyrics—it was their long hair. Youths were thrilled. Adults were annoyed. The Beatles gave young people their most powerful symbol of rebellion, long hair, even though they did not refer to it until a lyric of 1969—'Come Together'.

The impact of dress symbols, not just the long hair of the Beatles, was revolutionary. When the Beatles, Dylan, the Rolling Stones and The Who started in 1965 to appear in multi-coloured clothes, these were readily adopted by their youthful followers. The more teachers and parents objected, the more determined were the followers. By 1967, clothes that were flamboyant yet casual had become, like long hair, a most popular way to attack conformity to drab, dark suits, school uniforms, and short Establishment haircuts.[10]

Not surprisingly, therefore, the most distinctive symbols of identity and belonging among the working-class tribes of Britain are those of dress. Each successive group seems to outdo its predecessors in the flamboyancy of its dress symbols in an effort to shock the wider society. For example:

- Punk in 1976–77 broke on to the London scene. For Punks, the world is absurd and the only way to cope with it is with unusual clothing, blazing music and thoroughly outrageous behaviour. So Punk followers appear with their bodies perforated by safety pins, their hair spiky and garishly dyed, and their necks draped with all kinds of symbols geared to shock society, e.g. the swastika. Their music bands, also named to shock, e.g. The Sex Pistols, The Stranglers, The Damned, specialize in loudness and obscenities.

136

- The Bikers, for their part, cultivate dirt and chains in contrast to the Mods, who stress neatness and order.

## 3. Symbols of gender/violence/non-violence

Reactions, especially in Britain, to adult society diverge on the basis of class (see Figure 8.1 on p. 134). Working-class youth subculture is geared for action. For the Mods, it might be the action of dancing. For Teds, Skinheads, Bikers and Soccer Tribes, it is the action of violence; they actually seek violence as a way out of their considerable frustrations. And in these working-class movements, it is the male that dominates.

Passivity—often aided by drugs, not violence—is the emphasis for many within youth subculture of the middle class. Young people became frustrated or exhausted after trying to achieve changes in the adult world that they are expected to join. Hence, the hippie world of the middle class evolved, especially in the 1960s/1970s. If the wider society could not be changed, then an entirely new world would be built alongside of it. The new world would be created not by people doing anything special, but just by people 'being themselves', being open to their inner selves first and then to one another. New realms of selfhood were to be opened up and explored through the use of psychedelic drugs, sex, and communal living.

By way of summary, the following characterized the hippie world:

- barriers between the sexes disintegrated;

- especially in North America, the passive resistance to war and to the impersonalism of the capitalistic system: love will conquer all injustice;

- withdrawal from institutions, e.g. universities, and the voluntary acceptance of poverty;

- expressivity: work and play should be one; immediate personal gratification is essential;

- subjectivity: the need to enter into oneself, aided by drugs, for 'mystical' or religious experiences;

- individualism: one must be concerned first with one's self-fulfilment in order to avoid being lost in the faceless masses.[11]

## 4. The return of boundaries: 1980s

### Middle-class youth subculture

The hippie movement did not survive. It could only flourish if there was an economy with sufficient financial surplus and full employment to allow people to move in and out of work with ease. Once the economic recession hit, it was no longer so easy to find work without adequate training and experience. Not only did people of the middle-class youth subculture stop escaping into the hippie world, they also opted out of campaigning for social justice. Overall, the emphasis is now on obtaining the official certificates, e.g. university qualifications, for entrance into the uncritically accepted adult world of business and power. Leisure pursuits must not interfere with this emphasis.

The new middle-class youth tribe is called the 'yuppies'. Within Britain, a more elite tribe is referred to as the 'Sloane Rangers', the sons and daughters of the upper middle-class. They remain, like their parents, wealthy, landed, horsey, snobbish and secure in their friends, their schools and their lives. For example, men are expected to prove themselves in the army, the financial world, the Foreign Office, the legal profession or Parliament, but it would be thought unbecoming to be too obviously successful at any of them. Thus, intellectual pretensions are definitely discouraged by authentic Sloaners.

## Working-class youth subculture

People of the working-class youth subculture, as they especially experience the burdens of unemployment with its horrible monotony, boredom, and crippling loss of self-esteem, remain actively involved in fostering or supporting new, generally aggressive protest movements. Even those with employment may feel alienated from the wide class-ridden society. The violence and other antisocial symbols (e.g. of racism, nationalism) are evident in the behaviour of British 'soccer tribes', when they have attended games in Continental Europe in recent years.

# 5. The complexity of youth subculture

As this description implies, youth subculture is a complex reality, so much so that it is preferable, as noted earlier, to speak of various expressions of youth subculture. At a particular time and place, one expression may predominate or grip public attention, e.g. the hippie movement in the 1960s/1970s. In Table 8.1 there is a summary version of F. Milson's helpful typology of possible youth subcultures;[12] it should be studied alongside the overview given in Figure 8.1.

The reality is that most young people today are *ritualists*; they conform to adult values, though they may pass through some periods of rebelliousness.

The socially rejected, however, may never find it possible to accept their inferior position. They are powerless, removed from the possibility of using the institutions, e.g. educational services, employment, that are ultimately the only avenues for partici-

---

A. *The assenters–conforming groups:*
    a. Privileged: youth uncritically conforming to the adult society, e.g. yuppies
    b. Ritualists: conforming, but at times critical of it
    c. Hedonists: primarily seeking pleasure and enjoyment, e.g. 1960s' cultural revolution youth

B. *The experimenters:*
    a. Political revolutionaries: e.g. student civil-rights movements 1960s
    b. Personal revolutionaries: e.g. hippies, youth witnessing by simple lifestyle for a just world

C. *The socially rejected:*
    a. Delinquent youth
    b. Escapists: e.g. drug-takers
    c. Disgruntled/protesters: e.g. Punks, Skinheads, Soccer Tribes

**Table 8.1** Types of youth subculture

pation in, and control of, the adult society. The following example, however, shows that individuals will not *necessarily* remain in one particular type of youth subculture. In the example, of course, the young person, unlike the socially rejected, comes from a background that allowed him with some ease to make decisions about his life.

---

*Example*:
Joseph, from New York, comments: 'I come from a wealthy family and in my early youth I accepted without question that I would enter the world of finance [*the privileged*]. After a couple of years of university study and reflection on the Gospels in a prayer group, I began to question within myself some of the values of the world I had come to accept, but I still did nothing about my life [*ritualist*]. My friends asked me to prepare a report for them on the plight of Chicano (Mexican immigrants) grape pickers in a part of California. I was shocked at the degree of exploitation. Then I joined my friends' social justice group and became very active in official protests to employers and government [*political revolutionary*]. Now I work full time for this group and try hard to live simply to identify with the poor for whom I campaign [*personal revolutionary*]. It all started with Gospel reflection and then involvement with the poor.'

---

# Youth subculture: a Christian initiation rite?

Youth is a primary experience of death—the death of childhood (M. Harris).[13]

Youth subculture is one of the few most critical stages in the journey of life. It provides the cultural space in which young people are challenged to move away from the ways of childhood, and to prepare themselves through attitudinal/behavioural changes and skills for the responsibilities of adulthood. Ideally, this process of giving up the past and taking on an adult identity can be termed an initiation rite, a rite of passage.

Traditionally, in initiation rituals (see Chapter 6, pp. 106–108, and Chapter 4, pp. 74–77), the initiates are physically or symbolically separated or secluded from ordinary life and social relations, entering the phase which was referred to in Chapter 4 as *liminality*. That is, the initiates of the youth subculture have the status neither of children nor of adults. They are in the betwixt and between stage. Participants in initiation rites should eventually be reincorporated into the wider society in their new status, and this reincorporation is generally referred to as a symbolic rebirth. Thus in the youth subculture there is to be death to the ways of childhood and rebirth into adulthood.[14]

St Paul is referring to this human experience of transition from childhood to adulthood, which should also be a faith event, when he writes: 'When I was a child I used to talk like a child. When I became a man I put childish ways aside' (1 Cor 13:11).

The process of dying to the old identity and taking up the new can be most painful, the initiate experiencing periods of psychological and spiritual confusion, disorientation, chaos. Again, St Paul frequently refers to the process of conversion in initiation terms, and how painful and mysterious it can be, e.g. through reference to death/life, suffering/joy. Of himself he writes: 'we were crushed to the point of despairing of life. We were left to feel like men condemned to death so that we might trust, not in ourselves, but in God who raises the dead' (2 Cor 1:9).

I will now describe:

- how a youth subculture *should* be a Christian initiation ritual, whereby young people are formally aided to enter the world and the faith community as responsible evangelizers (see Figure 8.2);

- why it is becoming increasingly difficult in the contemporary Western world for a youth subculture to be used as a Christian initiation rite (see Figure 8.3).

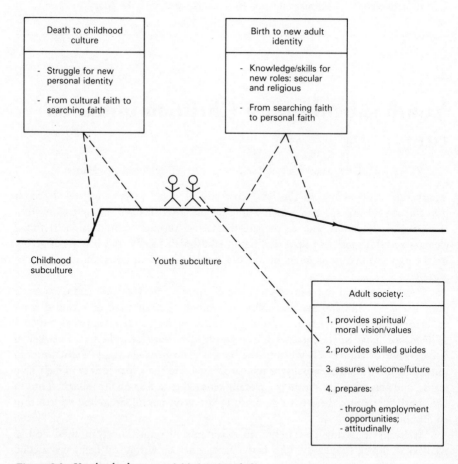

**Figure 8.2** Youth subculture as an initiation rite: ideal

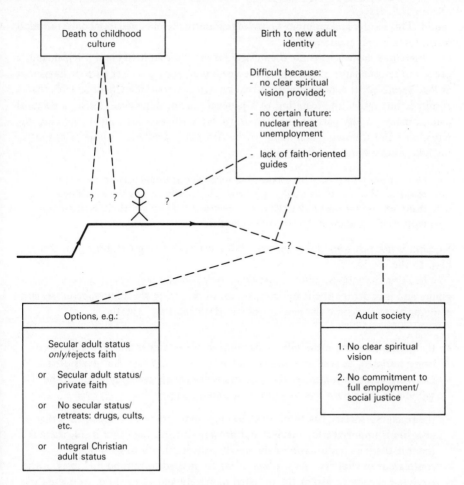

**Figure 8.3**  Youth subculture: initiation rite frustrated

## Youth subculture as a Christian initiation rite: ideal

In Figure 8.2, there is set out in summary form what should happen in a youth subculture from a Christian viewpoint. Notice that significant adjustment is required on the part of:

- the *initiates*, who must leave the childhood ways behind and adopt the necessary attitudes and skills for adult responsibilities;

- and *adults*, who must prepare themselves and their own culture attitudinally to receive the new adults.

Initiates need information and formation if they are to enter adulthood. *Information* refers to the knowledge and skills needed to participate in and contribute to the adult world. This secular and religious knowledge is normally obtained in schools, technical institutes and universities.

*Formation*, however, is for the initiate far more difficult to obtain. It demands a process of *personal* faith conversion to the Lord, with the agonies of faith darkness that St Paul speaks of. It is not just intellectual knowledge *about* the Christian faith that is required, but rather the fostering of a *personal* relationship with Christ, a personal commitment on the part of the initiate to act with and for him in building the Kingdom. The following comment by the Australian Catholic Bishops' Committee for Education emphasizes this point:

> Until recently there was the tendency to focus almost exclusively on the assent of the mind to the truth taught by Christ. This is *balanced* now by an insistence that faith also includes *trust* in Christ; *commitment* to Him; a personal relationship with Him, a communion with Him in love.[15]

So, faith is not just something we have, but a way of relating to Christ and, through him, to the world.

In initiation rituals, adults must be involved in two key ways: some as trusted guides and instructors of the initiates, others in preparing the adult subculture/faith community to welcome the new members. Both roles are crucial:

- the guides must have the gift of listening to the anxieties and hopes of those being initiated, as well as being able to articulate the vision and goals of the receiving adult community; these guides will instruct *primarily* through the witness of their own lives—words alone are powerless.[16]

- the receiving society has ambivalent feelings about its task; it recognizes that new life is important for survival and growth but, on the other hand, there is the fear that the enthusiasm of the newly converted will disturb their complacent mediocrity. So *prophetic adults* are needed to remind members of the receiving society to accept the initiated positively and, if need be, to make the necessary structural changes so that the initiated are able to use their talents socially, economically and spiritually for the good of the total culture.

---

## Youth subculture as a Christian initiation rite: the reality

Figure 8.3 sets out what can happen when a youth subculture is unable adequately, or at all, to realize its function as an initiation rite for one or more of the following reasons.

## 1. Lack of clear vision

Adult society can fail to offer initiates a clear and challenging vision of itself, since it is immersed in materialism, consumerism, greed, self-centredness. According to Allan Bloom, author of the best-selling book *The Closing of the American Mind*, the central problem in American society is widespread relativism. Hence, young students are taught that all ideas of the good life are equally valid; no absolute principles of morality exist.[17]

Why, some young people ask, should we try to enter the adult world when it is so utterly confused about what is good or bad?

## 2. Fear of nuclear holocaust

There is fear that society has no future because of the nuclear threat. Many young people say that the possibility of nuclear war is a major concern to them. It is a threat that overshadows their learning, their relationships and their growth.

They have reason to be concerned about the future: in the mid-1980s, American and Soviet arsenals contain about 18,000 strategic, thermonuclear warheads which, if exploded, could produce the equivalent of 500,000 Hiroshimas![18]

If the world is threatened with destruction, what is the use of being initiated into a society that has created such a threat?

## 3. Fear of unemployment

There is well-founded fear that there will be no employment for a significantly high percentage of young people; they have been offered no adequate training for work, or, if they have, there are no openings for them. Society is unwilling, or unable, to make the necessary attitudinal and structural changes to allow for employment possibilities to expand. Reflect on the following unemployment statistics:

- In Australia, 19 per cent of young people between 15 and 24; a further 4 per cent have part-time work only.

- In Britain, 1.2 million youth between 15 and 24 or about 23 per cent of the labour force under 25; in Bradford, 80 per cent of Asian migrant males of 16 to 19.

- In France, 28 per cent of those 15 to 24.

Unemployed youth in Western Europe are more likely to commit suicide, more open to drug abuse, more liable to break the law than working youth. For example, in 1985 in Belgium the suicide rate among 15- to 24-year-olds had more than doubled between 1970 and 1981; officials relate unemployment to the rising crime rate in the city's subway system, where they blame gangs of idle youths for a 79 per cent increase over a three-year period in muggings and assaults.[19]

---

*Example*:
Vince, aged 21, Liverpool, UK, left school at 15, but has never had a job: 'I really want to work. I'd take anything. No one wants me. One of my friends, like me, never having worked, committed suicide. Why blame him? Man, it is terrible not ever to be wanted! I am a nobody.'

---

# 4. 'Hypocrisy/indifference' of Churches

Youth surveys frequently show that the Churches are seen as 'hypocritical, apathetic or irrelevant, and clergy are accused of being either so remote or so trendy that any serious discussion with them is impossible'.[20] They claim not to see in the Churches an adequate number of adults to inspire them to live integrated faith/justice lives. There is the feeling that the Churches are so confused about their own identity that they are unable to respond to the special needs of the youth subculture.

Given these fears and perspectives of young people today, what happens to them when their time for leaving their youth subcultures occurs? These are some of the possibilities:

a. *either* they achieve the secular status of adulthood by obtaining employment, conforming to secular values but rejecting the faith and membership in any Church;

b. *or*, achieving secular status through employment, they conform to secular values uncritically, but develop a very private faith with no commitment to social justice;

c. *or*, achieving no secular adult status, because they can find no adequate employment, they seek to opt out of society through seeking a meaning system in world-rejecting sects, drugs and alcohol, or through a refusal to let go of adolescent pursuits.

d. *or*, co-operating with the grace of the Lord, they develop a deep personal relationship with Christ, committing themselves to work in a spirit of faith/justice for the Kingdom of God. They may or may not be able to obtain employment, but their status as adults comes first and foremost from their union with Christ the Leader, the Compassionate One, the Saviour of the little people of this world.

# Pastoral response: guidelines

> Separate youth work, which does not aim at a reconciliation of the generations and does not make this aim visible in its activities, does not belong to the Church. . . . A youth ministry should . . . never become a nervous effort to keep young people in or win them for the Church. A style of life which is inspired by the Gospel and a genuine care for a new generation is all that is required. The message of good news is strong enough to excite, engage and commit those of all ages (World Council of Churches).[21]

The following guidelines need to be followed, if we are to respond to the pastoral needs of contemporary youth:

1. Inculturation requires that we pastorally respond to people at *their* point of need, not the point of need that evangelizers think they should be at.
   The express concerns of youth are:[22]

- fear of unemployment;

- fear of nuclear war;

- relationships with one another and the adult world;
- the meaning of life.

2. Youth subculture is primarily a liminal period in which young people must struggle to move away from childhood and win a new identity for entrance into an adult world. It is a period of uncertainty/tension because of:

- the pull of the past;
- fear of an unknown future;
- the struggle to come to terms with their own sexuality.

3. Youth subculture can be a Christian initiation rite, whereby the young are inducted into the adult subculture/faith community as responsible Christians, with a maturing personal faith.

4. For this induction to take place, however, there are required
—*guides* who, primarily through the power of their own gospel-oriented–integrated lives, can inspire the young

- in *hope* to develop a personal faith/justice commitment to Christ and the world,
- to *minister* to one another with courage and zeal.

> Do not say, 'I am a child'.
> Go now to those to whom I send you.
> Do not be afraid of them,
> for I am with you to protect you –
> It is Yahweh who speaks (Jer 1:7f.)

—*prophetic* people, who challenge the wider society to develop socio-economic–political attitudes/structures that permit the newly initiated to exercise their adult rights in faith/justice.

5. There is considerable urgency to foster within People of God communities (families, Basic Christian Communities, parishes) the emergence of adults who have these faith-oriented, prophetic qualities. The future of society and the Church depends on them.

# Reflection questions

## To the reader

1. Do you agree that youth subculture exists in contemporary Western cultures? If you agree, can you identify different types? What symbols identify them?

2. Young people are often said to lose their faith. What does this mean? Share your answer with a friend.

## To a discussion group

1. How many young people *could* be attending your parish church worship? How many do attend? Why?

2. In what way did God call and empower various young people in the Bible? Before answering, read:

- 1 Samuel 3:1–21.

- Jeremiah 1:4–19.

- Luke 1:26–28.

How can you help young people in your parish to discover the energizing power of Christ in their lives:

- within a month?

- within six months?

- within one year?

# Suggested reading

Bloom, A., *The Closing of the American Mind: How Higher Education has Failed Democracy and Impoverished the Souls of Today's Students* (New York: Simon & Schuster, 1987).

Brake, M., *Comparative Youth Culture: The Sociology of Youth Culture and Youth Subculture in America, Britain and Canada* (London: Routledge & Kegan Paul, 1985).

Chambers, I., *Urban Rhythms: Pop Music and Popular Culture* (London: Macmillan, 1985).

Cohen, S., *Folk Devils and Moral Panics: The Creation of the Mods and Rockers* (Oxford: Martin Robertson, 1980).

Greeley, A., *Come Blow Your Mind with Me* (New York: Doubleday, 1971), pp. 166–179.

Hall, S., and Jefferson, T. (eds), *Resistance through Rituals: Youth Subcultures in Post-War Britain* (London: Hutchinson, 1976).

Harris, M., *Portrait of Youth Ministry* (New York: Paulist, 1981).

Kett, J. F., *Rites of Passage: Adolescence in America 1790 to the Present* (New York: Basic Books, 1977).

Stow, P., and Fearon, M., *Youth in the City: The Church's Response to the Challenge of Youth Work* (London: Hodder & Stoughton, 1987).

Turnbull, C. M., *The Human Cycle* (London: Jonathan Cape, 1984), pp. 81–170.

Warren, M., *Youth and the Future of the Church: Ministry with Youth and Young Adults* (Minneapolis: Seabury Press, 1982).

# 9 Inculturation, prejudice and discrimination

Racism is an evil which endures in our society and in our Church (US Catholic Bishops, 1979).[1]

Racial disadvantage is a fact of current British life . . . Urgent action is needed if it is not to become an endemic, ineradicable disease threatening the very survival of our society (Lord Scarman, 1981).[2]

## Introduction

'I am', wrote Charles Lamb (1775–1834), 'in plainer words, a bundle of prejudices—made up of likings and dislikings.' He speaks for all of us. So often we fail to see the virtues of others, the richness of their insights or the sufferings and even joys around us, simply because we are blinded by prejudice.

Prejudice is a feeling, favourable or unfavourable, towards a person or thing, prior to, or not based on, actual experience. At the very centre of prejudice is a *pre-judgement*. We make a judgement *before* we allow ourselves to be open to the person or thing as it really is.[3]

Prejudice interferes with how we approach and understand God and the world around us. So often, it is the cause of wars; it has even instigated the mass killings of millions of people.

This chapter, therefore, is about the most fundamental of all human problems:

- the nature, and main types, of prejudice/discrimination;

- how Jesus Christ confronted prejudice;

- practical suggestions about how we ourselves can help remove prejudice.

## Understanding prejudice

Prejudice—the jumping to conclusions without wanting to consider the facts—has two dimensions: the meaning and feeling aspects.

# The meaning aspect

The meaning aspect is commonly referred to as a stereotype. A stereotype is a pre-formed image or picture that we have of things or people; it is a shorthand, but faulty, method of handling or grasping a complex world. By placing things and people into pre-formed categories, I feel I am controlling a world that threatens my sense of order or meaning.

For example, I categorize bananas as tasteless, simply because I ate a certain type of banana years ago that had not ripened properly. On the basis of this one experience, I label *all* bananas, no matter what type they may be, as tasteless. Similarly, in cultural prejudice, some English people see *all* Irishmen as 'red-haired, stubborn, prone to excessive use of alcohol'. Some Irishmen, on the other hand, see *all* Englishmen as 'snobbish, arrogant, sour'. Yet there are Irish and English people who in no way exemplify these characteristics of behaviour!

The stereotype may not be entirely false. It may rest on a grain of truth. For example, concert pianists are said to be temperamental. By and large, they are forced to practise a highly sensitive craft in a setting (e.g. in draughty halls) where there are many possibilities of interference in the intensity of concentration their artistry requires. No wonder it is said that they are temperamental. But the error is in expecting *all* concert pianists to act in this way, or expecting *all* Irishmen, or *all* Englishmen, to act according to preconceived images. The stereotype is a *pre-judgement*. It is the judgement that I make without first checking the facts about things or people.

# The feeling aspect

Prejudices are not just made up of stereotypes; they are stereotypes motivated by strong, and often powerful, feeling impulses (see Figure 9.1). The feeling aspect forces the prejudiced person to see only what he or she wants to see, even to see things that are not there at all.

---

*Examples:*

An amusing story is told of two elderly Catholic ladies in Dublin who were passing by a lawn on which an elderly clergyman was throwing a ball to a dog. Said one lady: 'That's the Archbishop of Dublin'. The other said: 'Ah, the dear old gentleman, simple and innocent as a child, playing with his little dog'. The first said: 'It's the Protestant Archbishop, you know!' The second said: 'Ah, the silly old fool, wasting his time with a pup'.[4] The feeling aspect of prejudice is evident in the second lady's comment.

Jesus, on one occasion, spoke of how the people received John the Baptist and himself: 'For John came, neither eating nor drinking, and they say, "He is possessed". The Son of Man came, eating and drinking, and they say, "Look, a glutton and a drunkard, a friend of tax collectors and sinners" ' (Mt 11:18f.). No matter what Jesus does, his enemies will only see evil in him.

---

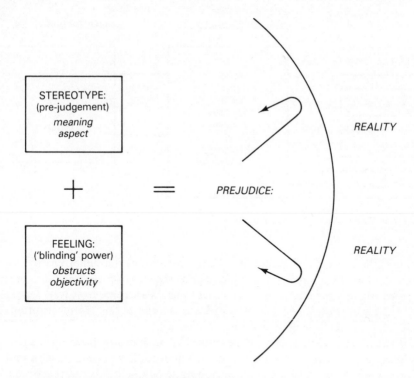

**Figure 9.1** The twofold dimensions of prejudice

# Prejudice and discrimination

Within this section, the following points will be clarified:

- the types of prejudice;
- the relationship between prejudice and discrimination (Figure 9.2).

## Types of prejudice

### 1. Cultural or ethnic prejudice

People of every culture or nation tend to think that their way of doing things is right; other ways of acting are stupid, crude, uncivilized, unreasonable, evil or superstitious.[5]

This type of prejudice, in favour of one's own group, is what is technically called *ethnocentrism*. In its mild forms, ethnocentrism is normal, reasonable and serves a useful purpose. Group or what can be termed *ethnic* identity requires a feeling of pride in the group's achievements, the feeling that other ethnic groups have something to learn

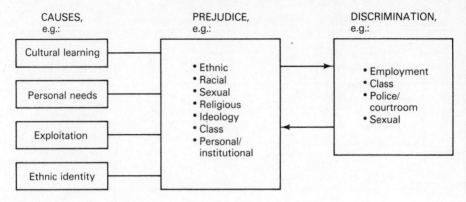

| CAUSES, e.g.: | PREJUDICE, e.g.: | DISCRIMINATION, e.g.: |
|---|---|---|
| Cultural learning | • Ethnic<br>• Racial<br>• Sexual<br>• Religious<br>• Ideology<br>• Class<br>• Personal/<br>  institutional | • Employment<br>• Class<br>• Police/<br>  courtroom<br>• Sexual |
| Personal needs | | |
| Exploitation | | |
| Ethnic identity | | |

**Figure 9.2**   Causes of prejudice/discrimination

from my ethnic or cultural group. We call this patriotism. But, unfortunately, such patriotism is apt to evaporate, as our group pride takes us over the brink into prejudice; then ethnocentrism ceases to be a positive value. We become excessively nationalistic. The assumption is that 'our way of life is *the* way of life'. Members of other ethnic groups have nothing of any value to offer us!

Ethnic prejudice, therefore, can be defined as 'an antipathy based upon a faulty and inflexible generalization. It may be felt or expressed. It may be directed toward a group as a whole, or toward an individual because he is a member of that group.'[6] Notice the reference to 'faulty and inflexible generalization', that is, to the two aspects of prejudice: the meaning and feeling dimensions.

---

*Example*:
One evening, while visiting a Fijian village, I heard my hosts laugh every time they mentioned a person they called 'the backhome man'. On asking about him, I was told: 'He is the New Zealander who has come to help us build a water supply for our village. That is good. But whenever he speaks, he starts like this: "*Back home* in New Zealand, we have the best road network in the world . . . the best education system . . and so on!" He is not interested in anything Fijian.'

Despite the genuine concern this New Zealander had to help the less fortunate, he was suffering from an overdose of ethnocentrism or ethnic prejudice. He assumed New Zealanders had nothing to learn from the Fijians.

---

## 2. Racial prejudice

*Race* is a highly confusing word. It is used in at least three main ways:[7]

a. To indicate an ethnic group:
People who share distinctive cultural qualities are referred to as belonging to this or that race, e.g. the American *race*, the English *race*. So, the expression *race relations* refers here to an interaction between two or more ethnic groups.

b. To indicate a distinct biological group:
Commonly, in English, *race* connotes a group of people who share common *physical* qualities and form a discrete and separable population category. Understood in this sense, the term has *no* scientific validity whatsoever; no fixed or discrete racial categories exist in the world.[8]

c. To indicate superiority/inferiority:
The term *race* is here used by people of some ethnic group to refer to another group of people, who may or may not have a sense of belonging together as an ethnic group, in ways that proclaim the superiority of the former and the innate biological inferiority of the latter. There is *no* scientific foundation for this belief.

A basic assumption of human inequality that pervaded the emergence of colonialism in the West and came to be called *racism* has remained in the popular imagination ever since. The belief in the inferiority of some groups of people, or *races* as they were named, has been transferred from one generation to the next, and continues to haunt contemporary 'race-relations situations'. These races are distinguished by real or imagined physical characteristics, e.g. the colour of the skin. Racism existed before the development of colonialism, but in a less dramatic and organized way.

---

*Definition of racism*:

By racism we mean

ethnocentric pride in one's racial group and preference for the distinctive characteristics of that group;

belief that these characteristics are fundamentally biological in nature and are thus transmitted to succeeding generations;

strong negative feelings towards other groups who do not share these characteristics,

coupled with the thrust to discriminate and exclude the outgroup from full participation in the life of the community (World Council of Churches, Uppsala Report, 1968).

---

Thus racism includes the belief that race determines intelligence, cultural and moral qualities, e.g. the Nazis branded *all* Jewish people as a separate ethnic group, even though Jews had no feeling of forming such a separate group, and considered them as innately/biologically inferior as human beings. When people are considered *nonhuman*, they can be discriminated against, even killed, by the oppressing group with impunity, a reality so tragically true for Jews in Germany under Hitler.

A contemporary form of racism is the system of *apartheid* in South Africa. The South African Roman Catholic Bishops' Conference condemned apartheid for precisely its racist assumptions: 'The basic principle of apartheid is the preservation of what is called white civilisation. This is identified with white supremacy. . . . It is a purpose dwarfing every other purpose, an end justifying any means.'[9] Today less than one-quarter of the population hold all political power and nearly all civil rights.

# 3. Sexual prejudice

Sexism, as a prejudice, is the assumption that a person is inferior in some way or other as a human being because he or she belongs to a certain biological category. Sexism, like racism, assumes that members of a particular sex are objects to be freely used for the pleasure and the preservation of the dominant position of the other sex. Anti-female prejudice, for example, is extremely common in most cultures of the world; women are falsely considered to be intellectually and emotionally inferior, and childlike when compared with men. Women are depicted as helpmates to men, incapable of participating equally with men in making decisions that concern them and society.

Christians must be alive to the fact that anti-female prejudice is to be found within various books of the Bible. The writers reflect the male-centred cultures of their times. For example, in the book of Genesis, in the created order the female is depicted as subservient to the male. Often in the Old Testament women are presented as dangerous to the male's 'rightful position as the superior being', e.g., as seductresses, sorcerers, betrayers. In the writings of St Paul, there are some passages that reiterate the contemporary culture's assumption that the female must be always subordinate to the male (e.g. Eph 5:22–33); the duty of the male is that of order and love in society, that of the female—as with slaves and children—is to be obedient and submissive to the male (e.g. Col 3:18–22).

# 4. Religious prejudice

Once a religious group believes it has the monopoly of truth concerning salvation, that is, that it has nothing to learn from any other religion, then there is prejudice. Thus, for centuries Roman Catholics looked on Protestants as thorough heretics, lost to Christ; Protestants in their turn thought the same of Catholics.

Religious prejudice can be used to support a political system that is itself discriminatory towards minority groups. Such is the case today, for example, among some extreme Protestant groups in Northern Ireland; for them, Catholics are evil, the Pope is Anti-Christ.

---

*Examples*:
Dr E. P. Groenewald, a leading Dutch Reformed Church theologian, wrote in 1947, in support of apartheid: '[Purity of blood] is as necessary for a nation to do the will of God as is holiness for the individual if he wants to serve God wholeheartedly. . . . If a nation guards its separateness, it will enjoy the blessings of God.'[10]

William Johnston writes on Northern Ireland: 'Religion was shamelessly tied to ideology and culture. It became axiomatic that to be a good Protestant one must fanatically wave the Union Jack and to be a good Catholic one must reverently salute the Tricolor.'[11]

---

# 5. Ideology as prejudice

Ideology is an action-oriented, dramatic understanding of the person and the world. A person is emotionally and entirely controlled by an ideology, and it becomes for him or her a dogmatic faith the truth of which can in no way be questioned. The ideologist *pre*-judges everything according to this faith, and he or she will not listen to any argument that in any way throws doubt on the truth of the pre-judgement. For example:

- An ideological Marxist sees conflict in all things, and is so blinded by this belief that the presence of any form of consensus without conflict is completely ignored.

- A Scriptural fundamentalist assumes that the Genesis story of creation is literally true; he or she will refuse to accept the contrary insights of Scripture scholars.

- Pilate, on the other hand, claimed to be an open Roman ruler, a so-called liberal thinker, but he was also a vigorous ideologist; ' "Truth?" said Pilate, "What is that?"'; and with that he went out again to the Jews' (Jn 18:38). In other words, he was so committed to the view that no objective, unchanging truth can exist that he refused to listen to any view to the contrary. He asked his question of Jesus, but immediately rushed off to avoid hearing the answer.[12]

# 6. Social class prejudice

A social class is any portion of a people that is marked off from the rest by a distinction of social status; in a system of social classes, there is a hierarchy in the listing of the classes, i.e. some are thought to be superior or inferior to others within the system.

A wide range of prejudices (and discriminations) makes it extremely difficult for people, especially in the lowest class, to move upwards, because they have little or no access to the power that is held by the middle and upper classes. When this situation is combined with the prejudice of racism, the problem of upward mobility is made yet more difficult.

---

*Example*:
In Britain, despite the fact that there have been almost twenty-two years of anti-discrimination legislation, the 2.4 million blacks (including Pakistanis and Indians) remain at the bottom of the socio-economic pyramid. The average non-white worker earns only 85 per cent of the income of all workers. Non-white unemployment stands at 20 per cent, twice the figure for the 95 per cent of the population that is white. The pressure of class prejudice against the upward socio-economic mobility of blacks within Britain is enormous.

---

# 7. Personal/institutional prejudice

In 1967, two black activists in the USA, Stokely Carmichael and Charles V. Hamilton, introduced the term 'institutional prejudice', as opposed to individual racism, to highlight the fact that anti-black attitudes had become entrenched in key institutions of society, e.g. education, justice, government. Hence, black people are obstructed at all levels from obtaining their civil rights. Similarly, we can also speak of *institutional* religious or anti-feminist prejudice. Instead of the word 'institutional', sometimes the terms 'structural', 'structures of sin' or 'sinful structures' are used.

---

*Examples:*

Tessa Blackstone argues that institutional prejudice makes it difficult for women to be engineers in Britain today, e.g. the teaching profession tends to hold to stereotypes about what girls can and cannot achieve; the profession does not imagine them as engineers. This institutional attitude is transferred to girls, who are then less likely to see themselves as engineers.[13]

Recently, Sister Joan Chittister, when writing on institutional prejudice against women, commented that 'nowhere are women actually equal, either in Church or society, and everywhere male systems define, restrict and exclude women from their inner sanctums' in which decisions are made, even about women.[14]

---

## Prejudice/discrimination and causes

---

# 1. Causes of prejudice

The causes of prejudice are many. However, it is possible by way of summary to pin-point several important roots of prejudice:

## a. Cultural learning

Rudyard Kipling grasped, in a few brief lines, the power of ethnocentric thinking, e.g. the feeling of our cultural or sexual superiority:

> All good people agree,
> And all good people say,
> All nice people like Us, are We
> And everyone else is They.[15]

We learn that 'All nice people like Us, are We . . .' first and foremost through absorbing, so often *unconsciously*, the prejudices of our own nation about other peoples or things.

## b. Particular personality needs

Deeply insecure people achieve for themselves a sense of self-esteem simply by down-grading the abilities of other people, e.g. if I believe that blacks have lower IQs than whites, then I as a white person feel superior to blacks, and I therefore feel good.

The process, or ritual, of 'scapegoating' (see Chapter 6, pp. 102–103) exists in race and ethnic relations. It is a simplistic and unreal way of solving or avoiding complex problems. Usually, visibly identifiable minorities, e.g. blacks, Mexicans and Asians in the USA, are seen as the causes of my personal or group's misfortunes. Invariably, the scapegoated people are powerless to protect themselves.

---

*Example*:
Stephen Castles *et al.* reflect on what happened to migrant workers in Europe from Third World countries once the economic recession began, following the oil crisis of the mid-1970s: 'As living conditions there [in the cities] deteriorated, indigenous workers often came to blame the immigrants, and far-right groups took the opportunity to fan the flames. The result was outbreaks of racial violence.'[16]

---

## c. To legitimize socio-economic exploitation

Historically, prejudice has been used to rationalize, for economic and political gain, the oppression of minority groups by dominant cultures. In contemporary South Africa, the white minority elite feels threatened economically and culturally, but the assumption of superiority enshrined in apartheid allows it to dominate ruthlessly and economically the republic's black and Coloured ethnic groups.[17]

## d. Maintenance of ethnic identity

In order to maintain or further intensify a group's sense of belonging and security, leaders can encourage an excessive nationalism, which may well slip into a form of racist superiority. Today, indigenous Fijians fear the economic and political influence of the numerically stronger descendants of the Indian migrant workers of the nineteenth century. Under articulate, highly nationalistic leadership, indigenous Fijians are about to reduce the Indian Fijians to the status of second-class citizens.

# 2. Forms of discrimination

Discrimination is the differential treatment of people, who have been assigned through prejudice, to a particular social category. In other words, discrimination is the acting out of one's prejudice. Not everyone, however, who is prejudiced, will automatically allow that prejudice to flow over into forms of discrimination. The following are some forms of discrimination.

## a. Educational discrimination

Prejudice can lead, often insidiously, to discriminatory behaviour against minority ethnic groups. The following extract from an official inquiry shows why West Indian children in British schools are poor achievers:

[We] are convinced from the evidence that we have obtained that racism, both intentional and unintentional, has a direct and important bearing on the performance of West Indian children in our schools. . . . [It] has repeatedly been pointed out to us that low expectations of the academic ability of West Indian pupils by teachers can often prove a self-fulfilling prophecy. Many teachers feel that West Indians are unlikely to achieve in academic terms but may have high expectations of their potential in areas such as sport, dance, drama and art. . . . [Teachers] may be led to encourage pupils to pursue these subjects at the expense of their academic studies.[18]

## b. Employment discrimination

Research in Britain in 1966 pinpoints what happens when prejudice leads to discrimination in employment. Three subjects, an Englishman, a Hungarian and a West Indian, all with exactly the same qualifications, applied for the same forty jobs. The Englishman was accepted thirty times, the Hungarian seventeen, and the West Indian three.[19] Discrimination continues. Sylvester Monroe reported recently that 'Many British employers, however, are reluctant to employ blacks in even the most menial capacity. Thus most poor blacks are forced to fall back on . . . community service, such as picking up rubbish along the Thames.'[20]

## c. Housing

In their efforts to obtain accommodation in an English city, a West Indian researcher was told thirty-eight times that the accommodation was already taken, even though two white researchers were informed that it was still available. The minority ethnic group or person so often feels powerless to act against discrimination, as is clear in the following example.

*Example*:
There is a Los Angeles real estate agent who customarily takes Chicano clients only to the poorest housing sections and deliberately inflates the prices. These clients often lack the education and the language to see the discriminatory act, though they may feel 'something is wrong'.

## d. Class discrimination

The Report of the Archbishop of Canterbury's Commission on Urban Priority Areas (1985) pinpoints what happens to people in the lowest class in a society simply because they are poor: 'Poverty is at the root of *powerlessness*. Poor people . . . are trapped in housing and in environment over which they have little control. They lack the means and opportunity—which so many of us take for granted—of making choices in their lives.'[21]

## e. Police and courtroom discrimination

Not infrequently, members of minority ethnic groups, rightly or wrongly, feel that the police force and the courts exist to serve only the interests of the dominant group in the society. The 1981 Brixton disorders illustrate this point. In his report on these disorders, Lord Scarman considered that the intensity of the violence was due in part to 'the ill-considered, immature and racially prejudiced actions of some officers in their dealings on the streets with young black people. . . . It may be only too easy for some officers . . . to lapse into an unthinking assumption that all black people are potential criminals.'[22]

In other words, Scarman is referring to the problem of labelling or stereotyping that was explained earlier in this chapter; individuals were judged as dangerous, simply because they *looked* like West Indians.

---

*Example*:
A researcher in New Zealand comments: 'The judicial system labels a large proportion of Maori males as having a criminal character, and this would lead the public and police to give any Maori male the label of "criminal" even *before* he acquires an official record. This would help to explain also the increased likelihood of prosecution of Maori youths at the first offence.'[23]

---

## f. Male/female sexual discrimination

Sexual oppression, springing from deep anti-female prejudice, may not only be the oldest form of human domination; it is possibly also, says Rosemary Radford Ruether, the most entrenched type of prejudice/discrimination in society. Ruether believes that 'the domination of women is the most fundamental form of domination in society, and all other forms of domination, whether of race, class, or ethnic group draw upon the fantasies of sexual domination.'[24] This is as true in the West as in many Third World countries, e.g. Pakistan, Korea, Iran.[25] In the West, women have customarily been accorded a lower status, and in consequence they suffer discrimination; under pressure, especially from women themselves, prejudice/discrimination is somewhat lessening.

Some statistics illustrate society's widespread discrimination against women. For example, women make up a third of the world's formal labour force (and most of its non-formal workforce), yet receive a tenth of the world's income. They own less than 1 per cent of the globe's property. Two-thirds of the illiterate people in the world are women. Practically the entire training and technical know-how for improving the world's agricultural production is made available to men only. However, about 50 per cent of the agricultural production and almost all of the food processing is the duty of women. Little apartheid, 'the system' or 'sinful structures' keep it that way.[26]

In the 1960s, within the Western world in particular, the struggle intensified for the rights of women. As more and more women entered the labour force, they increasingly recognized the discrimination against them and that it could be removed only through concerted action on their part. Feminism has now become for many a symbol of liberation from centuries-old male prejudice/discrimination. For others, especially for those who find the symbols of male dominance congenial, feminism evokes only anger and confusion.

Men, for their part, can become the victims of their own male-centred stereotypes. In New Zealand, over 85 per cent of traffic casualties are male. This is scarcely surprising. A dominant stereotype of the nation's male is that a man must be physically tough, highly sceptical of intellectual attainments, determined, and prepared to prove his manhood through *ample* doses of alcohol.[27] In Australia,[28] the image is that of an even more rugged individual—unemotional, *hard-drinking*, thoroughly able 'to keep women in their place'. Men who are interested in the arts or intellectual pursuits are considered in both countries as 'rather strange—just not with it'.

## g. Ecclesiastical/liturgical discrimination

Patriarchy, which in recent decades has come to mean not just male rule, but male-instigated oppression over women, has deeply affected the Churches for centuries. Scripture has been misused to support patriarchy and the Churches have too readily uncritically accepted the male-centred cultures in which they exist. Certainly, within the Roman Catholic Church patriarchy has helped foster:

- *clericalism*, that is, the belief and practice that only the clergy should be involved in proclaiming the word of God and in ecclesiastical administration; lay people—especially women—must be submissive, dependent receivers.

- *male-oriented*, or sexist, liturgical language. For centuries, in the language of the Church, women did not exist; they were non-persons. God comes to save *men*. Hence, when the English translation of the Eucharistic Prayers first came out after Vatican II, we read: 'This is the cup of my blood . . . shed for you and for *all men*'. 'Men' is a most powerful symbol. It has come to connote, for women, patriarchal domination, male superiority/female inferiority. Patriarchy in any form is a 'sinful structure'.[29]

# Jesus confronts prejudice

Jesus, sensitively aware of prejudice and discrimination within the culture of his time, quite deliberately attacks these crippling vices in various ways.

## 1. By accepting the Samaritans

Jews looked on Samaritans in a racist manner; they were pictured as stupid, lazy and heretical. And the Samaritans had similar views of their Jewish neighbours. Scripture commentator J. McKenzie points out that: 'there was no deeper break of human relations in the contemporary world than the feud of Jews and Samaritans, and the breadth and depth of Jesus' doctrine of love could demand no greater act of a Jew than to accept a Samaritan as a brother'.[30]

Hence, when Jesus told the story of the Good Samaritan, his listeners would have been left in no doubt about its meaning for them (Lk 10:29–37). A man is left to die on the roadside. Some very important people in the Jewish hierarchical social-status system see him dying, but excuse themselves from any obligation to do anything because they are too busy. But the one considered by the Jewish people to be stupid and uncouth—a Samaritan—sees the dying Jew and immediately goes to his aid. Jesus' listeners must have been stunned to hear him say: 'Go, and do the same yourself' (v. 37). They could not live as Christians and at the same time hold on to ethnic or racist prejudices. The choice is dramatically clear.

In the second story, this time a personal event in Christ's life, Jesus again reminds his disciples, and all those who wish to follow him, that prejudice must have no place in their lives. Jesus journeys through Samaria, a country normally avoided by Jews (Jn 4:1–42). He pauses at a well and asks a Samaritan woman for a drink of water. The woman is obviously startled by such a request, for the prejudiced bitterness between the two peoples is such that one would never ask or receive even a drink of water from the other: 'What? You are a Jew and you ask me, a Samaritan, for a drink?' (v. 9).

The disciples, when they find Jesus talking to the Samaritan woman, are startled and embarrassed: they 'were surprised to find him speaking to a woman, though none of them asked, "What do you want from her?" or, "Why are you talking to her?"' (v. 27). Thus, by word and example, Jesus attacks the racist prejudice of his day.

## 2. By associating with the marginalized

Contrary to the behaviour of the Pharisees, Jesus associates with 'sinners', that is, with those who are publicly known to be violators of the Jewish moral and ritual code: 'The tax collectors and the sinners, meanwhile, were all seeking his company to hear what he had to say, and the Pharisees and the scribes complained. "This man" they said "welcomes sinners and eats with them"' (Lk 15:1–3).

## 3. By dialoguing with the rejecting elite

While strongly disagreeing theologically with the scribes and Pharisees, he nonetheless remains friendly, open to them, or unprejudiced towards them. We even see him dining with a Pharisee, overlooking at first the fact that his host had given him no special welcome. Jesus uses the occasion to point out gently what true conversion means; he reflects on the deep repentance and love of the woman who washed his feet with her tears and 'wiped them away with her hair' (Lk 7:44).

## 4. By respecting the dignity of women

According to Jewish culture at the time of Jesus, in many ways women are considered inferior to men. However, often in his daily life, Jesus expresses concern for the welfare of women, but in ways that are not condescending or prejudiced; he heals sick women, and forgives sinners among them. And he appears to Mary Magdalene before he reveals himself to the apostles; she is charged to carry the news of his resurrection to the disciples (Jn 20:11–18).[31]

# The Churches and prejudice

It is impossible briefly to provide an overview of how the Churches have fostered, or actively hindered, the development of prejudice, especially of cultural and racial prejudice/discrimination. Several comments, however, may be helpful.

## 1. Early Christian communities

These communities accept the 'class- and male-biased household regulations of contemporary, upper class Hellenistic society, and legitimize them by making these expressions of God's will',[32] e.g. the submission of wives to their husbands, the necessity of slaves being obedient to their masters (Col 3:18, 22–24). We also recognize now just how these early Christian communities fostered a strong anti-Jewish prejudice, which helped form the foundation for a later vicious anti-Semitism, that has affected the Churches for centuries. When Vatican II stated that 'The Church repudiates all persecutions against any person . . . deplores the hatred, persecutions, and displays of anti-Semitism directed against the Jews at any time and from any source',[33] the Council was at last publicly admitting, and asking forgiveness for, the many times that the Church had been responsible, over the centuries, for anti-Semitic behaviour.

## 2. Colonial and missionary expansion

We also must admit that Christianity played an important role in fostering Western colonialism, with its associated racist and paternalistic attitudes and oppression, throughout the world.[34]

The decree of 1445 of Pope Nicholas V (1397–1455), with its approval of the subjugation of infidels to the Church 'for their own good', laid the foundation for Spanish and Portuguese colonialism. The decree helped to encourage the Portuguese slave trade. The gross destruction of human rights, in the New World, however, led Pope Paul III to condemn in 1537 the enslavement of Indians. Tragically, however, the ruthless colonial suppression of human rights continued. C. D. Rowley, writing on the influence of Protestant Churches in British colonies, comments that the 'discounting [of] the native systems of belief, paved the way for more debased ideologies of colonialism'.[35] Without necessarily any deliberate ill-will on their part, many evangelizers over the centuries just accepted, and supported uncritically, the cultural and racist prejudices of their times.

## 3. Recent years

The Churches, over the last thirty years, have become more aware of cultural and racial prejudices of the societies in which they live:

- The World Council of Churches initiated in the 1960s a vigorous, educational programme against world racism.

- Many Churches within South Africa have become publicly critical of the apartheid system.[36]

- The theology of liberation has called the oppressed—those economically and politically prejudiced and discriminated against for centuries—to become actively involved in their own liberation.

- Within the USA, the Roman Catholic Bishops, in a pastoral letter of 14 November 1979, bluntly stated the reality: racism remains, even within the Church:

---

Racism is an evil which endures in our society and in our Church . . . Racism is a sin: a sin that divides the human family, blots out the image of God among specific members of that family, and violates the fundamental human dignity of those called to be children of the same Father . . . Many of us have been prisoners of fear and prejudice. We have preached the Gospel while closing our eyes to the racism it condemned. We have allowed conformity to social pressures to replace compliance with social justice.[37]

---

# Pastoral responses

Prejudice is commonly thought to precede, and be the cause of, discrimination. However, discrimination may also precede prejudice and be a cause of it. In fact, because prejudice and discrimination feed on each other, it is essential that both evils be attacked *simultaneously*. The following are some practical suggestions.

## *Action against prejudice: personal/group work*

### 1. Self-knowledge

Even though we may not be aware of it, the *potential* for prejudice (and discrimination) against peoples of different ethnic groups remains within each one of us. Reflect on the following example.

---

*Example*:
A few years ago, in a multi-cultural Catholic training institute in Asia, a group of Japanese students were enthusiastically preparing to display symbols of their Japanese culture for other cultural groups to enjoy. Before breakfast one day, they attached a large Japanese flag to the wall in the dining room. Filipino students later came into the room, took one look at the flag, experienced intense feelings of anger and hatred against everything Japanese, and immediately fled. They were puzzled and embarrassed by how they had reacted.

---

These students had not been alive during the war years, but the memory of the vicious and bloody occupation by Japanese troops remained vivid in the cultural history of the Philippines. The flag symbolized this experience and triggered off the feelings of bitter hatred, revulsion and indignation. The Filipinos, before the incident, would have loudly claimed that they had no feelings of bitterness against their former colonial masters. If they had not been helped to understand the power of prejudice, they might have unwittingly discriminated against their Japanese fellow students.

---

St Augustine prayed: 'That I may know myself, that I may know Thee, O Lord'. We can extend this prayer to: 'That I may know my prejudices—all that blinds me to seeing You in others, for then I will know You better'. Knowledge of oneself is not only the most difficult experience, but it happens to be also inconvenient, for it so often demands change in oneself. Anyone wishing to help others discover their prejudices must first be prepared to undergo thorough self-analysis of his or her own prejudices. The blind cannot lead the blind to light.

## 2. Avoid ethnic jokes

Ethnic jokes are common in most societies. Are they really funny? Reflect on the following:

> How do you make an Irishman laugh on Monday?
> Tell him a joke on Friday!

On careful examination, however, it will be seen that the object of an ethnic joke, like the above, is 'to put down' members of other cultures. At the same time, one's own group is presented as normal and superior. Ethnic jokes can be most painful, and unjust, to members of minority groups, who, if they are present when the jokes are told, are expected to laugh obediently and accept the ascribed expression of inferiority.

---

*Example*:
I once gave a seminar on the evils of prejudice to a group of professional people. Everyone said that they now understood the dangers of prejudice. At a formal dinner to end the seminar, a participant wanting to entertain the group said: 'Have you heard the latest Polish joke?' With that, a descendant of a Polish migrant shouted: 'Stop! I am deeply offended. I am fed up with these jokes. Why don't you learn?' Yes, we can be slow to learn.

---

Sometimes one hears the defensive comment: 'I know members of minority groups who really enjoy the jokes and they even retell them to one another. So why all the fuss about the jokes?' When minority members retell ethnic jokes about themselves, it is frequently to deprive the jokes of their emotional power. By retelling jokes, they hope to build up an immunity to the prejudices inherent in them, thus curbing their anger and aggressive instincts towards members of the dominant culture.

The practical conclusion is: do not retell ethnic jokes! Take the right chance to explain to others why such jokes can be unjust and deeply offensive, even if we do not intend the jokes to be such.[38]

## 3. Avoid offensive and sexist words

Derogatory language involves not just jokes about other ethnic or minority groups, but also the use of emotion-charged words, e.g. in North America, whites have favourite expressions for blacks—'spades', 'niggers', 'jungle bunnies'. These are powerful symbols of inferiority for blacks.

The same can be said of sexist language. Our male-centred culture is filled with words that assume the inferiority of women, and we can be using these words without realizing their offensive/unjust connotations.

---

*Example*:
In the mid-1970s, after lecturing to an international group, I sat down expecting considerable praise to come my way for all the work I had done on the paper. One lady in the audience stood up and vigorously attacked me: 'You are a sexist! You used the word "man" thirty times!' She was right. I had spoken in a highly insensitive way.

---

We simply must avoid these symbols of unjustifiable male domination. Not easy! But, justice and the example of Christ require that we do so. Remember, spontaneous and relaxed communication develops when a person has learned the language of prejudice. Over a period of time, this person eliminates from his or her vocabulary phrases and expressions that might be offensive to groups that are prejudiced against in society.

## 4. Complain about mass-media stereotyping

Various forms of the mass media (e.g. television programmes, newspapers) commonly articulate and reinforce a culture's prejudices about minority groups. For example, in studies of newspaper reporting in New Zealand, it was found that headlines often identified criminal offenders as Maori, but rarely were white New Zealanders designated as such.[39] Watch how minority groups are reported in your mass media. If you see a prejudicial bias against them, then complain.

## 5. Be critical of prejudiced textbooks

Formal education is one of the major transmitters of culture from one generation to the next. In a study of texts used in Australian schools in the early 1970s, it was found that children were being exposed to learning material that showed Asians and Aborigines in a highly negative and prejudiced manner, e.g.:

> Each year more and more Aborigines are learning to live the way we do. They find it easier to live that way. They are being helped by the white people to find good jobs and live in clean houses.[40]

## 6. Avoid testimonials to minority groups

Sometimes a member of a dominant ethnic group, who genuinely wants to be liked and accepted by a member of a minority ethnic group, tries to prove his or her lack of prejudice by assuring the person that 'you're as good as I am', or 'some of my best friends are from your ethnic group'. But these testimonials are patronizing gestures and mature people resent them.

## 7. Reflect on prejudice only in small groups

Prejudice, in all its forms, is potentially a highly emotional topic, because, as we have seen above, people's identity or security can be so dependent on the maintenance of their prejudices of superiority. From experience of helping groups to be sensitive to their prejudices, I recommend the following approach:

- *never* directly confront large groups of people with what you know, or feel to be, *their* prejudices; there may well be public, emotional and hostile reactions of denial, thus further reinforcing the prejudices;

- work in small groups, where people can feel less threatened, and thus more open to admitting that they are prejudiced.

## 8. Provide motivation

The battle against prejudice is a challenge to a personal conversion, to justice and love in the Lord. Recall that racial intolerance or male domination do not rest always on ignorance, but on the desire to manipulate or control people for one's advantage.

Hence, the mere knowledge of how prejudice works in and through me will do nothing of itself to destroy it. I must be motivated to attack the sinful roots of prejudice within myself. Therefore, when helping Christian groups to become sensitive to the power of prejudice in their own lives, I strongly suggest that sessions always begin in an atmosphere of faith and prayer, e.g. by reading incidents of prejudice in the Gospels and how Jesus confronted it. Encourage people to pray for conversion to truth, and for the ongoing release from their prejudices.

---

## Action against discrimination

---

Prejudice breeds on discrimination, e.g. in housing, employment, education. Often, only governments can effectively act in particularly difficult areas of discrimination, but individuals and concerned groups in a society also have power on their own initiative to:

- identify and publicize areas of discrimination;

- pressure governments to act (see example below);

- develop anti-discrimination programmes, e.g. in housing, education.

---

*Example*:
A group in New Zealand complained in 1976 to the Race Relations Office about a competition for the best Irish jokes in a supposedly reputable weekly newspaper. After the official complaint, the paper ceased immediately to publish such jokes. This shows that concerned people can be effective.

---

# Reflection questions

## To the reader

1. Why is racial prejudice unjust? What other types of prejudice would you consider unjust? Why?

2. Why is self-knowledge so difficult to obtain?

3. Ethnic jokes are common in our cultures. Explain to a friend why they should not be retold.

4. As you watch television over the next week, note down on a pad the stereotypes that are projected about:
   men;
   women.

5. Why does prejudice strike at the very heart of what inculturation means?

## To a discussion group

1. What minority groups in (a) your city (b) your parish, are discriminated against in employment, education and housing? What can *you* do to help remove this discrimination over the next six months?

2. Read Galatians 3:27f. What is St Paul speaking about?

3. Can you devise an *educational/motivational* plan for a six-month period aimed at helping the people in your parish discover:

- the existence of an example of prejudice/discrimination within your parish boundaries;

- that Jesus Christ condemned prejudice;

- that, personally and corporately, we must act against prejudice/discrimination.

# Suggested reading

Ballara, A., *Proud to be White: A Survey of Pakeha Prejudice in New Zealand* (Auckland: Heinemann, 1986).

Benyon, J., *Scarman and After: Essays Reflecting on Lord Scarman's Report, the Riots and their Aftermath* (Oxford: Pergamon, 1984).

Centre for Contemporary Cultural Studies, *The Empire Strikes Back: Race and Racism in 70s Britain* (London: Hutchinson, 1982).

Dundes, A., *Cracking Jokes: Studies of Sick Humor Cycles and Stereotypes* (Berkeley, CA: Ten Speed Press, 1987).

Mbali, Z., *The Churches and Racism: A Black South African Perspective* (London: SCM Press, 1987).

Miles, R., *The Women's History of the World* (London: Michael Joseph, 1988).

National Conference of Catholic Bishops (USA), *Partners in the Mystery of Redemption: A Pastoral Response to Women's Concerns for Church and Society*, 1st Draft (Washington, DC: NCCB, 1988).

Parvey, C. F. (ed.) *The Community of Women and Men in the Church: The Sheffield Report* (Geneva: World Council of Churches, 1983).

Pilkington, A., *Race Relations in Britain* (Slough, UK: University Tutorial Press, 1984).

Rose, P. L., *They and We: Racial and Ethnic Relations in the United States* (New York: Random House, 1981).

Ruether, R. R., *Sexism and God-Talk: Toward a Feminist Theology* (Boston: Beacon Press, 1983).

Yarwood, A. T., and Knowling, M. J., *Race Relations in Australia: A History* (Sydney: Methuen, 1982).

# 10 Inculturation: migrants and adjustment

[The] angel of the Lord appeared to Joseph in a dream and said, 'Get up, take the child and his mother with you, and escape into Egypt . . . So [they] left that night for Egypt' (Mt 2:13f.).

The problems of migration are in reality a test as to whether the Church does not only *preach* the Universal Church, but *lives* as part of the Church Universal (W. A. Visser 't Hooft, WCC).[1]

## Introduction

The brevity with which the evangelist describes how Joseph, Mary and the child Jesus became both migrants and refugees from terror obscures the human drama of the event. Fear of the unknown would have gripped them and anti-Jewish prejudice would have confronted them wherever they went. Like their ancestors in exile, this young couple would have felt the desperate pangs of homesickness: 'Beside the streams of Babylon we sat and wept at the memory of Zion' (Ps 137:1). The Israelites would have readily understood this description of what migration can involve:

> When an immigrant . . . moves into the mainstream of [host] life, the resulting 'contact of cultures' is not an abstract concept, but a high order of human drama. . . . [The] plot and its cross currents, its motives and motifs, are played out by a ghostly cast of hangers-on, by prejudice, longing, fear.[2]

Migration through the centuries is an intensely human process where individuals and ethnic groups risk the loss of identity and human dignity itself. This chapter, therefore, aims to:

- define the meaning of migration/migrant;

- describe what happens to people who migrate;

- describe how host societies react to migrants;

- suggest ways in which evangelizers may aid migrants.

# Defining migration/migrant

Migration can be viewed geographically and/or culturally:

- *geographically*, that is, as a movement by individuals or groups from one place to another; *internal*, if the movement is within the limits of a single state; *external*, if international boundaries are crossed giving rise to *emigration* and *immigration*.

  Most migrations are a voluntary response to an expectation that the movement will lead to an increase in overall gratification, or a lessening of deprivation. Some migrations are forced, e.g. refugees from religious or political persecution or war. Tragically, refugees often find themselves in countries where they are not at all acceptable. There are about 15 million refugees in the world at present; only 15 per cent have been given shelter in the First World, 85 per cent in the Third World.

- *culturally*, and more importantly, as any interaction in which an individual comes into contact with people of another culture, particularly if the latter culture is a dominant and technologically more powerful one. In this sense, migration should be seen as 'a high order of human drama'. Understood in this way, people do not have to move geographically in order to be migrants. In this chapter, we are concerned primarily with this cultural definition of migration/migrant.

---

*Example*:
For over 150 years, the indigenous Maori in New Zealand have lived side-by-side with the white, politically and economically dominant immigrants from the West; their sense of belonging and self-respect have been systematically attacked and undermined: 'They have passed . . . as a people through almost every kind of negative experience, save total extermination, that could possibly be'.[3]

---

One final introductory clarification. Already in this book, the term *minority group* has been used. The term, or sometimes simply *minority*, is generally used as a synonym for ethnic, racial and religious groups; it implies that a group is suffering various forms of deprivation, e.g. economic, social, educational. There is a tendency in literature, on the other hand, to use the term *ethnic group* when invidious distinctions are not under consideration.

# Models of migrant reactions

On the basis of the cultural definition given above of migration/migrant, it is possible to distinguish several different types or models of migrants. The adjustment problems of migrants are so humanly complex that no one model is able to explain fully the challenges migrants face when they are confronted by a more dominant or overpowering culture, and their reactions to it. However, generally one of the following models will predominate in a particular situation, while aspects of other models may be present at the same time (see Figure 10.1). Strategies for pastoral care will differ depending on what model is the most vigorously present.

## Model 1: Self-confident adjustment

Migrants retain their cultural identity; they are open to learn from other cultures, even the dominant culture, and are encouraged to do so without any undue pressure from all concerned. People who belong to migrant cultures that are close in kind to the dominant culture are apt to experience little sense of confusion or malaise, e.g. New Zealand or Australian migrants in Britain, British in the USA.

In the following models, the close cultural similarities between migrant and dominant societies do *not* exist.

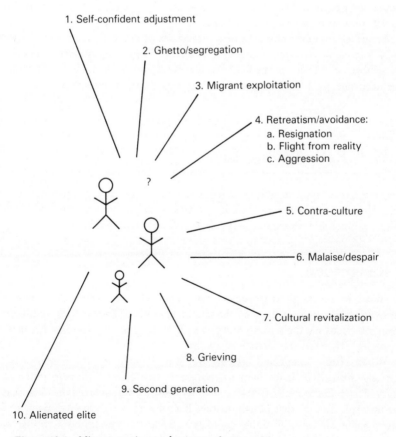

**Figure 10.1** Migrant reactions to dominant culture: models

169

## Model 2: Migrant ghetto/segregation

Migrants have withdrawn into ghettos, either because they cannot make the adjustment to the new cultural setting, or because they are forced, through ethnic or racist prejudice against them on the part of the dominant society, to live isolated from the latter. Catholic migrants from Italy, for example, faced this type of discrimination on entering the USA in the nineteenth and early twentieth centuries. West Indians face the same isolation today in Britain. More dramatically, the policy of apartheid in South Africa forces black and Coloured peoples into ghetto enclaves.

## Model 3: Migrant exploitation

Millions of Asians from India, Pakistan, Bangladesh and the Philippines now live abroad, working mainly in other Asian countries, e.g. Saudi Arabia, Iraq, Taiwan. Roughly 250,000 legal or illegal migrant workers leave the Philippines alone each year for other parts of Asia, the USA and Europe. Most are forced to migrate temporarily or permanently, because of the poverty of their own countries. For the year 1983, it is conservatively estimated that Filipino migrant workers remitted to their own country $US 950 million to aid relatives and friends.

Tragically, migrant workers, of whatever sex or nationality, are easily exploited, especially in Arab countries. The plight of legal or illegal migrant farm workers from the Caribbean or Mexico in the USA has been well documented: there is 'exploitation by growers and crew leaders who have almost total control over their lives'.[4]

## Model 4: Retreatism/avoidance

Group retreatism/avoidance shows itself in the following ways: resignation to inferior status, obsessive sensitivity to prejudice, forms of escape from reality, and aggressive actions against the dominant society. Each will be considered in turn.

## 1. Resignation

Individuals or the migrant group *internally* and *externally* accept the stereotype of inferiority levelled against them by the dominant culture. They become indifferent to, or even oblivious of, their status and poverty. Having no will to resist because 'they are inferior', they fall into a state of apathy.

When people accept and actually live out the stereotypes of inferiority, it is extremely difficult to help them to recognize their sense of human potential and dignity. Blacks in the southern states of America had so interiorized the view that they were humanly inferior that Martin Luther King found it extremely difficult to foster support there for his civil-rights campaign. César Chávez found a similar apathy among Chicanos (Mexican-Americans) in his efforts to organize them to press for workers' rights as farm labourers.

170

Ruth Fink reported that some Aboriginal people in Australia had 'an aggressive assertion of low-status; it seems to say "Look at me—I'm coloured and I'm dirty, drunken, lazy and irresponsible, like they say—that's my privilege, because I'm coloured—I can do as I like, because that's what they expect of me anyway"'.[5]

In 1976, in a study of attitudes of senior Maori college students in New Zealand, I found that 73 per cent accepted the dominant culture's view of their inferiority, by agreeing to the statement that 'Maoris have above-average gifts for manual or semi-skilled work'. Teachers said that when these students of average or above-average ability found their studies hard, they would quickly lose confidence in themselves, saying: 'What's the use! We Maoris don't have the skills anyway.'

Migrants may, on the other hand, accept the image of inferiority *only* externally, inwardly rejecting it. For the sake of peace he or she sees that it is useless to do anything about the situation. Internally, however, the constant reminder of 'inferiority' creates a 'time-bomb situation'. Violence could well erupt when the migrant 'has had enough', as happened in Brixton, London, in 1981, or in the Watts black ghetto of Los Angeles in 1965. Of the latter, Milton Viorst writes: 'Nobody wanted a riot, nobody plotted to start it. . . . But, as if they had been coiled for a signal, ten thousand blacks took to the streets that week to loot and to burn.'[6]

## 2. Obsessive sensitivity to prejudice

After negative treatment by the dominant society, migrants may sense prejudice against them everywhere, even when it is not there.

*Example*:
Reflect on this experience of an Australian Aboriginal: 'I feel self-conscious wherever I go if there are whites around. People look at you. Their eyes follow you. . . . Whites think we are going to steal something. . . . Even if they're nice, you know they are thinking that you are black.'[7]

## 3. Escape from reality

### a. Excessive consumption of alcohol

Alcohol is one way for migrants to escape the humiliations they experience. An Australian Aboriginal comments: '[If] you had to live as we do, you'd get drunk too. Just to forget. [We] drink because [we] want to get away, to forget how [we] are living in scum, treated like pigs.' Excessive drinking in fact can assume a desired status within a deprived minority group, especially if the traditional status structures have been undermined. Of Aborigines it is said that: 'Boys of twelve or thirteen, feeling themselves on the verge of manhood, begin to talk of getting "full" [drunk] and going to jail'.[8]

## b. Absenteeism

A high rate of absenteeism can exist among migrants of average or above-average ability who are forced, through prejudice or lack of sufficient education or opportunity, to work at tasks that are in no way personally fulfilling.

## c. Religious revivalist cults

Religious movements that have a strong stress on emotional release and experience can permit the individual to become immersed in a collectivity of ecstasy or exuberance in which daily frustrations arising from minority inferiority can be temporarily forgotten.

# 4. Aggression against the dominant society

Here the feelings of frustration with inferiority break out in forms of aggressive behaviour.

## a. Against the dominant society

The people verbally or physically attacked may in no way be responsible for the misery, but they symbolize the dominant society and its oppressive structures and attitudes. Rape can be one form of aggressive release. Eldridge Cleaver comments: '[The] particular women I had victimized had not been actively involved in oppressing me or other black people. I was taking revenge on them for what the whole system was responsible for.'[9]

## b. Deflected aggression

An especially tragic form of release is for migrants to vent their anger against the dominant society through an indirect method, most commonly through attacking the very people they love most.

---

*Example:*
I interviewed a Maori in New Zealand, imprisoned because of assaulting his wife and child: 'I was good at work as a building labourer. My white companions seemed to accept me, but so often told funny stories about my people. One day after one of these "jokes", I became so angry that I went home and bashed my wife and child, saying all the time: "I love you, I love you". I hoped they would understand!'

---

# Model 5: Contra-culture reaction

Members of minority cultures, in order to express their bitterness at the dominant society, actually adopt symbols or action that are despised by the latter. It is a way of annoying or getting revenge on dominant society members and of achieving a sense of group identity.[10]

For example, in New Zealand a gang leader commented: 'We dress ourselves as dogs [like wearing Nazi insignia] because society treats us like dogs, so we live like dogs. . . . The law will never be on our side no matter what we do, so why should we try [to conform to the dominant way of life]?'[11]

# Model 6: Malaise–despair

Human dignity can't be subjected to endless indignities and remain intact (F.J. Thwaites).[12]

Migrants experience deep confusion, malaise, *loss of hope*, a sense of traumatic loss of meaning, because their cultural identity and sense of human worth have been so undermined. People just give up trying to cope with the endless pressure of prejudice, poverty, unemployment. They just exist, cease to try for change, with no hope for any future change. What is said earlier in this book about the Culture of Poverty also describes this model.

# Model 7: Cultural revitalization

(See Chapter 4, pp. 72–73.) Migrants deliberately struggle to rediscover their cultural roots to build for themselves a more satisfying culture, or meaning system, and the feeling of human worth. It can be a very exclusive type of movement, highly nationalistic, e.g. the Black Muslim movement in the USA, and, in more recent times, the Rastafarian movement among blacks in several parts of the world, including Britain.

*Examples*:
These are autobiographical comments by:

a West Indian carpenter in Britain: 'I decided to quit the disenchantment, the uncompassionate, yet impolite monstrosity of the white man's society. . . . I began to intermingle with my own people. . . . I felt wanted and desired by my own people. . . . I belonged.'[13]

a black in the USA: 'Once I used to think I'm the same as everybody else. But then I started realizing. The first time was in 1965 when they had the riots in

Watts (Los Angeles). I started looking at all the things in the world and realized I got to act like a black man and got to be proud of it and everything.'[14]

---

In 1946, several evangelizers within the Roman Catholic Church in New Zealand encouraged Maori Catholics to come together for a week of religious, debating and sporting events within a Maori atmosphere. Maori culture had been, for over a century, increasingly undermined by the dominant white culture. The gathering (*hui*) was so successful that it became an annual event. Now Maoris travel from all over the country to be present at what is an annual cultural revitalization experience for several thousand people. I recorded various representative comments of participants. These personal testimonies convey the power and sense of cultural self-worth that cultural revitalization programmes can generate:

> I have been coming for years. Without this week of Maori music, singing and dancing, I do not think I would ever survive the year living in a white world.

> I have never been able to learn my Maori language properly. But here, I hear it spoken and I just feel proud to be a Maori.

> For a whole week, we can forget the importance of the white New Zealander's clock and just enjoy being Maori. Maori values come alive for us as never before and they give us strength and pride in our culture.

> I am 65 years old. All my life I was told that Maori culture is worthless. Now I feel here that is totally false. I am proud now to be a Maori. Let no white New Zealander tell me that Maori culture is dead!

---

## Model 8: Grieving reaction

(See Chapter 6, pp. 103–105.) Migration can result in the destruction of a people's way of looking at life, its meaning system (symbols, myths and rituals). People feel the loss of the old; there is a loneliness that grips them, a nostalgic yearning for the past. Even though, humanly speaking, the past may have been oppressive, at least it was a world that had meaning or a sense of order.

---

*Examples*:
Some of the families who were moved from the East End of London slums to a suburban housing estate later complained of loneliness and a coldness in their new neighbourhood. Wives would remain within their new homes crying or go back to wander through the old estate.[15]

The Israelites, as migrants, grieved: 'And the whole community of the sons of Israel began to complain against Moses and Aaron in the wilderness and said to them, "Why did we not die at Yahweh's hand in the land of Egypt, when we were able to sit down to pans of meat and could eat bread to our heart's content! As it is, you have brought us to this wilderness to starve this whole company to death"' (Ex 16:2f.).

# Model 9: Second generation

Second-generation migrants may experience considerable difficulties in adjustment. Often they must inhabit two cultural worlds at the same time: that of the school, or the workplace, where they feel aliens, and that of the home, where they are thought by their parents to be forgetful of the traditions of their ancestors. It is a dualism filled with tensions. Jawaharlal Nehru, first Prime Minister of India, described how he experienced these tensions in his own life. He was educated away from the traditions of his country of origin: 'I have become a queer mixture of the East and the West, out of place everywhere, at home nowhere. . . . I am a stranger and an alien in the West. I cannot be of it . . . But in my own country also, sometimes, I have an exile's feelings.'[16]

The more parents insist on family traditions, the more the migrant children feel alienated from the society they wish to adjust to, but which keeps refusing to accept them. Sometimes parents and children are unable to communicate easily with each other, simply because they have no common language; parents have been too busy working to learn the new language (e.g. English) well, and the young too uninterested to learn the language of their parents. Thus young people may live in a kind of cultural 'no-man's land'.

Boys sometimes try to escape the tensions by joining gangs that are often anti-dominant society. They find there a much-needed sense of belonging.

*Example*:
Minh, aged 18, was a small boy when he escaped to the USA with his parents from Vietnam: 'I do not understand myself. I am not accepted by the Americans because I am a foreigner. But I do not feel comfortable with my parents or with other Vietnamese migrants either. I am embarrassed when other people see my parents. Their English is poor, their clothes are not really American. They keep telling me that I must learn their language better, but it makes no sense here. Last year I, with other gang members, were in trouble with the police. I am just so angry, but I do not know why.'

The difficulties and needs of second-generation migrants are so significant, that one can rightly consider them to form a special type of migrant.[17]

# Model 10: Alienated elite

Commonly, in the estimation of members of the dominant culture, the educated and/or economic elite of the migrant culture are able to speak authoritatively for that culture. In fact, the elite who feel 'they have made it in the dominant society's culture' may have lost all sympathy and feeling for the migrant culture.

*Example*:
I was once asked to lecture on racial prejudice to police officers of a particular country. The officers of the indigenous culture were far more racist about their own people than the representatives of the dominant society present. The former desperately felt a need to be accepted by the latter and this led to the zealous adoption of the negative prejudices.

These models of migrant cultures illustrate how complex the reactions of migrants can be when they are in contact with dominant societies. The human dimensions of this interaction are poignantly portrayed by one observer:

> There is a difference between a felled tree and a felled human being. The tree
> . . . is doomed. . . . An uprooted human being may be equally powerless, but
> he is conscious of his fate. . . . An experience of such traumatic severity leaves
> physical and mental marks which are indelible.[18]

# Educational underachievement: reality

Within this section we summarize:

- two case studies of educational underachievement among minority ethnic groups;
- the reasons for educational underachievement.

## Case Studies

The following are summaries of educational underachievement of ethnic minorities in Britain and New Zealand. Similar levels of underachievement will be found in many migrant groups throughout the world.

*Britain*
about 3 million British citizens now belong to recognizable ethnic minorities;

of those unemployed, the rate is twice as high among those of West Indian origin and one and half times as high among Asians;

of the ethnic minorities, West Indian children particularly show signs of educational underachievement, e.g. only 1 per cent of West Indians go on to study at university compared with 3 per cent of Asians, 3 per cent of other school-leavers in the six local authorities surveyed, and 5 per cent of all 'maintained' school-leavers in England;[19]

in the inquiry following the 1981 Brixton race riots, it was concluded that 'the educational system has not adjusted itself satisfactorily' to the needs of ethnic minority groups.[20]

*New Zealand*
Maoris comprise a disproportionately large percentage of the unemployed. Whereas in 1986 Maoris were some 7 per cent of the total New Zealand labour force, they made up 20 per cent of all unemployed people;

of all Maori students leaving secondary school in 1984, about 65 per cent of males and 60 per cent of females had no formal qualifications; non-Maori percentages respectively were male 32 per cent and female 25 per cent.

---

## Reasons for educational underachievement

The following summarizes the reasons normally given for underachievement. However, many factors are involved in causing educational underachievement, and the desire to look for the *one* cause must be resisted.

## 1. The socio-economic conditions of ethnic minorities

Two problems arise because of the socio-economic background of ethnic minority children. First, parents are apt to have a poor self-image arising from their own failure to achieve, e.g. their inability to find regular employment. This poor self-image affects the motivation and self-image of the children. Secondly, parents have not the skills—or time, if both are working—to teach their children English from their early years.

## 2. Racism in the schools

Children are exposed to the pressures of racism from all sides—from remarks on the street, the mass media, teachers, the lack of obvious examples of success in politics and business concerns by blacks. All this reminds children that they are not expected to succeed.[21]

---

*Example*:
George, an unemployed 45-year-old Maori of above-average intellectual ability, comments: 'When I first went to school, the teachers and the other kids laughed at me because I spoke funny English. It made me angry. I tried hard but, over the years, teachers said to me that I was fit only for manual work, like other Maoris. I felt they were wrong, but the more I tried, the more difficulties and lack of encouragement I experienced. Then I decided to leave school as fast as possible. I know my teachers were wrong about we Maoris and myself. But it is too late for me to do anything.'

---

# 3. The academic atmosphere of the school

The school is of critical importance in the achievement rating of ethnic minority pupils; as one American study asserts: 'The achievement of minority pupils depends more on the schools they attend than does the achievement of majority pupils'.[22]

Two conditions must be fulfilled if a school is to improve the achievement pattern of minority pupils:

• the curriculum of the school must take into account where pupils come from, that is, their home and cultural backgrounds, as well as the opportunities that should be open to them because of their God-given talents;

• teachers must be alive to how prejudice operates, both within themselves and in the educational system, and be prepared to counter such negativity.

The pupil who comes from an ethnic minority requires a curriculum that aims to fit him or her into the life of the wider society, but in a way that takes into account their experiences at the same time. For example, the style of English spoken by the pupil on arriving at the school may be a dialect, and cannot be considered just 'bad English'; for the pupil, it connotes a sense of identity and belonging to a group. If teachers indiscriminately attack this dialect, they may well undermine whatever self-esteem the pupil may have left. Hence, a rightly structured curriculum will give dialects a respected place.

Similarly, much of the material used in schools is middle-class oriented, and so has little or no meaning for the young of poor socio-economic backgrounds. It makes them feel at a disadvantage from the start, so the wise teacher will make sure that experiences or examples that pupils can readily identify with are brought into the teaching process.

In summary, if the school is to facilitate improved minority achievement rates:

• what is needed is *compensatory education*, that is, educational equality of opportunity, which demands that pupils of ethnic minorities be accorded not the same consideration as peoples of the dominant culture, but *additional* opportunities, in order to assist them to reach a stage of integration, self-respect and true equality.

---

*Example*:
In New Zealand, the Roman Catholic and Anglican Churches staff several high schools for Maori students from culturally dispossessed backgrounds.
Academically, the schools have had generally better results than schools where the needs of Maori students are not specifically catered for. The schools assume the principle: only from a position of cultural strength will young people be able to develop a positive self-image. Hence, a strong emphasis is given to the learning of the Maori language, cultural symbols and mythology. Here are some representative comments on the value of these schools by senior pupils:

'When I first came to this school, I did not know who I am. Now I am beginning to feel Maori and that makes me feel good.'

'Before I came I was shy in speaking to white New Zealanders. They seemed so much better than we Maoris. Now, I can look them straight in the eye for I know I have much to be proud of as a Maori.'

'Academically, I am now strong. Why? I think it is because I now know who I am. I am a Maori and this gives me confidence to work hard to learn more. The more I succeed with study the more I can help my people.'

---

- while sensitivity to the needs of ethnic minority pupils is paramount, pupils from the dominant culture must at the same time be trained to accept and value a multicultural society.

- despite the inevitable difficulties, e.g. problems of language, parents must be involved with teachers and educational authorities in developing adequate curricula for multicultural living.[23]

# Policies of dominant societies

The dominant society can act towards migrant cultures in one of several ways: by policies of annihilation, segregation, assimilation, multiculturalism and bi-culturalism. Each policy will be explained in turn (see Figure 10.2).

## 1. Annihilation

For example, the British relating to Aborigines in Tasmania, the Dutch to blacks in South Africa in the nineteenth century, the Nazis to Jews.

## 2. Segregation

There are two ways of achieving this: either through deliberate planning, e.g. as in South Africa, or through policies that indirectly lead to segregation, e.g. West Indians in Britain tend to congregate together because of kinship relationships and poverty.

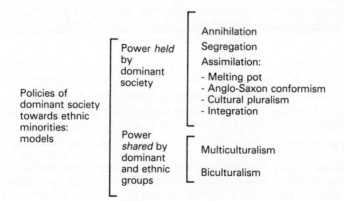

**Figure 10.2** Policies of dominant society towards ethnic minorities: models

# 3. Assimilation

Assimilation is the formal or informal policy whereby ethnic minorities are expected to acquire the symbols, myths and rituals of the dominant culture, so that minority distinguishing marks disappear. Several different types can be historically distinguished.

## a. 'Melting pot' policy

Up to the early 1920s in the USA, this policy flourished. The assumption was that all immigrants were to be thrown into the mainstream of American life, without concessions or supports, in order to pool their characteristics and develop together a *new* amalgam or 'American culture'. The reality was very different. No one was particularly interested in the customs and values of socio-economically poor migrants. They were in fact forced, for the sake of survival, to adopt as quickly as possible the existing way of life. The experience was devastating for the welfare of immigrants.

## b. Anglo-Saxon conformism

From the 1920s onwards, immigration into North America became restrictive; there was fear of an influx of what was thought to be inferior stock from Eastern Europe and the Mediterranean. Immigrants must now conform to the Anglo-Saxon dominant group. The policy became known as *Americanization*. Elsewhere, e.g. in Australia, New Zealand and Britain, the policy was called *Anglicization* or *Anglo-Saxon conformism*.

## c. Cultural pluralism

As the above policies seemed not to be working, cultural pluralism emerged as the favoured option: core values and customs of the dominant culture were to be acquired, but ethnic minorities could preserve values and customs *provided* these did not interfere with the core values of the dominant society. In Australia, for example, the policy meant that 'immigrants would be expected to agree publicly that all things Australian are best, to be greatly interested in sport and not to work too hard, and in return they would not be badgered if they privately practised their native culture'.[24] At heart, this policy of toleration of *non-essential* customs was merely an attempt to make cultural assimilation efforts, in places like Australia and Britain, a little less nasty or disruptive for the migrants. The long-term aim remained the same: ethnic minorities must adopt all aspects of the dominant way of life.

## d. Integration

In Britain in 1966 Roy Jenkins, then the Home Secretary, called the policy *integration*; it is to be seen not as a 'flattening process of assimilation but as equal opportunity, accompanied by cultural diversity, in an atmosphere of mutual trust'. Apart from the rhetoric, little was done to implement the policy. And the British Council of Churches in 1976 commented:

> To wish to integrate with that which alienates and destroys you, rendering you less than a person, is madness. To accept the challenge to join it and change it from within, when it refuses to accept that you are there in your fullness and refuses to acknowledge the results of interaction between you and it, is double madness.[25]

# 4. Multiculturalism

In Australia, New Zealand and Britain, the term 'multiculturalism' has recently become popular to express a new and richer dimension in dominant/migrant culture interaction.

Multiculturalism is a social system that is claimed to offer freedom of choice to those who want to be culturally different in one or several aspects, e.g. religious or political beliefs, occupation, and ethnic identity. The model aims to remove the pressures that prevent migrants from using their own cultural roots to develop their personalities and sense of group-belonging. As a system of action, it is founded on several assumptions:

- *First*, the meeting of different cultures can bring a richness in values to all, including the dominant culture. The stress is no longer on toleration (as is the case in cultural pluralism), but on fostering a spirit of *positive acceptance* of cultural differences.

- *Second*, the model assumes a duality of interaction; that is, positive adjustment is necessary, on the part of migrant *and* dominant cultures, through a process of positive, dynamic interaction.

- *Third*, multiculturalism assumes that only from a position of cultural strength will migrant peoples be able to move out to contact other cultures, with a sense of self-recpect and confidence.

If multiculturalism is to be realized, the dominant society must adhere to two guidelines:

a. Whatever will assist the emergence of a multicultural society is to be encouraged, e.g. additional educational programmes for migrant children to help bring them up to the standards of the dominant society; inter-cultural educational programmes for all; equality of opportunity programmes.

b. Migrants must be given the power to participate in decisions that intimately affect their own lives (see Figure 10.2). Without power-sharing, talk of multiculturalism is simply a political fad. And that is very much the situation in Britain today. For example, the electoral process has provided Britain's ethnic minorities with very little ability to be involved in fostering multiculturalism. They must rely on the goodwill of whites to eliminate institutional prejudice/discrimination, to guarantee legal and civil rights, and to obliterate poverty. Moreover, there is no way of ensuring that this goodwill will develop and be maintained.[26]

# 5. Bi-culturalism

A bi-cultural society is one where members of the *indigenous* culture contribute equally—that is, together with the members of the original colonizing culture—to policy and decision-making at all levels. The New Zealand government has recently committed itself to establishing such a society.[27]

# The Church and multiculturalism

> You are to divide it [land] into inheritances for yourselves and the aliens settled
> among you . . . since you are to treat them as citizens of Israel (Ezek 47:22).

## General comments

The Churches, having accepted inculturation, at least theoretically, are committed
consequently to multiculturalism in their pastoral concern for migrant peoples. For
example, while Vatican II did not use the expression *multiculturalism*, it accepted the
assumptions on which multiculturalism is founded. In 1969, Paul VI issued an instruction on the pastoral care of migrants and it enshrines key pastoral principles of ecumenical relevance:[28]

pastoral care must relate to people at *their* point of need (n. 24);

pastoral care must take into account the *total* human needs of migrants (n. 5),
and for this reason their culture must be respected;

pastoral structures must bend to suit the needs of migrants (nn. 33, 12).

John Paul II, speaking on the pastoral care of migrants, said in 1985 that the authenticity of the Church's preaching will depend, first and foremost, on its commitment to
multiculturalism within its own structures of power. There is pastorally required an
'openness, mutual respect, dialogue, exchange' and the participation of migrant peoples in all that concerns them.[29]

## Multiculturalism and power

If multiculturalism is to exist, three types of power must be exercised by dominant and
migrant societies:

*nutritive* power, that is, enabling power whereby people are given the chance to
develop their own inner capacities;

*integrative* power, that is, the working together of individuals or groups for the benefit
of all;

*relational* power, which is the willingness of all involved to learn from one another.

Christ himself exercised all three powers, symbolized in his role as the Servant of the
Lord, the listening One, the One open to respond to the deprived, the unwanted.
Thus the authentic multiculturalist is one who is open to hear, to dialogue with, to
learn from and to encourage people of different cultures. A most demanding challenge.

182

# 1. Britain

The Anglican Church, in recent years, has become increasingly conscious of its failure to relate better to the pastoral needs of the ethnic minority groups. The Archbishop of Canterbury's Commission on Urban Priority Needs advised the Church to make a clear response, not only to racism in society, but also to the alienation, hurt and rejection experienced by many black people in relation to the Church of England. Barriers to effective black participation and leadership at all levels of Church life had to be removed.[30]

The Roman Catholic Commission for Racial Justice stated in 1982 that 'we are inclined to believe that *most* Catholic schools are not at present oriented toward multicultural education. Even less often do they consciously incorporate a critique of racism and ethnocentrism beyond perhaps a brief mention in religious education or social studies.'[31] This is a serious criticism of Catholic education. Why is the Church so reticent to spearhead educational programmes against racism, or to respond creatively at a wider level to the pastoral needs of ethnic minorities?

I agree with the thesis of Antony Archer: the Roman Catholic Church in Britain has generally lost touch with the the working class, the poor, the marginalized, the dispossessed who were once its major supporters. It has become pleasantly middle-class, too uncritical of the institutional and personal racism in society;[32] it cannot continue to accept 'inaction and isolationism'.[33] I personaly believe that radical rethinking at the educational and pastoral levels is desperately demanded.

# 2. United States

Between 1820 and 1920, over 40 million immigrants, the vast majority being Roman Catholics, arrived in the developing United States.

In relating to this incredible influx of migrants, most Catholic leaders in America, at the turn of the century, had at least four objectives. They wanted the Church to grow and take firm root; they wished the Church to be seen as American and thus counter the attacks of those who questioned the loyalty of Catholics to the republic; immigrant groups were to be 'Americanized' if the second aim was to be realized; and the faith of the immigrants was to be preserved.

These objectives were frequently in conflict. Some leaders, holding firmly to the 'melting pot' principle, were worried when ethnic groups held on to customs that to non-Catholic eyes showed disloyalty to the republic's goals. Others, supporters of cultural pluralism, felt migrant cultures should be encouraged for a time in order to aid assimilation and the retention of the people's faith. The Church, therefore, drifted back and forth from the emphasis on rapid assimilation of ethnic groups to the fostering of migrant cultures through the establishment of ethnic parishes.[34]

Today, the Roman Catholic Bishops forthrightly speak out in pastoral letters on the adjustment problems of minorities of all kinds. However, these statements are widely ignored at the pastoral grassroots, a point strongly made by sociologist Joseph Fitzpatrick. Hispanic migrants feel alienated and unwelcome in the parishes, because the Church is 'now a middle-class institution' and 'has not yet discovered an effective method of ministering to the poor'.[35]

## 3. Australia

> As yet, the multicultural character of our [Australian] society has not been
> adequately reflected in major institutions. . . . [This] has resulted in a lack of
> justice for many.[36]

Since 1947, over 3.3 million people have come to Australia from more than a hundred countries; of this number, about 3 million have become permanent residents. Over 1 million children have been born to post-war migrants.

The dominant Anglo-Saxon culture insisted from the beginning that migrants accept the assimilation policy. The same policy, aided by a cruel racism, has condemned the indigenous Aboriginal people for two centuries to poverty, disease and despair. In very recent years, however, the government has acknowledged the need for a multicultural policy.

The reaction of the Roman Catholic Church to the post-war flood of migrants, which swelled its numbers by over a million, was that of the prevailing prejudice—conformism, assimilation. The good migrant is the one who 'fits into the parish as quickly as possible, learns English, avoids speaking foreign languages, regularly puts money on the plate on Sundays, and keeps funny devotions away from the church'. The territorial parish has remained the unchallenged agency for evangelization. Ethnic chaplains have been encouraged to visit migrant families and celebrate liturgies in their language, but beyond that they were given little or no authority.[37] Despite the official government support now for multiculturalism, the Roman Catholic Church still remains in practice committed to the pastoral policy of assimilation, not inculturation/multiculturalism. The particular cultural/religious needs of migrants continue to be widely unknown and neglected.

# Pastoral action: suggestions

> If a stranger lives with you in your land, do not molest him. You must count
> him as one of your own countrymen and love him as yourself—for you were
> once strangers yourselves in Egypt (Lev 19:33f.).

## General comment

(See Chapter 5, pp. 81–83.) Churches are able to act prophetically with and for the migrant poor at several levels:

- by gathering accurate information on the state of migrants in their regions;
- by using this information to speak to the nation and government(s)

  — against institutional and personal racism;

  — in favour of socio-economic and educational services for migrants.

- by condemning all forms of racism and migrant oppression within their own ranks

— through developing, among the faithful, educational programmes to explain the nature and Christian foundation of multiculturalism;

— through removing barriers to migrant participation within their own church structures;

— through fostering educational and social welfare services in favour of the migrants;

- by encouraging liturgies, and popular devotions, to develop according to the symbols, myths and rituals of the people.

# Reflection questions

## To the reader

1. What strikes you as the most important point in this chapter? Why?

2. In order to be involved in multiculturalism one needs to share power with migrant peoples. What does this mean?

## To a discussion group

1. Can you give some examples of prejudice and discrimination against ethnic minorities at work?
in schools?
within the parish?

2. Reflect on the following texts:
1 Jn 3:17;
Mt 25:31–46.
What are the implications of these texts:
for multiculturalism?
for yourselves?

# Suggested reading

Arora, R., and Duncan, C. (eds), *Multicultural Education: Towards Good Practice* (London: Routledge & Kegan Paul, 1986).

Campion, E., *Australian Catholics: The Contribution of Catholics to the Development of Australian Society* (Ringwood, Vic.: Viking Penguin, 1987), pp. 179–185.

Glazer, N., and Young, K., *Ethnic Pluralism and Public Policy: Achieving Equality in the United States and Britain* (London: Heinemann, 1983).

Macdonald, R., *The Maori of New Zealand* (London: Minority Rights Group, 1985).

McLemore, S.D., *Racial and Ethnic Relations in America* (Boston: Allyn & Bacon, 1980).

Martin, J. I., *The Migrant Presence: Australian Responses 1947-1977* (Sydney: George Allen & Unwin, 1978).

Modgil, S., *et al.* (eds), *Multicultural Education: The Interminable Debate* (Philadelphia: Falmer Press, 1986).

Puxon, G., *Roma: Europe's Gypsies* (London: Minority Rights Group, 1987).

Secretariat for Hispanic Affairs, US Catholic Bishops' Conference, *Prophetic Voices: The Document on the Process of the III Encuentro Nacional Hispano de Pastoral* (Washington, DC, 1986).

Swann, M., *Education For All: The Report of the Committee of Inquiry into the Education of Children from Ethnic Minority Groups* (London: HMSO, 1985).

Watson, J. L., *Between Two Cultures: Migrants and Minorities in Britain* (Oxford: Basil Blackwell, 1977).

Wilson, J., *Canada's Indians* (London: Minority Rights Group, 1982).

Working Party on Catholic Education in a Multiracial, Multicultural Society (UK), *Learning from Diversity: A Challenge for Catholic Education* (London: Catholic Media, 1984).

# PART 3
## Inculturation: the pastoral agent

# 11 Fostering inculturation: pastoral hints

Inculturation . . . presupposes a long and courageous process . . . in order that the Gospel may penetrate the soul of living cultures (John Paul II).[1]

Applied anthropology may sometimes look like common sense, but careful examination often discloses an uncommon sense (James L. Peacock).[2]

## Introduction

We have seen that 'Inculturation is not the purpose of evangelization. Properly understood, it *is* evangelization.'[3] It is the Good News *entering* into the very heart of a people's way of life; inculturation is not something that one adds to a culture, like paint on a house. This entering into the heart of a culture, however, is a slow and ever-challenging task.

If inculturation is so challenging, demanding such enormous courage and patience, the reader would be excused for crying out: 'It looks just so impossible. I can do nothing!' Take heart! In co-operation with the Lord, every reader has the ability to foster inculturation in some way or other. So this chapter offers some hints on ways in which this fostering can take place. We will:

- summarize some pastoral assumptions about inculturation from previous chapters;
- reflect on how in the New Testament inculturation was fostered;
- offer practical hints on how evangelizers can encourage inculturation.

## Inculturation: some assumptions

In summary form, these are some key pastoral assumptions:

1. *The Church evangelizes through conversion*
The Church evangelizes, when it seeks to *convert* the personal and collective consciences of people, their work, their cultures.[4]

2. *Conversion is sustained through the Christian community*[5]

3. *Role of pastoral agents*
Formally designated ministers are involved in 'vertical' ministry, i.e. celebrating the Eucharist; those people in a Christian community who freely minister to one another through love/justice and worship, supported and challenged by formally designated ministers, are involved in 'lateral' ministry. All are called to at least 'lateral' ministry. Both types of ministers can be called pastoral agents or workers, or simply evangelizers.[6]

4. *People inculturate, not the evangelizer for them*
Inculturation occurs through the free decisions of individuals and community; an evangelizer cannot make these decisions for people, but only encourage conditions to develop that foster the free involvement of others.

# Inculturation: New Testament hints

To appreciate better these assumptions, the following are some examples of the ways in which Jesus in particular fostered the process of inculturation. Notice how he uses events, e.g. misunderstandings about the use of power, as the occasions to instruct his followers about how his message does, or does not, fit in with the local culture.

## *Example 1: Community—the setting for inculturation*

One of the most striking aspects of the life of Christ is the emphasis he gave to the building of community with his disciples. And through the interaction within a community of faith, love and worship, he sought to evangelize his followers. He fostered community growth by sharing with them his own experiences with the Father, by encouraging them to share with each other their own apostolic experiences (Lk 10:17–20), by eating and spending leisure time with them. He spoke to them of the new commandment of love that must permeate all relationships within cultures (Lk 10:25–28); they have come to experience this love in their lives through him, and they must continue this bond of union when he is gone (Jn 13:34). Suffering and death to preserve this love will be the ultimate testimony of one's devotion to others (Jn 15:13).

## Example 2: Events—occasions for inculturation

Jesus aims to foster in his followers a type of leadership based not on domination or authoritarianism, so evident in the culture around them, but on humility, love and servanthood. He instructed not only through words but, most especially, by using events that occurred within the community.

- Take the incident of the still naive James and John, the sons of Zebedee. They approach Jesus, having in mind a very worldly type of kingdom, in tune with the political aspirations of many contemporary Jews: 'Allow us to sit one at your right hand and the other at your left in your glory' (Mk 10:37). Jesus explains once more the nature of his kingdom, and that he would himself be called to suffer for it, not to dominate others. The other apostles hear about it and become angry over the stupidity of the two. But Jesus again uses the occasion to explain the meaning of authentic leadership and how it is to differ from the coercive, political type of leadership: 'You know that among the pagans their so-called rulers lord it over them, and their great men make their authority felt. This is not to happen to you. . . . For the Son of Man himself did not come to be served but to serve, and to give his life as a ransom for many' (Mk 10:42, 43, 45).

- Earlier, the evangelist Mark describes how Jesus uses a child as a 'teaching aid' to emphasize the point that leadership demands openness and humility: 'He then took a little child, set him in front of them, put his arms round him, and said to them: "Anyone who welcomes one of these little children in my name, welcomes me; and anyone who welcomes me, welcomes not me but the one who sent me" ' (Mk 9:36f.).

- The more poignant event is the washing of the feet of the apostles, a most dramatic gesture aimed at fostering within the community what leadership must entail. Having washed their feet, Jesus sits down and explains why he did this, an action contrary (i.e. 'antistructure') to the local cultural expectations of a leader: 'I have given you an example so that you may copy what I have done to you' (Jn 13:15).

## Example 3: Inculturation demands listening

Again, Jesus uses an event to instruct his followers about the need to be open to the presence of the Spirit, even in the most surprising places.

Some of the disciples are troubled, since they find a man who is casting out devils in the name of Jesus, but 'because he is not with us, we tried to stop him' (Lk 9:49). Because of their special relationship with Jesus, they feel they alone should have this special gift. So Jesus uses the occasion to remind them that God distributes gifts freely, and he may speak to us in the most unusual events and people. Our task is to listen: 'You must not stop him; anyone who is not against you is for you' (Lk 9:50).

## Example 4: Inculturation through functional substitution

Earlier, we saw that functional substitution is a method whereby rituals of a culture are not destroyed through evangelization, but are given new meanings; since the structures of rituals remain intact, people do not experience undue cultural disorientation and personal confusion.

- Christ follows this method at the Last Supper. There he gives a dramatically new meaning to the Passover meal, for he becomes the meal itself: '. . . this is *my* body . . . this is *my* blood' (Mt 26:26, 28).

- The early Church continued to use functional substitution as an evangelical method of helping people to understand the Gospel message. It borrowed considerably from the secular world, in a way that today's theologians might turn to business-management insights to provide job descriptions of the Church's leadership roles; new Christian meanings were added to the existing forms of secular leadership. The term 'overseer' (*episkopos* in Greek), for example, was derived primarily from Greek culture and it meant a superintendent, one who would visit those he was responsible for. The term was modified by the early Christians to connote a ruler, whose task in the Church was to supervise the ministry of individuals, keep order, judge, and discipline if necessary. Unlike his or her secular counterpart, however, the Christian overseer was not to be someone aloof from the community, but one who would work side by side with people, just as Christ himself did with his disciples (1 Pet 2:25).[7]

## Example 5: Inculturation is a slow process

Inculturation is a slow process, because personal and cultural conversion is rarely dramatic. True conversion is a life-long striving towards self-transcendence, in the midst of failures and imperfections.

## Conversion of Peter

Jesus, in his relationship with Peter, highlights this point: the evangelizer needs to be challenging, instructing, waiting, encouraging people along the conversion journey. Simon Peter, with a burst of initial enthusiasm, 'left everything and followed him' (Lk 5:11). Yet we quickly find Peter not understanding the words and intentions of Jesus (e.g. Jn 13:6–11; 18:10f.), sinking because he lacks faith (Mt 14:28–31), being vigorously rebuked as 'Satan' (Mk 8:33), and finally denying Jesus after his arrest (Mk 14:66–72).

Through all this, Jesus is trusting, waiting for Peter's conversion to become more deeply rooted in his heart and actions. Finally, that trust is rewarded: 'and the Lord turned and looked straight at Peter . . . . And he went outside and wept bitterly'

(Lk 22:61f.). Peter becomes a true and faithful shepherd in imitation of Jesus the Shepherd.[8]

## Conversion of Paul

St Paul's journey of conversion is equally instructive. During the ten years after his initial conversion, and prior to Paul's first really successful mission to Cyprus and Asia Minor, people find him a very disturbing influence and are rather pleased to see Paul leave them: 'The churches throughout Judaea, Galilee and Samaria were now left in peace' (Acts 9:31). As Carlo Martini points out, in those years Paul experienced considerable loneliness and discouragement.[9]

Paul speaks of conversion, but his instinctive way of speaking and acting is still the pre-conversion Paul. He has yet to allow a spirit of detachment and trust in the Lord to affect *all* his faculties and senses; the Lord permits the negative reactions of the local Churches he visits to prod Paul into undergoing a much deeper conversion. Slowly, Paul discovers detachment at last. It is the Lord who converts, not the eloquence of Paul (1 Cor 3:5, 18).

---

*Example 6: Inculturation—faith venture/nurtured in prayer*

In the Gospels, the process of the Word becoming flesh and living among us ( Jn 1:14) occurs because the principal people involved are inspired and supported through prayer. The evangelist Luke focuses on the fact that prayer is at the heart of discipleship, to which we are all invited. If zeal for the apostolate, detachment from one's own cultural values, and an openness to hear what the Lord is saying are to be sustained, then the evangelizer must have the ability to pray and not to lose heart.

# Conversion: a multi-faceted process

The object of inculturation is conversion. But what is conversion? Sometimes, in popular literature or preaching, conversion is incorrectly presented in terms of a simplistic and instantaneous choice.[10] However, the stories of the conversion of Peter and Paul do more than hint that the conversion process is normally tortuously slow and complex.

It is possible to agree with 'born again' Christians that there may be a dramatic moment in life, a 'fundamental option', which goes into the deepest level of our being and our values, a commitment from which most of our subsequent choices flow. Peter and Paul experienced this when called by the Lord. But that experience must then enter into so many levels of our life, e.g. intellectual, emotional, social relations, and that is where obstacles to full or integral conversion can occur.

In the following section, we define conversion in general and then look briefly at its different types.

# Understanding integral conversion

Conversion connotes in general *self-transcendence*, that is, the leaving aside of self-centred attitudes that deny objective reality or the limitations of being human. In conversion, one assumes responsibility for the motives and consequences of one's own conduct.[11]

# Types of conversion

## 1. Intellectual conversion

This conversion occurs when one earnestly seeks objective truth and is prepared to accept it, even though the truth contradicts previously held views.

## 2. 'Trust' conversion

Trust conversion is when people, e.g. dispossessed migrants, develop faith in their own ability to do things themselves, *or* they learn to trust other people.

## 3. Moral conversion

This is a more complete form of self-transcendence than the above. This is the movement from just knowing to doing—a very difficult form of conversion, because choices must be made on the basis of definite values.

## 4. Affective conversion

Here one accepts responsibility for the health of one's personal and emotional development, e.g. to struggle against fear that obstructs intellectual conversion.

## 5. Community/justice conversion

The person recognizes his or her obligation to work for social justice.

## 6. Religious conversion

This is, as Bernard Lonergan notes, 'being grasped by ultimate concern. It is otherworldly falling in love. It is the total and permanent self-surrender, without conditions, qualifications, reservations. . . . For Christians it is God's love flooding our hearts through the Holy Spirit given to us.'[12]

Through faith, the religiously converting person is confronted with the mystery of the cross as the way that God chose to act in cultures and history; the freely offered call of Jesus invites the person to live out the mystery of the cross—through detachment, service, love, justice. The heart of conversion is not just turning away from evil and from sin. It is not just asceticism or fasting. First and foremost, it is the turning of the heart to God in the way of little children who permit themselves to be led without guile and with enormous trust (Mt 18:3). If this conversion is authentic, the person is moved to struggle for a sharpened sense of honesty in all other types of conversion.

## 7. Ecclesial conversion

In ecclesial conversion, the Church ceases to be an institutionalized 'they'. The converting person identifies with the Church as 'we', that is, as a community requiring full co-operation from its members, so that the mystery of God in Jesus Christ can be proclaimed.

Conversion, therefore, is a *life-long striving* towards self-transcendence in response to the call of the Lord. It is 'integral', when the individual struggles for conversion at all levels explained above.

# Inculturation: anthropological hints

Our task here is to clarify, in concrete terms, the role of a pastoral agent in the inculturation process. This means:

- identifying the *stages* of the inculturation process for individuals and communities;

- identifying *who* in fact inculturates;

- suggesting *ways* in which a pastoral worker can foster inculturation through community building.

## Stages in the inculturation process

There are four stages in the process. In the first three, individuals need a faith community, in and through which they can *evaluate* a culture according to Gospel/tradition values. Only at stage 4 does inculturation formally take place. The actual implementation of what has been decided is the result of the free faith-decision of individuals within the community.

*Stages in the inculturation process*:

1. Identifying aspects of a culture that are in *conformity* with Gospel values;

2. Identifying aspects of a culture that are *not* in conformity with Gospel values;

3. Choosing *how* to elevate, purify a culture, according to Gospel faith values;

4. Actually *implementing*, in response to God's grace, the plan that is chosen according to Gospel values.

---

The pastoral worker will be tempted to undertake all the stages alone, imposing his or her plan on the community, and placing pressure on individuals to act accordingly. This is *not* inculturation, even if the particular action undertaken finally by individuals under duress is according to Gospel values. Inculturation must flow out of the free, responsible faith-decisions of individuals who are converting to the Lord. No one—no matter how skilled or knowledgeable they may be—can make the decisions for others.

# Case Studies

---

1. *A village credit union, Fiji*
A credit union was established in a depressed village in Fiji, in 1961. Within three years, the morale of the villagers had improved considerably, people had returned to farming, and children attended school regularly.

A villager comments: 'We spent months learning about credit union and its philosophy of self-help before we decided to form one as a village. The instructor would ask us awkward questions like: "Do you see anything in Fijian culture that would cause credit union to break down or anything that would help it to grow?" Finally, we admitted two problems: the custom of "borrowing" money/things from other people without their permission. We could see that this made some of us very lazy and would make those who worked very angry. Secondly, we must do what our chiefs tell us. We could see that if we use these customs in credit union, then the credit union will fail. People will lose confidence in it, if their money is taken without permission by others—including the chiefs.

'We talked and talked about these problems. We prayed for more faith and Gospel courage to do the right thing. Then we said that we would start the credit union, and refuse to loan money to people without credit, no matter who they are. That is what the Gospel says about justice. And our credit union committees did just that. Never before have chiefs been refused, or friends told that "borrowing" Fijian-style is not for credit union! It is not Gospel!

'Our custom of sharing is now given better life. We hold on to our money individually in the bank, but the more we save the more other people can take out loans, not just in the village, but throughout Fiji. Now we understand what the Good Samaritan story and Christian brotherhood really mean.'

### 2. People Power Revolution, Philippines

Go back to Chapter 4, and re-read the description of what happened.

---

## Comments on the case studies

1. In the Fiji example:

- in preparing for the establishment of their credit union, all villagers went through the first three stages listed on p. 194. But only at stage 4 did inculturation occur, that is, when, through faith and courage, the committee members of the credit union refused to bow to the enormous pressures of tradition. They declined to loan money to relatives who wanted to 'borrow' according to Fijian custom and not pay it back; in two instances, chiefs were taken to court when they defaulted on loan repayment, something unheard of in the village before.

- the traditional Fijian notion of kinship, that is, relationship based on tribal affiliation, was purified by being given a richer Christian meaning. As one said: 'Now, I see that my brothers and sisters are all Fijians. The more I save, the more people all over Fiji can borrow in need. This is what Jesus means by charity.'

2. In the case of the People Power Revolution, the thousands of people prayed and reflected. The parents of six children told me: 'When the Cardinal called us to the streets to protect the anti-Marcos troops, we prayed for two hours to be sure of God's will. We decided to go, knowing that we might never see one another again. Then we prayed for strength to do God's will.'

The people opted for non-violence, even though culturally violence is a strong Filipino imperative in circumstances of such dramatic pressure. The actual carrying out of this decision not to have recourse to violence was *the* act of inculturation—stage 4 on p. 194.

3. Neither the instructor who taught the village people how to form a credit union, nor Cardinal Sin of Manila who invited the people on to the streets, caused inculturation. These two people definitely fulfilled an important role, by acting as catalysts for people to move through the first three stages. But they did not *cause* the inculturation. The people did.

What, then, is the role of the pastoral worker in the inculturation process? He or she can, e.g.:

- provide physical facilities, e.g. meeting rooms in which people can gather for reflection/prayer;

- provide information, e.g. theological, cultural, necessary for accurate discernment;

- foster community growth so that individuals can support one another, and be challenged to conversion and action according to Gospel values.

The last possibility is the most important and difficult, especially if people, as can occur in the West, have had little or no experience of what a community means.

## Fostering faith communities: guidelines

Applied cultural anthropology provides insights on how any form of community can be fostered, e.g. parish, Basic Christian Communities, youth club. The first insight of applied anthropology is: authentic community growth is extremely slow. There are no recipes for instantly successful mutual support or shared decision-making. If someone offers you such a recipe, turn it down, for it will never work! There is just no substitute for immensely patient informed listening and reflective action. The pastoral worker can foster community growth:

- *formally*, that is, by inviting a group of people to work together for a definite purpose, according to a certain pattern or structure, e.g. a parish council.

- *informally*, that is, the agent encourages individuals to develop their talents, which may later be used in the service of community building (Figure 11.1).

## 1. Formal community-growth projects

Guidelines for community building, and the fundamental aims behind all genuine community programmes, are now explained.

### Guidelines for action

Community growth depends on:

a. *Discovering the real felt needs of people*. It means finding out what really worries a group of people. This is far more difficult than may appear at first. And it is a guideline that is possibly the most overlooked.

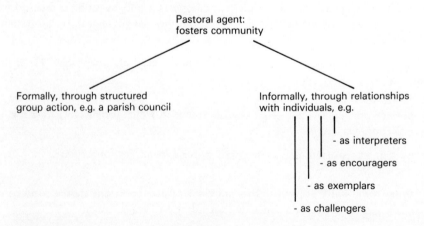

**Figure 11.1**   The pastoral agent and community

*Examples:*
*Goodwill is not enough*
Two lay American volunteers on a remote South Pacific island noticed how the women of the village had to climb and descend a hill before they could reach water to wash clothes. The two, with immense goodwill, decided to act. If the women had running water in the village, they would not have to travel to the river and wash there. They built two tubs, the same height as the average American tubs, in the heart of the village, and connected running water. They called the women to wash, which they did for one day, but the next day the women were down at the river again. The volunteers, annoyed at the 'ingratitude and lack of wisdom' of the women, demanded to know why: 'We are not used to standing up for washing, and the tubs are too high, for we are short people, so our backs ached badly', one said. 'And we want to gossip about the men, but cannot do that while washing in the village. We will be overheard', said another.

*A reflective evangelizer*
An Episcopalian priest built a small mission church in a remote part of the USA, with funds he procured from his rich family. After a few years, it needed repairs, so he asked the people to pay for them. They replied: 'No, you built the church. You pay for the repairs!' The deeply offended priest thought over the matter, and finally decided to do nothing at all. After months of putting up with leaky roofs, the people said: 'When are you to repair our church?' He replied: 'It is not your church. It is mine, since I paid for it, and I have no intention of paying for the repairs!'

After more months of rain, the people could take the situation no longer. So they went ahead without the priest to repair the church. Then they invited the priest back to 'their church' to celebrate the occasion.

*A wise pastor*
Shortly after his arrival in the parish, a pastor was approached by a delegation of parishioners. They asked for a parish school, and they said that they were prepared to work together to build it. The pastor said: 'Let's talk this over together!' (Secretly, the pastor thought it a good idea, but did not say so.) They did, over an eight-month period.

In the discussions, it became clear that the people did not have a *real felt need* for a school at all. The parish had been split by feuds for years, but some had finally recognized the need to work together. They immediately thought of a school, but did not stop to think if it was really needed, or how it could be financed. Their *real* felt need was to have an experience of working together. Eventually, they decided on a flag pole and built it. And, having seen what they could do together, they wanted to try something bigger. They did so. On their own initiative, and after lengthy discussions together and with the pastor, they planned and built a small experimental school for adult education. It is flourishing today!

*A detached evangelizer*
An American Jesuit priest, Marion Ganey, was brought in by the Fiji govenment in the early 1950s to establish the credit-union movement. Despite the limited time available to him, he refused to allow credit unions to be established until the people clearly expressed the desire for them. He would spend days in a village explaining what a credit union is, and move away if the people remained uncommitted.

# Reflections on the examples

- The first two pastoral agents involved were both intelligent men, yet they overlooked the need realistically to check out with the people whether or not the latter sincerely felt the need for the projects.

- In the second example ('A reflective evangelizer'), the pastor learnt from his mistake and deliberately held back from repairing the church, though he found it hard to resist rushing in.

- In the third example ('A wise pastor'), the pastor was sensitive to the importance of not taking the immediately expressed needs of people as the *real* needs. He invited them to dialogue, asked questions, encouraged them to question each other.

- In the last example, the Jesuit priest refused to shorten the process of discussion and decision-making, despite the inconvenience to himself.

In brief, the process of inculturation *must* begin at the point of needs of the people, not the needs as seen by the pastoral agent, no matter how objectively important they may be. If this basic guideline is neglected, any effort at community development is doomed to fail.

b. *A project must affect all in the group.* A change agent, wishing to help a community to develop, must seek to involve all sections. If not, factions will emerge and endanger whatever co-operation has emerged.

---

*Examples*:
*The over-anxious evangelizer*
The pastor decided to seek the help of the parish in establishing a parish council. With enthusiasm and speed, he invited twelve people, who he thought were leaders, to a meeting. And, acting on the advice of these people, he formed a successful council. After several months, some of the councillors kept missing meetings. On investigation, the pastor found he had hastily overlooked two leaders of factions in the parish. Deeply offended, these forgotten leaders began an effective campaign to undermine the council from the outside.

*A listening social worker*
Clare, a New Zealand parish social worker, noticed that a young Maori woman, Molly, was unemployed. Clare suggested a course in modelling and she accepted. Molly was immensely proud of her diploma and her new job. One day, Clare, noticing Molly deliberately avoiding her in the street, managed to catch up with her to inquire about her work. She replied in the midst of tears: 'I have left the job and torn up the diploma. When my friends, who have been unemployed for months, saw the paper and my job they ridiculed me so much that I could not take it any longer.'
  Clare had forgotten all the other members of the group, who saw in Molly's achievements a tragic reminder of their own failures. Clare then spent weeks with them, listening and challenging them. Eventually, they were able to discover talents they thought they did not have, and they all, including Molly, found employment. Later, the group asked Clare to help them establish a Gospel

reflection programme. They are now, with Clare, also helping unemployed youth in the district to discover unknown talents.

## Reflection on the examples

In both examples, the pastoral agents tried to move too fast. They did not take enough time to feel the power of the cultures of the people they were trying to work with.

c. *The project's stages must be clearly visible.* People are apt to lose interest, become discouraged or suspicious of others, if they are unable to see that each step in a project is related to the overall goals.

*Example*:
*Failure to maintain communication*
A parish council consulted widely, and over a long period, about the idea of building a new church. The parishioners appreciated the way in which the council explained the project, sincerely listened to suggestions, and finally voted in favour of the scheme. After the project got under way, the people were regularly asked for money, but they felt that they were not being kept informed about changes in plans; all kinds of rumours started about mismanagement, misuse of funds, authoritarianism. The project, instead of uniting the parish, was bitterly dividing it.

## Reflection on the example

It was impossible for the people to retain all the details of the proposed church when it was first presented to them. The parish council should have devised a method to allow those interested to see the project develop in small or comprehensible steps.

d. *On-going leadership structures must be established.* The temptation is for the pastoral worker to attempt to do everything himself/herself. Structures must be established by the people themselves, to facilitate the continuation of the project.

*Example*:
*Enthusiasm alone is insufficient*
Two dioceses, under the inspiration of two pastoral agents, joined together in sponsoring a conference on racism and how the Christians should respond locally. For months prior to the conference, surveys were conducted into attitudes, study groups met, and widespread enthusiasm was generated. The conference was voted a resounding success. One diocese formed a team to carry through the enthusiasm of the conference into action programmes, to be spread over a two-year period. The second diocese did nothing, because the pastoral worker in charge wrongly thought that the enthusiasm of the conference would generate, by its own momentum, ongoing, practical anti-racist programmes.

e. *Allow time for Gospel reflection/prayer.* Co-operation for common goals cannot be sustained by a group, if members are not offered a spirituality based on oneness in Christ.

---

*Example:*
*Secular values are insufficient*
A particular parish council in a London suburb started with considerable enthusiasm. Management training experts were brought in to teach councillors how to co-operate, in the light of clearly stated goals.

After several months, all kinds of divisive tensions developed between councillors. The Anglican pastor invited the council to reflect, over several weeks, on the causes of the tensions. Finally, one councillor concluded, and the others agreed: 'The management training experts were highly professional, but we forgot to ask them what values they believed in, because these values were being conveyed to us as the foundation of our work. I now realize their values of uncontrolled competitiveness and individualism conflict with the Gospel values of co-operation, discernment, faith.' The council decided to spend time, every month at their meetings, just on Gospel study/reflection. The council has now been functioning successfully for five years.

---

## Reflection on the example

Some of the values and techniques that can be used to animate a business operation conflict with Gospel assumptions. Fortunately, council members not only discovered this, but had the courage and faith to learn from the experience.

## Aims of community development

Pastoral agents must recognize that community development programmes exist:

1. *Primarily, to foster in people a spirit of self-confidence, or the conviction that they can work together for a common purpose.*
For example, when the people who built the flag pole in the church grounds wanted to tell me about it, they said very little by way of explanation. Instead, in silence, they guided me to the flag pole (not very professionally built), paused and just pointed to it. In a most powerful, non-verbal manner they conveyed to me their sense of achievement: after years of bitter feuding, they saw in this flag pole the symbol of their ability to work together as Christians.

Or consider the example of a group of Hispanic migrants in a Californian parish. Most men are unemployed. No shops would trust them with credit. Nor would they trust each other with credit. This changed with the introduction of their parish credit union. I asked one man what he had acquired by membership, expecting him to describe something material. He said: 'Before credit union came, no one trusted me. I started to save a little money each month, even though I have no work!' With tears rolling down his cheeks, he said: 'One day I said to myself: "I am a man now, for I can save money like anyone else". Then one day I asked for a small loan from my credit union. They gave it to me immediately, on the basis of my character alone. I have never been trusted before in my life. I feel a different man. Now I know what it means for my brothers and sisters to have the compassion of Jesus for one another. I no longer hear the Gospel read to me. I feel it around me!'

Once people learn to trust one another, through common action, they are then able to discover what it means to be Church, in the here and now. This is an example of 'trust' conversion.

2. *To help people to develop structures that can facilitate working together, and the solving of common problems, in the light of Gospel values.*
For example, the structures of credit union are liberating. They provide an objective framework that permits people to interact freely and with dignity. No one feels dependent on the fickle whims of other people. So also with a parish council. Unless there are clear structures, one or two people will dominate and begin to manipulate others.

---

*Example*:
An American evangelizer working in Korea has established a fine physical plant in his parish: church, kindergarten, school, small hospital. He thinks everyone is so happy with the efficiently run facilities. He is wrong. They feel humiliated, because everything is controlled by him. When he leaves, the plant will collapse. There are no structures through which the people own and manage the facilities. He does not allow the structures to emerge, simply because he never trusts the people. And they sense this. He speaks often of the need for Gospel co-operation, but he contradicts what he says by his paternalistic example.

---

3. *Primarily for the achievement of human dignity. The obtaining of material things, though important, may provide the initial focus for working together, but this will rarely be seen by people as the priority, once they discover the liberating experience of working together on the basis of Gospel values.*

---

*Example*:
*Standing tall*
A migrant people, without land, had to build their rough shacks over a lagoon in the Solomon Islands. Embarrassed by their poverty and their failure to obtain work, the men had turned to drinking dangerous methylated spirits.

Mick, a pastoral agent, would regularly visit them, to listen and question. They trusted him, and one day they asked him how to get a loan of money to buy a fishing net, so that food could be improved. They did not want a gift of money; it would remind them again of their loss of dignity. From the net, they caught more fish than needed, so they hired a freezer, established a small co-operative, and sold fish to other people under a sign: 'Auki Fish Co-operative'. I visited them and they took me to see the shop, pointed to it and said nothing! What could they say! Their dignity had been restored and no words could adequately convey this experience. They now had the necessary material things, but these were unimportant compared with the joy of achieving dignity.

---

One final, but crucially important, comment. Community growth is primarily about attitudinal change. But recall an earlier insight: such change is immensely slow because people need time and space to reflect on, or absorb, what is happening, what they must give up, or do next. Therefore, the axiom for pastoral workers: *to think big in community change, think small; foster growth through patient listening and challenging*. This axiom runs contrary to our cultural assumption: that change, to be effective and satisfying, must be large-scale, rapid and without pain.[13]

# 2. Fostering community growth informally

Here, pastoral workers do not aim *directly* to foster community growth, through working with several people together for this purpose. Rather, they relate immediately with individuals, e.g. as 'interpreters', 'encouragers', 'exemplars' or 'challengers', that is, in ways that may later encourage leadership for community growth.

## a. As interpreters

We can minister to culturally confused people by offering to interpret for them what is happening around them. For example, historians, anthropologists, and cultural counsellors can point out that what is occurring is not unique, and that there are ways through the chaos.

## b. As encouragers

Those people who have lost all confidence in their own gifts, e.g. disadvantaged migrants, desperately need sincere encouragement.

---

*Example:*
*A telephone evangelizer*
Pastor Frank uses a variety of means to keep contact with individuals, e.g. the telephone and visits—personally, or through others. People sense he respects them deeply, even when they let him down. One said: 'He says to me often that I have talents to learn and be educated. It took me years to discover that he is right, but he never gave up. Now I am a trained social worker, and I am building a network of people in need of being encouraged. We pray together and give each other confidence.'

---

## c. As exemplars

I owe my years of interest in community change first to my mother, not to research. During the Second World War, she quietly developed a free nursing service to villagers of all denominations, some of whom were vigorously opposed to her beliefs. No matter what the hour or the weather, if there was a need, she would be off on her pedal bicycle to tend the sick. At night, we would pray as a family and the sick were always included. Though she did not aim to do so, her example helped to break down barriers between different cultures and denominations.

### d. As challengers

Challengers are people with a gift of being able to point out to others, in a spirit of empathy, gentleness and respect, a particular gap in their lives between the Gospel ideal and the reality. Apostolic cultural challenging can take many forms, e.g.:

### Confrontational

This dramatic method of challenging is seen as the only way in which the gap in people's lives can be pointed out. The prophets were skilled at this. For example, Amos condemned the Israelites for price-rigging, weight-cheating, short-changing and their hypocritical devotions: 'Listen . . . you cows of Bashan . . . oppressing the needy. . . . I hate and despise your feasts' (Am 4:1; 5:21). Similarly, the Irish Roman Catholic Bishops confront people with their injustices: 'A new laxity of conscience seems to be growing. . . . Any way of getting money or goods . . . seems all right to them, so long as they can get away with it.'[14] The Archbishop of Canterbury's Commission on Urban Priority Areas confronts the government, to break 'the present conspiracy of silence' over the injustices of overtime working of employees.[15]

No one should challenge through confrontation, unless the following conditions are observed:

- the person confronting must know the facts;
- criticism is not sufficient; an alternative response must be proposed;
- there is no less dramatic/public way of stating the truth effectively;
- the confrontation must be done with charity and justice.

Amos, as with all the prophets, offered Yahweh's option, e.g. love and justice towards the poor. John the Baptist condemned the Pharisees and Sadducees as hypocritical, but he gave them the alternative: ' "Repent, for the kingdom of heaven is close at hand" ' (Mt 3:2).

### Questioning/dialogue

The challenger sees the gap, but wishes to lead the people to recognize this themselves, through a process of question and answer. Jesus exercises this gift in his discussions with the two discouraged disciples on the road to Emmaus (Lk 24:13–32).

# Culture jolt/shock hints

In 1968 I went to a small group of islands, the Chatham Islands, off mainland New Zealand, to research the pastoral needs of 500 inhabitants. Within a few days of arrival, I became annoyed with the climate and the food, and highly judgemental about the people and what I felt were their ridiculous customs. 'If only they acted like other New Zealanders, then', I said to myself, 'they would not be so poor!' I rejoiced in having a heavy cold, for that meant I could stay in my room and avoid the people! I was suffering from culture jolt/shock, and evasive action was urgently needed.

It is inevitable when we meet cultures different from our own that we are at times surprised, even jolted, by what people do. The unfamiliar leaves us perplexed; we simply don't know how to handle the situation. For example, Filipinos commonly will avoid telling me something that I should know but, if told, will make me sad. I am just not used to this 'failure' to communicate. However, unless I learn to cope with attitudes or customs I am not used to, the initial surprise or culture jolt can change into *culture shock*.

## Understanding culture shock

The expression *culture shock*, in general, is a label for a wide variety of different possible responses to culture-contact stress, which may include disorientation, depression, apathy, irrational or inappropriate responses, and so on. More particularly, it is 'a reaction that is blind and unreasoned, a reaction that is but a subconscious flight or escape from a culturally disagreeable environment'.[16] Culture shock can generally be expressed (see Figure 11.2):

* *either* through arrogant ethnocentric reactions, e.g. racist or paternalistic comments/actions.

---

*Examples*:
A pastor was transferred, after years of working in a rural parish, to a city parish in Dublin. Within a few weeks he was saying: 'The people in this parish have no faith like my rural people. They are arrogant, they will not listen to what I say to them as their priest. As for the youth, they are lazy, good-for-nothing, uninterested in anything but themselves.' Since his views remained the same, if not stronger, two years later, the pastor was happily assigned back to a rural parish.

An Episcopalian priest was appointed to an Hispanic apostolate in California, after a highly successful work among the youth at a university. After a few weeks, the priest found that the rectory needed painting and he personally did

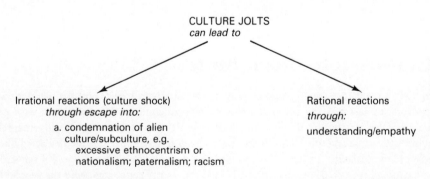

CULTURE JOLTS
*can lead to*

Irrational reactions (culture shock)
*through escape into:*
  a. condemnation of alien
    culture/subculture, e.g.
      excessive ethnocentrism or
      nationalism; paternalism; racism

  b. cultural romanticism

Rational reactions
*through:*
understanding/empathy

**Figure 11.2**  Culture jolt/shock

the job. Next, the garden needed digging. . . . To an understanding friend he said: 'You know, these Hispanics are really incapable of doing anything for themselves. That is how they were meant to be!' He also had to be reassigned.

---

Both evangelizers in the examples suffer culture shock when confronted by the city parish and Hispanic subcultures they cannot cope with. Both are educated persons, yet both fall into racist or paternalistic reactions. In the second example, the evangelizer seeks to escape from the frustrating situation by becoming excessively busy about apostolically unimportant matters.

* *or* through culturally romantic attitudes/actions.

The evangelizer, in order to cope with the culturally frustrating situation, and yearning for acceptance by the people, dramatically attempts to discard his or her own culture. The culture to be evangelized is considered to be 'perfect'.

---

*Examples*:
Ruby is a devoted social worker, working among West Indian immigrant families in an area of London. At staff meetings with social workers asigned to other migrant groups, Ruby refuses to listen to any criticism of West Indians. 'They may have some problems, but absolutely nothing like us English people. They share with each other. We don't.' Her fellow workers do not attempt now to offer advice.

John, aged 35, is a volunteer parish youth-club worker. He believes that in order to 'get close to the youth, one must act and dress like the youth. If I do this, then they feel I am one with them and I can really be their equal. If the oldies could only see how good the youth are!'

---

Ruby and John are cultural romanticists. Ruby cannot relate to any group outside 'my migrant people'; they give her a much needed sense of belonging and so she is blinded to their defects. John is the same. Tragically, he is unaware of the fact that he has lost all contact with the youth. They laugh at his efforts to be young.

Thus we do not need to leave our own country to experience culture jolt/shock. As pastoral agents, we come into frequent contact with all kinds of different subcultures/cultures, e.g. youth, senior adult, parish, parish council, migrant.

We can react irrationally, in a culture-shock manner (as just described), or rationally. If *rationally*, then we will struggle to understand why people are acting in ways that apparently make no sense to us. It is often a difficult task. But people feel our empathetic concern for them, and generally they will repond positively to our efforts to understand them. They know that their culture is not perfect, and they expect that we will be critical, but understanding, of it.

## Practical advice to evangelizers

1. Don't be surprised if you experience culture jolts. They commonly occur when we meet unfamiliar cultural situations.

2. We can all experience culture shock. It can happen when we least expect it, e.g. after many years of successfully living in a culture that is not our own.

3. If evasive action is not taken, culture shock can become chronic, that is, it can unknowingly cripple the evangelizer's apostolic effectiveness for years.

4. Seek advice from others from time to time about how they see your attitudes and actions, if you are working in a culture/subculture that is foreign to you.

5. Ponder the spiritual qualities that should characterize the pastoral worker, as described in the following chapter.


# Reflection questions

## To the reader

1. Can you think of other examples in the New Testament where the process of inculturation is described?

2. Can you identify, in your own life, an example of culture jolt and shock? What did you learn from the experience?

## To a group discussion

1. Go back to Chapter 2, and read again the description of the folk/associational culture types. What type most fits the culture of your area? What values/customs of this culture conform to, or diverge from, Gospel values?

2. If your group decided to go about fostering community change in your parish, what practical steps would you take? When could you plan to start?


# Suggested reading

Augsburger, D. W., *Pastoral Counseling across Cultures* (Philadelphia: Westminster Press, 1986).

Boyack, K. (ed.), *Catholic Evangelization Today: A New Pentecost for the United States* (New York: Paulist, 1987), pp. 99–159.

Egan, G., *Change Agent Skills in Helping and Human Service Settings* (Monterey: Brooks/Cole, 1985).

Ely, P., and Denney, D., *Social Work in a Multi-Racial Society* (Aldershot, Hants: Gower, 1987).

Freire, P., *Pedagogy of the Oppressed* (New York: Herder & Herder, 1971).

Greenleaf, R. K., *Servant Leadership: A Journey into the Nature of Legitimate Power and Greatness* (New York: Paulist, 1977).

Lohfink, G., *Jesus and Community: The Social Dimension of Christian Faith* (London: SPCK, 1985).

Luecke, D. S., and Southard, S., *Pastoral Administration: Integrating Ministry and Management in the Church* (Waco, TX: Word Books, 1986).

Niklas, G. R., *The Making of a Pastoral Person* (New York: Alba House, 1981).

Schein, E. H., *Organizational Culture and Leadership: A Dynamic View* (San Francisco: Jossey-Bass, 1987).

Whitehead, E. E. and J. D., *Community of Faith: Models and Strategies for Developing Christian Communities* (New York: Seabury Press, 1982).

# 12 A spirituality for 'refounding the Church'

A Church caught up in mission is a Church on the move, taking fresh
initiatives, exploring new beginnings (John Tiller).[1]

The failure of the Church today is not just a failure to respond to need; it
is—perhaps still more—a failure to attend to the voices, the experience and the
spiritual riches of the 'poor' in its midst (The Archbishop of Canterbury's
Commission on Urban Priority Areas).[2]

## Introduction

Spirituality is the *style* of a person's or a community's response to Christ, before the
challenges of everyday life, in a given historical and cultural environment.[3] Down
through history, there have been many particularly significant responses to Christ by
individuals and communities. Hence, there are many different forms of spirituality,
e.g. monastic, Dominican, Ignatian, Wesleyan.

Why do we speak of a spirituality of inculturation? What is there *special* or *new*
about it? In brief, we Christians are now looking outwards, to a degree unimagined
thirty years ago, to the world and its evangelical needs. From being ghetto Churches,
jealously guarding our separate frontiers and fearful of the world, we are to be
Churches *for* others, for the world of cultures. Previous spiritualities, helpful though
they be, are insufficient to sustain us in this uncharted faith journey into a world of cultures that are receptive or unreceptive to the Good News. We need a new spirituality,
a spirituality of inculturation or of 'earthing the Gospel'.

To explain the background to this spirituality a little further: the Churches, in
recent decades (e.g. as is evident in the documents coming from the World Council of
Churches, the Anglican and Roman Catholic Churches), are returning to two truths
that are at the heart of the New Testament:

* that the Church is the People of God; all—pastor and laity—share a common
  baptism and mission in Christ; we are all called to ministry, that is, to respond
  to the pastoral needs of the members of the community.[4]

- that the People of God are to be no longer concerned only with their own growth in Christ, but they must strive to respond to the pastoral needs of the world.

## 'Refounding the Church'

('Refounding' in this chapter refers not to the institution of the Church but to its methods of proclaiming the Gospel in a world in rapid change.)

The world is in a chaotic state—with its tragic division between the rich and the poor, and the threat of nuclear destruction (see Figure 12.1, p. 210). The challenge to relate to it is so humanly daunting, frightening and *newly defined*, that we can realistically speak of a call to *refounding the Church*—a Church vibrantly alive within a world that does not know, or does not want to know, the justice and love of Christ. In order to refound the Church, we need a new spirituality—a spirituality of inculturation or refounding.

It is a spirituality:

- for faith community action to make known the Good News as the fulfilment of every legitimate human aspiration;

- that releases and liberates the poor, and enables them to define, analyse and come to grips with their situation;

- that rescues the rich and poor, inspired by hope in the risen Lord, out of the great moral avalanche set in motion by evil and oppressive attitudes/structures;[5]

- for today's world, not a support for a nostalgic escape into a ghetto Church of a former age. The Second Isaiah is as relevant today as he was when he spoke to those Israelites who wanted to escape the challenges of revitalization by dreaming of the glories of a former age:

> No need to recall the past,
> no need to think about what was done before.
> See, I am doing a new deed,
> even now it comes to light; can you not see it? (Is 43:18f.)

In this chapter, therefore, we will reflect on:

- the general qualities of the spirituality of refounding;

- some of the particular qualities required of refounding people within the contemporary Church.

# Characteristics of a spirituality of refounding

Recall that a spirituality is a special way of responding to Christ, within a particular historical and cultural environment. What are some of the notable characteristics of our environment? There is chaos, but there are also signs of hope (see Figure 12.1).

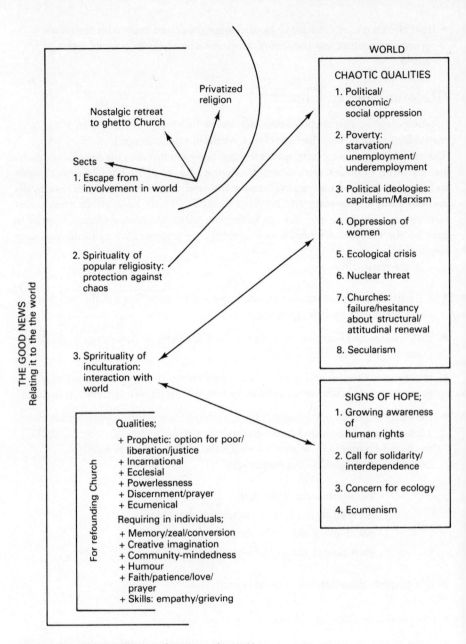

THE GOOD NEWS
Relating it to the the world

Privatized
religion

Nostalgic retreat
to ghetto Church

Sects

1. Escape from
   involvement in world

2. Spirituality of
   popular religiosity:
   protection against
   chaos

3. Sprirituality of
   inculturation:
   interaction with
   world

For refounding Church

Qualities;

+ Prophetic: option for poor/
  liberation/justice
+ Incarnational
+ Ecclesial
+ Powerlessness
+ Discernment/prayer
+ Ecumenical

Requiring in individuals;

+ Memory/zeal/conversion
+ Creative imagination
+ Community-mindedness
+ Humour
+ Faith/patience/love/
  prayer
+ Skills: empathy/grieving

**Figure 12.1**　The Good News: relating it to the world

# The world: chaos and hope

## Chaos

In previous chapters, we have described aspects of a world in a chaos of poverty, various forms of oppression, and twisted values. For example, nuclear missiles can travel from Western Europe to Moscow in six minutes, but the average rural housewife in Africa must still walk several hours a day for a family's water supply.[6]

How are Christians responding to these evils? By radical attitudinal and structural changes?

- We are not without *challenging* statements, e.g. the 1971 Synod of Roman Catholic Bishops bluntly wrote: 'Our examination of conscience now comes to the life-style of all:. . . . In the case of needy peoples it must be asked whether belonging to the Church places people on a rich island within an ambience of poverty.'[7]

- Nor do we hesitate to *plan*. Since 1948, there has been, as David Barrett points out, 'a vast mushrooming of 5,300 significant congresses or conferences— Catholic, Protestant, Ecumenical, Evangelical, Charismatic—dealing with evangelization at national, regional, continental, or global levels'.

With such massive planning, one might have expected some dramatic impact on the world of chaos. Not so! An estimated '99.9 per cent of all Christians' income is still spent on themselves, including 2.9 per cent on the Christian world around them at home; only 0.1 per cent goes on outreach abroad, and under one-tenth of this goes on outreach to the unreached, non-Christian world'.[8]

## Some signs of hope

In contrast with the chaos, there are some signs of hope in the world, e.g. the increasingly vocal demand that human rights be respected. People are also now recognizing the growing ecological crisis in the world. Finally, the ecumenical movement is helping to break down bigotry, useless rivalry, and centuries-old structures that contradict our statements of a common faith in Jesus Christ.[9]

## Qualities of a spirituality of refounding

A spirituality of refounding will have the following characteristics:[10]

# 1. Prophetic: concern for liberation/justice

The love that impels Christians to communicate to all peoples a 'sharing in the grace of divine life, also causes (them) . . . to . . . promote an integral liberation from everything that hinders the development of individuals'.[11] The liberation is at three levels:

---

liberation from absolute poverty: that is, freeing people from starvation and lack of shelter, through relief aid.

liberation from oppressive cultural, economic and political attitudes/structures that prevent or hinder people from being the agents of their own integral development.

liberation from conditions, e.g. ignorance and sin, that prevent people from knowing the fullness of Christ's revelation.

---

# 2. Incarnational

The world is God's creation. God is present in people, things and events, and we are called to co-operate with him to develop what is good and just. This means working with all peoples who yearn for truth/justice in every sphere of life, e.g. in science, at the workplace.[12]

# 3. Ecclesial

The early Church especially understood itself as the sacred people of God's possession, a people with a way of life which differed from that of the cultures around them, a people supportive of one another for life *and* mission:

> Do all that has to be done without complaining or arguing and then you will be innocent and genuine, perfect children of God among a deceitful and underhand brood, and you will shine in the world like bright stars (Phil 2:14f.).

A spirituality of refounding will powerfully motivate Christians to struggle to build a community of believers, a church, who will foster in one another an effective desire for ongoing conversion; at the same time, they will be a sign of prayer/love/reconciliation to those who do not know Christ. St Paul admonishes Christians to *be* church: 'warn the idlers, give courage to those who are apprehensive, care for the weak and be patient with everyone . . . pray constantly' (1 Thess 5:14, 17).

# 4. Powerlessness

Christ is present in many ways to us. In particular, he speaks to us in the Gospels, in the faith-inspired example of his followers, and in the sufferings of the poor and oppressed.

Identification with Christ in the poor is to be a special quality of this spirituality. It is a task that excludes no one nor any institution: 'our faith demands of us a certain sparingness in use. . . . If the Church appears to be among the rich and the powerful of this world, its credibility is diminished.'[13] The Church must be present to all groups, even to the middle and upper economic sections, but it is a question of the *how* of this presence. Our task is to draw these sections to an awareness of their social obligations—based not on charity alone, but on justice. We cannot do that if we live as the worldly live, or use power as they do to enhance their own status.[14]

## 5. Discernment/prayer

Pastoral needs change rapidly. In order to discover *what* and *how* to react, there is required a heart open to the Spirit in the silence of frequent personal prayer: 'That is why I am going to lure her and lead her out into the wilderness and speak to her heart' (Hos 2:14).

## 6. Ecumenical

The mainline Churches are committed to the cause of inculturation. An earnest desire to share resources, to work and pray together for justice, will authentically witness to the presence of Jesus the Unifier, the Just One.

# Refounding person: qualities

Now I am making the whole of creation new (Rev 21:5).

The Church needs today *refounding* persons, that is:

- people who have the gifts of the Lord to grasp the heart or vision of the Gospel message,

- and can imaginatively, and creatively, relate it especially to the dramatically new needs of today's world,

- drawing others, through conversion and commitment to the vision, into a believing, worshipping and evangelizing community.

Refounding people are the gifted persons that every age needs, our age of chaos in particular. They are the type of people Paul speaks about: the prophets, evangelists, pastors, teachers, encouragers, interpreters, reconcilers, community builders, so that the body of Christ may be built up until we all reach unity in faith (Eph 4:11f.).

People who are called by the Spirit to foster the ongoing refounding of the Church, will have, in addition to the above qualities, particular personal gifts. We see these gifts in the prophets of the Old Testament and in Christ himself.

The Israelites are in and out of chaos. They drift away from Yahweh, become seduced by riches and false gods of the cultures that surround them; they become arrogantly self-sufficient, yet think that Yahweh will always be with them. They are cast into exile, and learn the bitterness of loneliness and foreign oppression. Yet Yahweh remains faithful. His prophets are sent to call the people back to an intimate covenant relationship with him. Despite the immense diversity in talents and character, these prophets have certain key gifts in common.[15]

# 1. Memories of hope

In the midst of the people's forgetfulness and denial, the prophets are living and vital memories of Yahweh's abiding love for the nation and what he demands from them—justice and love. Through this memory, they can energize people with hope: no matter what they have done, the Lord still loves them. Listen to Yahweh giving to Jeremiah the powers of memory and energy:

> Tell them, 'Yahweh, the God of Israel, says this: Cursed be the man who will
> not listen to the words of this covenant which I ordained for your ancestors
> when I brought them . . . out of the land of Egypt. Listen to my voice . . .
> carry out my orders, then you shall be my people and I will be your God'
> (Jer 11:2–4).

# 2. Creative imagination

Imagination is the creative, intuitive capacity to see connections, between things or events, that others just do not see. The prophets were gifted with creative imagination. They could break through the darkness of materialism and idolatry around them, not just by condemnation, but by creatively pointing out the way the people should journey, in order to return to a love of, and a just relationship with, God.[16]

# 3. Community-oriented

The prophets are no loners. Even if they are banished by an ungrateful people to the margins of the Israelite society, they earnestly and persistently call the Israelites into a deep covenant communion with one another and with Yahweh.

# 4. Sense of humour

Humour is that *sense* within us which sets up a kindly contemplation of the incongruities of life. The most authentic humour is when people recognize that, despite their own sinfulness, God still loves them. Humanly speaking, this is a very incongruous situation.

The prophets have this gift of humour. They see their own lack of gifts and reluctance to serve Yahweh on the one hand, but on the other, Yahweh loves them and still wants them to be his messengers. A highly incongruous situation! Jeremiah has a profound gift of humour, for he sees himself as being a perfect example of incongruity. Despite his acknowledged reluctance to get involved with Yahweh, he is 'seduced' by Yahweh (20:7). After being made a laughing-stock by the Israelites, he tries to break away from Yahweh. No luck! He is 'seduced' again (20:9). He sees the incongruity of the event: wanting to flee from Yahweh, but Yahweh repeatedly finds him: 'You have seduced me . . . you have overpowered me: you were stronger' (20:7).

Prophets also use comedy to draw attention to the stupidities of people's behaviour. Elijah, for example, laughs at the priests of Baal, who think that the louder they rant and shout, the more likely it is that Baal will hear them (1 Kings 18:27).[17]

# 5. Men of faith, courage, patience, and prayer

The prophets are tempted to escape from their burdensome task, and even to flatter people with lies, to avoid having to tell them the truth (Is 30:10f.). But they do not fail the Lord, because they are radically converted to him and to his service in faith and love.

The prophets work hard, suffer and are often marginalized, because the message they offer is rarely acceptable to a nation that has avidly run after materialist and selfish values (Hos 9:7). Their courageous acceptance of suffering, in fact, is a mark of their authenticity.

The prophets pray. It sustains them in their vocation, for in prayer they repeatedly discover their own nothingness before the Lord and the immensity of his mercy towards them. Jeremiah moves to prayer the more he realizes the enormity of the response expected of him: 'A curse on the day I was born. . . . But Yahweh is at my side, a mighty hero. . . . For I have committed my cause to you' (20:14, 11f.).

# 6. Skilled in grieving/empathy

Jeremiah sees that his city and culture are to be destroyed and his people dragged into exile. He mourns the loss of the familiar: 'I mourn, and dismay has taken hold of me' (8:18). But the Israelites refuse to hear about what is to happen to them, and this causes further pain to the prophet. They, in their stubbornness (Jer 18:12), deny the death of the once familiar world around them. Therefore they will not join with Jeremiah in grieving. Yet if they do not grieve and express their dependence on Yahweh, they will not receive the new and revitalized relationship with Yahweh (1:10).[18] (See Chapter 6, pp. 103–105).

Empathy is the ability to put oneself in another person's shoes and comprehend his or her needs and feelings. The prophets have this gift. They can see, behind the façade of arrogant self-confidence of a people, a deep uncertainty and insecurity about life. Or, they can feel the pain of a people whose sense of belonging has been utterly shattered in exile, and offer them hope. Thus the prophet Ezekiel can speak for Yahweh: 'Yes . . . I have dispersed them to foreign countries . . . I will gather you together . . . I will put a new spirit in them' (Ezek 11:16, 17, 19).

215

# Jesus Christ: Church-founding qualities

There are several qualities that Jesus, *the* evangelizer and prophet, personally exemplified, and these need to be stressed.

## 1. Empathy/listening/respect

Reflect on the ways in which Jesus sensitively relates to known sinners or outcasts of society, e.g. his warm approach to Zacchaeus (Lk 19:1–10); his acceptance of Peter, though the latter had just denied him (Lk 22:61).

Often Jesus, out of respect for the freedom of the person, goes out of his way to avoid imposing his power on people, e.g. he knows the sick man at the Pool of Bethesda had been ill for decades, but still he asks him 'Do you want to be well again?' (Jn 5:6). Or consider the empathetic warmth of feeling that Jesus conveys to people in the midst of his own agonizing death: for those who were murdering him, Jesus prays, 'Father, forgive them; they do not know what they are doing' (Lk 23:34); and for the welfare of Mary, his mother, and John, his beloved disciple (Jn 19:26f.).

## 2. Creative imagination

Jesus repeatedly and creatively uses his imagination in teaching, e.g. in his use of parables, and his vivid descriptions of nature and human experiences (Lk 6:39).

## 3. Commitment to community

See Chapter 11, p. 188.

## 4. Apostolic adaptability

Ponder his remarkable adaptability, in the service of his Father, e.g.:

- teaching in the synagogues (Mt 4:23),

- in the Temple at Jerusalem (Mk 14:49),

- involvement in highly technical arguments with the prominent scholars of his day (Lk 20:19–44),

- using a fishing boat to preach to people on the shore (Mk 4:1),

- preaching to ordinary people in ways they could readily understand (Mk 12:37).[19]

In his teaching and life, Jesus highlights the pastoral guideline: *do whatever is helpful in preaching the Good News*; it may be an apparently small but powerfully significant action, e.g. giving a cup of water to a stranger, visiting a prisoner, or it may be something visibly dramatic, e.g. giving up one's life that others may have life.

# 5. Sense of humour

Tragically, this fundamental virtue of Jesus has been downplayed, or ignored, for centuries. Holiness has been falsely presented as synonymous with gloominess. Jesus had a sense of the incongruous, and he would use it in word and in action to help people understand his message. Often difficult things can be said and not rejected when they are recounted with humour, e.g. in exposing the hypocrisy of the Pharisees: 'You blind guides! Straining out gnats and swallowing camels!' (Mt 23:24).

Or consider his own life—he would have seen it as a joke of divine proportions! He, the King of kings, is born in a stable, and dies on a cross! Nothing could be more incongruous—a life of 'divine incongruity'! Yet nothing could be more powerful in conveying the truth of his words: 'I have come so that they may have life and have it to the full' (Jn 10:10).[20] And the source of Christ's humour? His detachment from self, his humility: 'His state was divine, yet he did not cling to his equality with God but emptied himself to assume the condition of a slave' (Phil 2:6f.).

# 6. Ability to grieve

Happy you who weep: you shall laugh . . .
Alas for you who laugh now: you shall mourn and weep (Lk 6:21, 25).

Jesus, like the prophets before him, has the gift of mourning; he recognizes there must be death before there is life: 'As he drew near and came in sight of the city, he shed tears over it. . . . Yes, a time is coming when your enemies . . . will leave not one stone standing on another within you—and all because you did not recognise your opportunity when God offered it!' (Lk 19:41, 42, 44). He is sad. Israelites refuse to read the signs of the times. But out of Jerusalem's destruction there will come life to peoples beyond Israel.

# 7. Prayer

To pray is to acknowledge the suffering and misery of the world within oneself and without. And Christ does just that to his Father: 'In his anguish he prayed even more earnestly, and his sweat fell to the ground like great drops of blood' (Lk 22:44). Prayer is also a listening to him, a being with him; this Jesus does, as a necessary part of the rhythm of his life (Lk 9:28–36).

---

## Contemporary Church refounding persons: qualities

Go, and do the same yourself (Lk 10:37).

All the qualities as described, and lived, by the prophets and Christ are especially needed today. For example, consider:

- *empathy*, or the ability to listen to people, not just to their words, but also to the pauses, their hesitations, the nuances of their speech or actions.

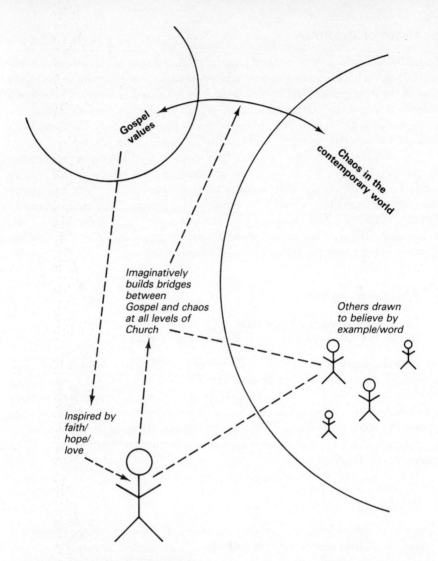

**Figure 12.2** 'Refounding the Church'

I asked a group of villagers once in Fiji why they thought Marion Ganey was so successful in fostering credit-union development among them. One summarized what the village thought: 'When he comes into our village, we all feel ten feet taller and ten years younger! Even without saying anything to us, we feel he believes in us.' Through non-verbal language, he could convey to the people his empathetic respect for them, born of years of meditative reflection on the example of Christ. As he once wrote: 'You will never do very much for people until you realize in your whole heart and soul that you are not doing them a favour by being with them. They do us a favour by permitting us to enter their lives; we are their servants, not their bosses.'

- *courage?* We face a world that is not just actively opposed to the message of Christ, but increasingly 'tone deaf' to, or simply uninterested in, Gospel values. Little wonder that the evangelizer is tempted to spiritual/apostolic fatigue,

218

disenchantment, loss of hope. Without the Christ-given gift of courage, we simply cannot maintain our enthusiasm for preaching the Gospel.

- and *humour?* True humour, as C. S. Lewis remarks, is a sense of proportion and the ability to see oneself from the outside.[21] It is recognizing the incongruity that exists within me: that I am a sinner, yet the Lord still loves me beyond anything I can ever imagine. If I have this gift, then I, like the prophets before me, can truly laugh at myself. I can rejoice to see others grow and no longer depend on me. If I have the spiritual gift of humour, then I am truly detached, that is, I have an inner freedom that comes from being 'dominated' by Christ, and not 'corrupted by following illusory desires' (Eph 4:22) of materialism, status seeking and worldly power.

  The pastoral worker lives in a culture that exalts the self-perfectibility of each man and woman; there is nothing that cannot be done through individual effort and a competitive spirit. This behavioural emphasis can leave people exhausted, joyless, with a hollowness or void inside.[22] The Church desperately needs people today with the gift of humour, who can, by their relationship with the Lord, undermine the self-important seriousness or pomposity of our secularist culture and attract the joyless to an authentic peace.

  An elderly lady, bedridden for years and in constant pain, yet with an infectious gift of humour, or inner peace born of prayer, would receive countless visitors supposedly to cheer her up. In fact, roles were reversed. The visitors would pour out their inner pain and loss of meaning to her; she would listen, smile, console and slowly encourage them to begin to pray.

- *grieving?* In our Western cultures, bereavement is surely the most ill-prepared of all the adjustments to loss with which we are faced; facing up to loss begins only, if at all, after it has happened. There is a desperate need for people who have come to terms with death in their own lives; they can gently help others to discover the liberating gift of acknowledging death, in all its forms, as the preface to new life in the Lord.

- *prayer?* Without prayer, there can be no courage, no humour, no grieving. In prayer, I discover my own inner nothingness, emptiness, narrowness of vision, powerlessness, my absolute need of the Lord.

- *listening?* The word we find most often used in the Scriptures is the name of God, with his many titles. Coming a close second is the word 'listen' and its many expressions, e.g. 'hearken', 'attend', 'open your ears'. Why is the word used so frequently? Simply because listening, really listening, is tough and grinding work, especially in a world where there is so much stress on being busy doing things. The evangelizer is called, like the prophets of old, first to listen to God in prayer, in events: 'If only you would listen to him today, "Do not harden your hearts"' (Ps 95:7f.). The more we listen to God, the more of course we discover just what must change in our lives personally and in the world around us. The evangelizer is called to listen to what people are saying of their joys, their hopes, their frustrations and pain. This active listening demands patience, courage, faith.

- what of *imaginative adaptability?* The creatively imaginative evangelizer will turn to anything, in imitation of Christ, that will help to relate the Gospel to cultures, thus helping the process of refounding the Church (see Figure 12.2).

219

# Reflection questions

## To the reader

1. The Second Isaiah warned the Israelites not to be tempted to retreat nostalgically into the past, when they faced an uncertain and difficult future (43:18f.). Does his admonition apply also to you?

2. What are signs of an *authentic* sense of humour?

3. What is prayer? Why is it so crucial for the refounding of the Church?

## To a group discussion

1. Why is the spirituality of refounding new in the Church?

2. What should the call to refound the Church mean for us:
   In our parish?
   At work?
   In the home?

3. Read again the qualities to be found in the prophets and in Jesus Christ. Of all the characteristics listed, which do you think are most urgently needed by your group?

# Suggested reading

Arbuckle, G. A., *Strategies for Growth in Religious Life* (New York: Alba House, 1987), pp. 67–87.

Arbuckle, G. A., *Out of Chaos: Refounding Religious Congregations* (New York: Paulist/London: Geoffrey Chapman, 1988), pp. 46–62.

Beker, J. C., *Suffering and Hope: The Biblical Vision and the Human Predicament* (Philadelphia: Fortress Press, 1987).

Bruggemann, W., *Hopeful Imagination: Prophetic Voices in Exile* (Philadelphia: Fortress Press, 1987).

Cassidy, S., *Sharing the Darkness: The Spirituality of Caring* (London: Darton, Longman & Todd, 1988).

Conn, J. W., *Women's Spirituality: Resources for Christian Development* (New York: Paulist, 1986).

Green, T. H., *Weeds Among the Wheat: Discernment—Where Prayer and Action Meet* (Notre Dame, IN: Ave Maria Press, 1984).

Gutiérrez, G., *We Drink from Our Own Wells: The Spiritual Journey of a People* (London: SCM Press, 1984).

Hughes, G. W., *God of Surprises* (London: Darton, Longman and Todd, 1985).

O'Collins, G., *The Second Journey: Spiritual Awareness and the Mid-Life Crisis* (New York: Paulist, 1978).

Sullender, R. S., *Grief and Growth: Pastoral Resources for Emotional and Spiritual Growth* (New York: Paulist, 1985).

# References

## Introduction

1. See D. Adams, 'The Monkey and the Fish: Cultural Pitfalls of an Educational Adviser' in *International Development Review*, vol. 2, no. 2 (1960), pp. 22–24.

2. See E. Hall, *The Silent Language* (New York: Doubleday, 1959), *passim*.

3. In the USA the expression 'cultural anthropology' is preferred, but in other English-speaking countries 'social anthropology' is the more common terminology. The technical differences between the two expressions are of no importance here. Either expression connotes an *in-depth* reflection on culture(s).

4. 'Toward an Evangelical Theology of the Third World' in *International Bulletin for Missionary Research*, vol. 7, no. 2 (1983), p. 58.

5. A. Carr, 'Theology and Experience in the Thought of Karl Rahner' in *Journal of Religion*, vol. 53, no. 4 (1973), p. 373.

6. *The Blessed Rage for Order* (New York: Seabury Press, 1975), p. 15, n. 5.

7. *Religion and the Rise of Capitalism* (New York: Mentor, 1954), p. 157.

8. *The Tablet* (11 July 1987), p. 740.

9. See A. Illig, 'Why Fewer Converts?' in *Evangelization and Initiation* (Washington, DC: Paulist National Catholic Evangelization Association, July–August 1985), p. 2.

10. 'Defection among Hispanics' in *America* (30 July 1988), p. 62.

11. 'The Evangelical–Roman Catholic Dialogue on Mission, 1977–1984: A Report' in *International Bulletin of Missionary Research*, vol. 10, no. 1 (1987), p. 16.

12. See G. A. Arbuckle, 'Theology and Anthropology: Time for Dialogue' in *Theological Studies*, vol. 47, no. 3, (1986), pp. 445–447.

## Part 1: Inculturation: theoretical considerations

## Chapter 1 Understanding mission, evangelization and inculturation

1. See A. R. Tippett, *Introduction to Missiology* (Pasadena: William Carey, 1987), pp. 183–202.

2. See A. J. Chupungco, 'Liturgy and Inculturation' in *East Asian Pastoral Review*, vol. 18, no. 3 (1981), p. 264.

3. See A. J. Mason (ed.), *The Mission of St Augustine to England according to the Original Documents, Being a Handbook for the Thirteenth Centenary* (Cambridge, UK: Cambridge University Press, 1897), pp. 89f.

4. See 'Liturgy and Inculturation', op. cit., p. 264.

5. See A. J. Chupungco, *Cultural Adaptation of the Liturgy* (New York: Paulist, 1982), p. 7.

6. 'Christianity as Faith and as Culture' in *East Asian Pastoral Review*, vol. 18, no. 4 (1981), p. 310.

7. G. Voss, 'Missionary Accommodation' in *Missionary Academic Study No. 2* (New York: Society for the Propagation of the Faith, 1964), p. 17.

8. 'Instructio Vicariorum Apostolicorum ad Regna Synarum Tonchini et Cocinnae Proficiscentium' in *Collectanea Sacrae Congregationis de Propaganda Fide*, vol. 1 (Rome, 1907), p. 42.

9. Ibid.

10. See G. Minamiki, *The Chinese Rites Controversy from its Beginning to Modern Times* (Chicago: Loyola University Press, 1985), *passim*.

11. See A. Dulles, *Models of the Church* (New York: Image Books, 1978), pp. 39–50.

12. F. Redwood, as cited by L. G. Keys, *Philip Viard: Bishop of Wellington* (Christchurch, NZ: Pegasus, 1968), p. 203.

13. In 1919 Benedict XV rebuked those missionaries who are concerned 'not so much to extend the kingdom of God as to increase the power of the missionary's own country': 'Maximum Illud' in R. Hickey (ed.), *Modern Missionary Documents and Africa* (Dublin: Dominican Publications, 1982), p. 37.

14. Allocution in *Acta Apostolicae Sedis*, vol. 45 (6 December 1953), p. 794.

15. Cited by L. Luzbetak, *The Church and Cultures* (Techny, IL: Divine Word, 1970), p. 343.

16. Encyclical Letter 'Evangelii Praecones' in *Modern Missionary Documents and Africa*, op. cit., p. 99.

17. Ibid., pp. 83f.

18. Encyclical Letter 'Princeps Pastorum' in *Modern Missionary Documents and Africa*, op. cit., p. 143.

19. See 'The Church in the Modern World' in W. M. Abbott (ed.), *The Documents of Vatican II* (London: Geoffrey Chapman, 1966), pp. 199f. and *passim*.

20. 'The Dogmatic Constitution on the Church', ibid., p. 25.

21. 'On the Missions', ibid., p. 608.

22. See 'The Constitution on the Sacred Liturgy', ibid., p. 151.

23. 'The Church in the Modern World', ibid., p. 246.

24. See 'On the Missions', ibid., p. 612.

25. See 'Declaration on Religious Freedom', ibid., pp. 678f.

26. See 'On the Missions', ibid., p. 616.

27. See 'The Dogmatic Constitution on the Church', ibid., p. 79.

28. See 'Medellín Documents' (1968) in J. Gremillion (ed.), *The Gospel of Peace and Justice* (Maryknoll, NY: Orbis, 1976), pp. 471–476.

29. Paul VI, *Evangelii Nuntiandi* (Vatican, Sacred Congregation for Evangelization, 1975), paras 20, 63.

30. Ibid., paras 28–38.

31. Ibid., para. 34.

32. Ibid., para. 18.

33. J. Aixala (ed.), *Other Apostolates Today: Selected Letters and Addresses* (St Louis, MO: Institute of Jesuit Sources, 1981), p. 173. For background on inculturation, see A. R. Crollius, *What is New About Inculturation?* (Rome: Gregorian University, 1984), pp. 1–18.

34. M. de C. Azevedo, *Inculturation and the Challenge of Modernity* (Rome: Gregorian University, 1982), p. 11; for an overview of how inculturation emerged, see G. A. Arbuckle, 'Inculturation and Evangelization: Realism or Romanticism?' in *Anthropologists, Missionaries and Cultural Change* (Williamsburg: Studies in Third World Societies, 1985), pp. 171–207.

35. A. R. Tippett, 'Contextualization of the Gospel in Fiji: A Case Study from Oceania' in J. Stott and R. Coote (eds), *Gospel and Culture* (Pasadena: William Carey, 1979), p. 390.

36. See L. Newbigin, 'Mission in the 1980s' in *Occasional Bulletin of Missionary Research*, vol. 4, no. 4 (1980), pp. 110f.

37. Final 'Relatio', in *L'Osservatore Romano*, weekly Eng. edn (16 December 1985), p. 9.

38. See *Evangelii Nuntiandi* op. cit., para. 18.

39. See John Paul II, 'Bringing the Authentic Gospel to the African Cultures', address to Zairean Bishops, in *John Paul II: African Addresses* (Bologna: EMI, 1981), p. 39.

40. John Paul II, *The Church is a Creator of Culture: Address to the Pontifical Council for Culture* (Melbourne: ACTS, 1983), p. 6.

41. *Evangelii Nuntiandi*, op. cit., para. 28.

42. See John Paul II, Encyclical Letter, *Sollicitudo Rei Socialis* (London: CTS, 1988), paras 36f.

43. *Evangelii Nuntiandi*, op. cit., para. 36.

44. See R. J. Sider, 'Five Conflicting Viewpoints' in *International Review of Mission*, vol. 64, no. 255 (1975), p. 255.

45. Cited by Sider, ibid.

46. Cited by R. O. Costa in R. O. Costa (ed.), *One Faith, Many Cultures: Inculturation, Indigenization, and Contextualization* (Maryknoll, NY: Orbis, 1988), p. xii.

47. 'Mission and Evangelism: An Ecumenical Affirmation' in *International Review of Mission*, vol. 71, no. 284 (1982), p. 438.

48. See A. F. Glasser, 'The Evolution of Evangelical Mission Theology since World War II' in *International Bulletin of Missionary Research*, vol. 9, no. 1 (1986), pp. 9–13.

49. See, for example, C. Kraft, *Christianity in Culture: A Study in Dynamic Biblical Theologizing in Cross-Cultural Perspective* (Maryknoll, NY: Orbis, 1979), *passim*.

50. J. Falwell, *Strength for the Journey* (New York: Simon & Schuster, 1987), p. 290.

51. See D. McGavran, *Understanding Church Growth* (Grand Rapids, MI: W. B. Eerdmans, 1970), p. 198.

# Chapter 2 The world of meaning: culture

1. *The Heretical Imperative: Contemporary Possibilities of Religious Affirmation* (New York: Doubleday, 1980), p. 47.

2. Paul VI, *Evangelii Nuntiandi* (Vatican: Sacred Congregation for Evangelization, 1975), para. 63.

3. *The Interpretation of Cultures* (New York: Basic Books, 1973), p. 89.

4. 'I am not a Camera' in W.H. Auden, *Collected Poems*, ed. E. Mendelson (London: Faber & Faber, 1976), p. 630; see G.A. Arbuckle, 'Communicating through Symbols' in *Human Development*, vol. 8, no. 1 (1987), pp. 7–12.

5. See V. Turner, *The Ritual Process: Structure and Anti-Structure* (Ithaca, NY: Cornell University Press, 1977), pp. 94–203.

6. See M. Douglas, *Purity and Danger: An Analysis of Concepts of Pollution and Taboo* (Harmondsworth, Middx: Pelican, 1970), pp. 41–53.

7. See V. and E. Turner, *Image and Pilgrimage in Christian Culture: Anthropological Perspectives* (Oxford: Basil Blackwell, 1978), p. 247.

8. See C. Lane, *The Rites of Rulers: Ritual in Industrial Society—the Soviet Case* (Cambridge: Cambridge University Press, 1981), pp. 224–228.

9. See introductory explanations by E. Leach, *Lévi-Strauss* (London: Fontana, 1970), pp. 36–53.

10. See reflections by J. Moltmann, *The Power of the Powerless* (London: SCM, 1983), *passim*.

11. See M. Douglas, *Natural Symbols: Explorations in Cosmology* (New York: Pantheon Books, 1970), pp. 37–53.

12. For fuller explanation and references, see G.A. Arbuckle, 'Mythology, Revitalization and the Refounding of Religious Life' in *Review for Religious*, vol. 46, no. 1 (1987), pp. 14–43.

13. See M.T. Kelsey, *Myth, History and Faith: The Demythologizing of Christianity* (New York: Paulist, 1974), p. 5 and *passim*.

14. *The Masks of God* (4 vols; New York: Viking Press, 1970), *passim*.

15. See comments by C.S. Kirk, *Myth: Its Meaning and Functions in Ancient and Other Cultures* (Cambridge: Cambridge University Press, 1970), pp. 275–280; and P.S. Cohen, 'Theories of Myth' in *Man: Journal of the Royal Anthropological Institute*, vol. 4, no. 3 (1969), p. 340.

16. See C. Lévi-Strauss, *Totemism* (Boston: Beacon Press, 1963), *passim*.

17. See *The Ritual Process*, op. cit., pp. 96ff.

18. See I. Buruma, 'Who can Redeem Mother Filipinas?' in *New York Review* (16 January 1986), pp. 27f.

19. See T. Fawcett, *The Symbolic Language of Religion* (Minneapolis: Augsburg, 1971), p. 277.

## Chapter 3 Understanding different cultures

1. *The Anthropological Lens: Harsh Light, Soft Focus* (Cambridge: Cambridge University Press, 1986), p. 99.

2. See R.J. Smith, *Japanese Society: Tradition, Self and the Social Order* (Cambridge: Cambridge University Press, 1983), pp. 68–105.

3. See A.J. Marsella *et al.* (eds), *Culture and Self: Asian and Western Perspectives* (New York: Tavistock, 1985), pp. 91–138.

4. G.A. Arbuckle, *The Chatham Islands in Perspective: A Socio-Economic Review* (Wellington, NZ: Hicks Smith, 1970), *passim*.

5. See, for example, D. Pitt and C. Macpherson, *Emerging Pluralism: The Samoan Community in New Zealand* (Auckland, NZ: Longman Paul, 1974), pp. 22–49; J.I. Martin, *Community and Identity: Refugee Groups in Adelaide* (Canberra: Australian

National University Press, 1972), pp. 118–133; V.S. Khan, 'The Pakistanis: Mirpuri Villagers at Home in Bradford' in J.L. Watson (ed.), *Between Two Cultures: Migrants and Minorities in Britain* (Oxford: Basil Blackwell, 1977), pp. 76–78.

6. See H.J. Gans, *The Urban Villagers: Group and Class in the Life of Italian-Americans* (New York: Free Press, 1962), *passim*.

7. M. Young and P. Willmott, *Family and Kinship in East London* (London: Routledge & Kegan Paul, 1957), *passim*.

8. See M.R. Hollnsteiner, 'Reciprocity as a Filipino Value' in M.R. Hollnsteiner (ed.), *Society, Culture and the Filipino* (Quezon City: IPC, 1979), pp. 38–43; and S.N. Eisenstadt and L. Roniger, *Patrons, Clients and Friends: Interpersonal Relations and the Structure of Trust in Society* (Cambridge: Cambridge University Press, 1984), *passim*.

9. Cited by R. Firth, *Economics of the New Zealand Maori* (Wellington: R.E. Owen, 1959), p. 368.

10. See J. Metge, *The Maoris of New Zealand* (London: Routledge & Kegan Paul, 1976), pp. 67–70; and E.T. Hall, *The Silent Language* (New York: Doubleday, 1973), pp. 1–19.

11. See examples in P. Lawrence and M.J. Meggitt (eds), *Gods, Ghosts and Men in Melanesia: Some Religions of Australian New Guinea and the New Hebrides* (Melbourne: Oxford University Press, 1965), *passim*.

12. *Japanese Society* (Harmondsworth, Middx: Penguin, 1973), pp. 155f.

13. *Mateship in Local Organization* (Brisbane: University of Queensland Press, 1978), pp. 57f.

14. See *Japanese Society*, op. cit., p. 68; and *Japanese Society: Tradition, Self and the Social Order*, op. cit., pp. 90f.

15. *Custom and Conflict in Africa* (Oxford: Basil Blackwell, 1956), p. 48.

16. See M. Douglas, *Cultural Bias* (London: Royal Anthropological Institute of UK and Ireland, 1978), *passim*.

17. See O. Lewis, 'The Culture of Poverty' in *Scientific American*, vol. 215, no. 4 (1966), pp. 19–25; and comments by C.A. Valentine, *Culture and Poverty: Critique and Counter-Proposals* (Chicago: University of Chicago Press, 1968), *passim*.

18. See *Power and Innocence: A Search for the Sources of Power* (New York: W.W. Norton, 1972), pp. 99–119.

19. See P.S. Cohen, *Modern Social Theory* (London: Heinemann, 1968), p. 167.

20. *Sollicitudo Rei Socialis* (London: CTS, 1988), para. 36.

21. Ibid.

22. See J.L. Seymour, 'Social Analysis and Pastoral Studies: A Critical Theological Assessment' in *Pastoral Sciences*, vol. 4 (1985), pp. 51–181; and J. Holland and P. Henriot, *Social Analysis: Linking Faith and Justice* (Maryknoll, NY: Orbis, 1984), pp. 1–44.

## Chapter 4 Understanding culture change/chaos

1. Cited in A.D. Timpe (ed.), *Creativity: The Art and Science of Business Management* (New York: KEND, 1987), p. 103.

2. The model is a much adapted version of that devised by A.F.C. Wallace, 'Revitalization Movements' in *American Anthropologist*, vol. 58 (1956), pp. 264–281.

3. M.F. Kets de Vries and D. Miller, *The Neurotic Organization* (San Francisco: Jossey-Bass, 1985), p. 142.

4. For reflections on millenarian movements, see M. Barkun, *Disaster and the Millennium* (Syracuse, NY: Syracuse University Press, 1986), *passim*.

5. See R.H. Pells, *Radical Visions and American Dreams: Culture and Social Thought in the Depression Years* (Middletown, CT: Wesleyan University Press, 1984), p. 79.

6. See B. Martin, *A Sociology of Contemporary Cultural Change* (Oxford: Basil Blackwell, 1981), pp. 13–52.

7. See R.A. Viguerie, *The New Right: We're Ready to Lead* (Falls Church, VA: Viguerie, 1981), *passim*.

8. Cited by A. Kee, *Domination or Liberation: The Place of Religion in Social Conflict* (London: SCM Press, 1986), p. 111; see also D.L. Shields, *Growing Beyond Prejudices: Overcoming Hierarchical Dualism* (Mystic, CT: Twenty-Third Publications, 1986), p. 2.

9. See L. Cada, R. Fitz *et al.*, *Shaping the Coming Age of Religious Life* (New York: Seabury Press, 1979), *passim*; and G.A. Arbuckle, *Out of Chaos: The Refounding of Religious Congregations* (New York: Paulist/London: Geoffrey Chapman, 1988), pp. 65–187.

10. Cited by J.M. Lozano, *Discipleship: Towards an Understanding of Religious Life* (Chicago: Claret Center, 1980), p. 53.

11. See J. Padberg, 'The Contexts of Comings and Goings' in *The New Catholic World* (January–February 1988), pp. 41–46.

12. See M. Eliade, *Myth and Reality* (New York: Harper & Row, 1975), pp. 39–53, 184–193, and *The Myth of the Eternal Return* (Princeton, NJ: Princeton University Press, 1965), pp. 51–162.

13. *Time* (19 April 1982), p. 56.

14. *Time* (7 January 1985), p. 20.

15. See L. Morrow, *Time* (19 April 1982), p. 56.

16. See V. Turner, *The Ritual Process: Structure and Anti-Structure* (Ithaca, NY: Cornell University Press, 1977), pp. 94–203.

17. V. Turner, *The Forest of Symbols: Aspects of Ndembu Rituals* (Ithaca, NY: Cornell University Press, 1967), p. 106.

18. F.X. Clines, *The New York Times* (2 March 1986), p. 1E.

19. Post-Election Statement (14 February 1986) in *Pulso*, vol. 1, no. 4 (1986), pp. 336f.

20. F. Claver in *Pulso* op. cit., p. 389.

21. *Purity and Danger: An Analysis of Concepts of Pollution and Taboo* (Harmondsworth, Middx: Penguin, 1966), p. 117.

22. Claver, in *Pulso*, op. cit., p. 387.

*Part 2: Inculturation: pastoral issues*

## Chapter 5 The parish community: calling to inculturation

1. Cited by J. Tiller, *A Strategy for the Church's Ministry* (London: CIO, 1983), p. 65.

2. *American Community* (New York: Random House, 1956), p. 27.

3. *Social Relations in an Urban Parish* (Chicago: University of Chicago Press, 1954), p. 188.

4. *New Ministries: The Global Context* (Maryknoll, NY: Orbis, 1980), pp. 61f.

5. See J. Bodnar, *The Transplanted: A History of Immigrants in Urban America* (Bloomington, IN: Indiana University Press, 1985), pp. 144–168; G.A. Arbuckle, 'Migrants and Pastoral Care' in *The Jurist*, vol. 46, no. 2 (1986), pp. 464–467.

6. M. Winter, 'The Survival of the Parish Structure' in *The Clergy Review* (May 1970), p. 367.

7. See 'Dogmatic Constitution on the Church' in W. M. Abbott (ed.), *The Documents of Vatican II* (London: Geoffrey Chapman, 1966), ch. 2.

8. Apostolic Letter, *Evangelii Nuntiandi* (1975), para. 73.

9. Ibid., para. 70.

10. J. Gremillion and J. Castelli, *The Emerging Parish: The Notre Dame Study of Catholic Life since Vatican II* (San Francisco: Harper & Row, 1987), p. 3.

11. *Ecclesiogenesis: The Base Communities Reinvent the Church* (Maryknoll, NY: Orbis/London: Collins, 1986), p. 1.

12. G. Deelen in *Basic Christian Comunities in the Church* (Brussels: Pro Mundi Vita, 1980), no. 81, p. 5.

13. See D. Hoge, *Future of Catholic Leadership: Responses to the Priest Shortage* (Kansas City: Sheed & Ward, 1987), pp. 23f.

14. See M. Mason, 'Pastoral Leadership for Tomorrow' in *Australasian Catholic Record*, vol. 60, no. 1 (1983), pp. 35f.

15. *Habits of the Heart: Individualism and Commitment in American Life* (New York: Harper & Row, 1985).

16. See L. Mascarenhas in *Basic Christian Communities in the Church*, op. cit., pp. 30ff.

17. See 'The Challenge of the Movements' in *The Tablet* (19 March 1988), pp. 323f.

18. See *RENEW National Report to New Zealand Bishops' Conference* (March 1988), p. 1 and *passim*.

19. P. Delooz, *New Beginnings* (Brussels: Pro Mundi Vita, 1983), pp. 26ff.

20. *The Emerging Parish*, op. cit., p. 195.

21. See G. A. Arbuckle and F. J. Faisandier, *The Church in a Multi-Cultural Society* (Wellington: New Zealand Bishops' Conference, 1976), pp. 25/D, 43/D.

22. See *The Emerging Parish*, op. cit., p. 205.

23. *Partners in the Mystery of Redemption: A Pastoral Response to Women's Concerns for Church and Society*, First Draft (Washington, DC: National Conference of Catholic Bishops, 1988), para. 225.

24. See ibid., paras 219f.

25. See 'The Challenge of the Movements', op. cit.

26. *The Two Catholic Churches: A Study in Oppression* (London: SCM Press, 1986), pp. 104–187; for comments on this thesis, see M. Hornsby-Smith, 'The Church's New Face' in *The Tablet* (11 July 1987), p. 740. See also M. Douglas, *Natural Symbols: Explorations in Cosmology* (New York: Random House, 1970), pp. 37–53.

27. See 'Pastoral Leadership for Tomorrow', op. cit., pp. 3f.

28. See Report of the Archbishop of Canterbury's Commission on Urban Priority Areas, *Faith in the City: A Call for Action by Church and Nation* (London: Church House, 1985), para. 2.20.

29. Bishop P. Cordes cited by J. Holland in 'Beyond a Privatized Spirituality?' in *New Catholic World* (July–August 1988), p. 176.

30. *The Two Catholic Churches*, op. cit., pp. 211–227; and *The Catholic Pentecostal Movement: Creative or Divisive Enthusiasm* (Brussels: Pro Mundi Vita, 1976), pp. 12f. and *passim*.

31. J. P. Fitzpatrick, 'The Hispanic Poor in a Middle-Class Church' in *America* (2 July 1988), p. 11.

32. *Faith in the City*, op. cit., para. 5.56.

33. 'Pastoral Leadership for Tomorrow', op. cit., p. 36.

34. See F. W. Lewins, 'Wholes and Parts: Some Aspects of the Relationship between the Australian Catholic Church and Migrants' in A. Black and P. Glasner (eds), *Practice and Belief: Studies in the Sociology of Australian Religion* (Sydney: George Allen & Unwin, 1983), pp. 74–85.

35. See G. A. Arbuckle, 'Liturgies for the Culturally Dispossessed' in *Worship*, vol. 59, no. 5 (1985), pp. 428ff.; also *The Emerging Parish*, op. cit., p. 206.

36. V. Elizondo, 'The Catechumen in the Hispanic Community of the United States' in W. J. Reedy (ed.), *Becoming a Catholic Christian* (New York: William H. Sadlier, 1978), pp. 95f.

37. *The Emerging Parish*, op. cit., p. 141.

# Chapter 6 Inculturation and ritual

1. *A Preface to Paradise Lost* (New York: Oxford University Press, 1961), p. 21.

2. *Faith in the City: A Call for Action by Church and Nation* (London: Church House, 1985), para. 6.101.

3. See R. Bocock, *Ritual in Industrial Society: A Sociological Analysis of Ritualism in Modern England* (London: George Allen & Unwin, 1974), pp. 35–59.

4. From 'Archaeology' in E. Mendelson (ed.) *Collected Poems* (London: Faber & Faber, 1976), p. 501.

5. See C. Lane, *The Rites of Rulers: Ritual in Industrial Society—The Soviet Case* (Cambridge, UK: Cambridge University Press, 1981), pp. 153–188.

6. See comments by G. A. Arbuckle, 'Evaluating General and Provincial Chapters' in *Review for Religious*, vol. 47, no. 2 (1988), p. 183 and *passim*.

7. See V. Turner, *The Ritual Process: Structure and Anti-Structure* (Ithaca, NY: Cornell University Press, 1977), pp. 167–203.

8. See 'The Pornography of Death' in *Encounter*, no. 5 (October 1955), pp. 49–52, and *Death, Grief and Mourning* (London: Cresset Press, 1965), p. 42. For a clear analysis of why grief rituals are necessary in social life, see P. Marris, *Loss and Change* (London: Routledge & Kegan Paul, 1974), *passim*.

9. William Broyles, 'A Ritual for Saying Goodbye' in *US News and World Report* (10 November 1986), p. 19.

10. See *The Rites of Rulers*, op. cit., pp. 140–188, and R. N. Bellah and P. E. Hammond, *Varieties of Civil Religion* (San Francisco: Harper & Row, 1980), *passim*.

11. See M. Gluckman, *Custom and Conflict in Africa* (Oxford: Basil Blackwell, 1956), pp. 109–136.

12. *Blessed are Those Who Have Questions* (Denville, NJ: Dimension Books, 1976), pp. 62f.

13. *The Breaking of the Image: A Sociology of Christian Theory and Practice* (Oxford: Basil Blackwell, 1980), p. 100.

14. *Final Document of the Third General Conference of the Latin American Episcopate, Puebla* in J. Eagleson and P. Scharper (eds), *Puebla and Beyond* (Maryknoll, NY: Orbis, 1979), pp. 185f.

15. J. Gremillion and J. Castelli, *The Emerging Parish: The Notre Dame Study of Catholic Life since Vatican II* (San Francisco: Harper & Row, 1987), pp. 144f.

16. Ibid., pp. 88f.

17. See G. A. Arbuckle and F. J. Faisandier, *The Church in a Multi-Cultural Society* (Wellington: New Zealand Bishops' Conference, 1976), pp. 40/H–52/H.

18. See G. A. Arbuckle, 'Dress and Worship: Liturgies for the Culturally Dispossessed' in *Worship*, vol. 59, no. 5 (1985), p. 435.

## Chapter 7 Sects, 'The cults' and inculturation

1. 'Mainline Religion in Transition' in M. Douglas and S. Tipton (eds), *Religion in America: Spiritual Life in a Secular Age* (Boston: Beacon Press, 1982), p. 137.

2. R. Gill, *Beyond Decline: A Challenge to the Churches* (London: SCM Press, 1988), p. 66.

3. G. Wigoder in *The Tablet* (15 August 1987), p. 862.

4. P. Lernoux, 'The Advance of the Sects' in *The Tablet* (2 July 1988), p. 747.

5. *Secularism*, US Catholic Bishops' Conference (14 November 1947).

6. See B. Wilson, 'An Analysis of Sect Development' in *American Sociological Review*, vol. 24 (1959), pp. 3–15; and J. A. Beckford, *The Trumpet of Prophecy: A Sociological Study of Jehovah's Witnesses* (Oxford: Basil Blackwell, 1975), pp. 122–133.

7. See B. Wilson, *Religious Sects* (London: Weidenfeld & Nicolson, 1970), *passim*.

8. See W. S. Bainbridge, 'Science and Religion: The Case of Scientology' in D. G. Bromley and P. E. Hammond (eds), *The Future of New Religious Movements* (Macon, GA: Mercer, 1987), pp. 59–79.

9. 'Cargo Cults in the South Pacific' in *America* (3 September 1969), p. 96. For a background to Cargo cults, see K. Burridge, *New Heaven New Earth: A Study of Millenarian Activities* (Oxford: Basil Blackwell, 1969), *passim*; for comments on the Rastafarian movement, see E. E. Cashmore, *Rastaman* (London: Allen & Unwin, 1979), *passim*.

10. See J. M. Yinger, *Religion, Society and the Individual* (New York: Macmillan, 1957), p. 154.

11. See W. Appel, *Cults in America: Programmed for Paradise* (New York: Holt, Rinehart & Winston, 1983), pp. 1–21.

12. See J. A. Beckford, *Cult Controversies: The Societal Response to the New Religious Movements* (London: Tavistock, 1986), *passim*.

13. *Enthusiasm: A Chapter in the History of Religion* (New York: Oxford University Press, 1950), p. 1.

14. *Gates of Eden: American Culture in the Sixties* (New York: Basic Books, 1977), p. 213.

15. See excellent overview by B. Martin, *A Sociology of Contemporary Cultural Change* (Oxford: Basil Blackwell, 1981), *passim*.

16. G. Howard (ed.), *The Sixties: The Art, Attitudes, Politics and Media of Our Most Explosive Decade* (New York: Washington Square Press, 1982), p. 4.

17. Cited by M. Haralambos, *Sociology: Themes and Perspectives* (London: Bell & Hyman, 1985), p. 489.

18. 'Contra Blake' in E. Mendelsen (ed.), *Collected Poems* (London: Faber & Faber, 1976), p. 540.

19. P. Berger, *Facing Up to Modernity* (Harmondsworth, Middx: Penguin, 1977), p. 16.

20. See J. G. Melton, 'How New is New? The Flowering of the "New" Religious Consciousness since 1965' in *The Future of New Religious Movements*, op. cit., pp. 46ff.

21. See J. G. Melton and R. L. Moore, *The Cult Experience: Responding to the New Religious Pluralism* (New York: Pilgrim Press, 1982), pp. 31–35.

22. This helpful distinction is made by Martin in *A Sociology of Contemporary Cultural Change*, op. cit., pp. 202–233.

23. See P.C. Vitz, *Psychology as Religion: The Cult of Self-Worship* (Grand Rapids, MI: W.B. Eerdmans, 1977), *passim*.

24. See E.B. Rochford, 'Dialectical Processes in the Development of Hare Krishna: Tension, Public Definition, and Strategy' in *The Future of New Religious Movements*, op. cit., pp. 109–122.

25. See E. Barker, *The Making of a Moonie: Brainwashing or Choice* (Oxford: Basil Blackwell, 1984), *passim*.

26. *The Resilient Church: The Necessity and Limits of Adaptation* (New York: Doubleday, 1981), p. 11.

27. *A Sociology of Contemporary Cultural Change*, op. cit., p. 231.

28. See *The Catholic Pentecostal Movement: Creative or Divisive Enthusiasm* (Brussels: Pro Mundi Vita, 1976), pp. 29–34.

29. P.M. Arnold, 'The Rise of Catholic Fundamentalism' in *America* (11 April 1987), p. 298.

30. See D. Pipes, *In the Path of God: Islam and Political Power* (New York: Basic Books, 1983), pp. 321–330.

31. See *The Economist* (London) (16 May 1987), p. 24.

32. See M.E. Marty, 'Fundamentalism and Modern America' in G. Marsden (ed.), *Evangelicalism and Modern America* (Grand Rapids: W.B. Eerdmans, 1984), pp. 56–68.

33. See A. Kee, *Domination or Liberation: The Place of Religion in Social Conflict* (London: SCM Press, 1986), pp. 101ff.

34. *Faith in the Nation: A Christian Vision for Britain* (London: SPCK, 1988), pp. 50ff.

35. M.E. Marty, 'The New Christian Right' in *The Tablet* (23 April 1988), p. 462.

36. *Strength for the Journey* (New York: Simon & Schuster, 1987), p. 358.

37. *Domination or Liberation*, op. cit., p. 104.

38. See P. Steinfels, 'Neo-Conservatism: Social and Religious Phenomenon' in G. Baum (ed.), *Neo-Conservatism: Social and Religious Phenomenon* (New York: Seabury Press, 1981), pp. 39–42.

39. *The Capitalist Revolution: Fifty Propositions about Prosperity, Equality and Liberty* (New York: Harper & Row, 1986), *passim*.

40. See Baum, 'Neo-Conservative Critics of the Churches' in *Neo-Conservatism*, op. cit., pp. 43–50.

41. See 'The Rise of Catholic Fundamentalism', op. cit., pp. 297–302; and T.C. Ross, 'Catholicism and Fundamentalism', in *New Theology Review* (1988), pp. 74–87.

42. 'Evangelization in Latin America's Present and Future' (Puebla, 1979) in J. Eagleson and P. Scharper (eds), *Puebla and Beyond* (Maryknoll, NY: Orbis, 1979), p. 188.

43. T. Robbins and D. Anthony, cited by Hammond, in *The Future of New Religious Movements*, op. cit., p. 266.

44. See C.A. Fracchia, *Second Spring: The Coming of Age of US Catholicism* (San Francisco: Harper & Row, 1980), pp. 159–161.

45. See *The Tablet* (6 October 1984); (19 March 1988), pp. 323f.

# Chapter 8 Inculturation and youth subculture

1. *AwopBopalooBop AlopBamBoom: Pop from the Beginning* (St Albans, Herts: Paladin Books, 1970), p. 31.

2. S. Frith, *The Sociology of Rock* (London: Constable, 1978), p. 205.

3. See J. Kett, *Rites of Passage: Adolescence in America 1790 to the Present* (New York: Basic Books, 1977), p. 38; and M. Harris, *Portrait of Youth Ministry* (New York: Paulist, 1981), p. 32.

4. See *The Economist* (London) (15 August 1987), p. 32.

5. See M. Brake, *Comparative Youth Culture* (London: Routledge & Kegan Paul, 1985), pp. 72–82; K. Pryce, *Endless Pressure: A Study of West Indian Life-styles in Bristol* (Harmondsworth, Middx: Penguin, 1979), pp. 143–162.

6. See *Folk Devils and Moral Panics: The Creation of the Mods and Rockers* (Oxford: Martin Robertson, 1980), *passim*.

7. See D. Hebdige, *Subculture: The Meaning of Style* (London: Methuen, 1979), pp. 106–112.

8. See I. Chambers, *Urban Rhythms: Pop Music and Popular Culture* (London: Macmillan, 1985), p. 9.

9. See *Subculture: The Meaning of Style*, op. cit., pp. 33–39.

10. See N. Schaffner, *The Beatles Forever* (Harrisburg, PA: Cameron House, 1977), p. 73.

11. See *Comparative Youth Culture*, op. cit., pp. 99–102.

12. Cited by P. L. Selfe, *Sociology* (London: Pan Books, 1983), p. 93.

13. *Portrait of Youth Ministry*, op. cit., p. 36.

14. For a detailed description of the anthropology of initiation rites, see G. A. Arbuckle, *Strategies for Growth in Religious Life* (New York: Alba House, 1987), pp. 185–201.

15. Cited by M. Flynn, 'Evangelisation and the Development of Faith by Youth' in *Australasian Catholic Record*, vol. 56, no. 3 (1979), p. 274.

16. See Paul VI, Apostolic Letter, *Evangelii Nuntiandi* (1975), para. 41.

17. *Closing of the American Mind: How Higher Education has Failed Democracy and Impoverished the Souls of Today's Students* (New York: Simon & Schuster, 1987), *passim*.

18. See M. Warren, 'Young People and the Nuclear Threat' in J. Coleman and G. Baum (eds), *Youth Without a Future?* (Edinburgh: T. & T. Clark, 1985), p. 83 and *passim*.

19. See *Time* (19 August 1985), p. 15.

20. E. Barker, '"And so to bed": Protest and Malaise among Youth in Great Britain' in *Youth Without a Future?*, op. cit., p. 80; see also P. Delooz, *The Social Context of Youth Catechesis* (Brussels: Pro Mundi Vita, 1976), pp. 9f.

21. *Youth in God's World* (Uppsala, 1968), cited by A. J. van der Bent, 'Youth in the World Council of Churches' in *Youth Without a Future?*, op. cit., pp. 100f.

22. See Australian Council of Churches *et al.*, *It's a Rocky Road* (Blackburn: Dove, 1985), *passim*.

# Chapter 9 Inculturation, prejudice and discrimination

1. 'Brothers and Sisters to Us: A Pastoral Letter on Racism' (14 November 1979) in J. B. Benestad and F. J. Butler (eds), *Quest for Justice* (Washington, DC: NCCB, 1981), p. 373.

2. *The Brixton Disorders 10–12 April 1981* (London: HMSO, 1981), para. 9.1.

3. See G. Allport, *The Nature of Prejudice* (New York: Doubleday, 1958), pp. 6–10.

4. See F. J. Sheed, *The Church and I* (London: Sheed & Ward, 1975), pp. 57f.

5. See *The Nature of Prejudice*, op. cit., p. 24.

6. Ibid., p. 10.

7. See K. R. McConnochie, *Realities of Race: An Analysis of the Concepts of Race and Racism and their Relevance to Australia* (Sydney: ANZ, 1973), pp. 5–7.

8. See *The Race Concept: Results of an Inquiry* (Paris: UNESCO, 1951), pp. 15f.

9. See *The Church to Africa: Pastoral Letters of the African Hierarchies* (London: Sword of the Spirit, 1960), pp. 11f.

10. Cited by D. J. Bosch, 'Racism and Revolution: Response of the Churches in South Africa' in *Occasional Bulletin of Missionary Research*, vol. 3, no. 1 (1979), p. 16.

11. *The Wounded Stag* (London: Collins, 1984), p. 158.

12. See T. E. Clarke, 'Fundamentalism and Prejudice' in *The Way* (January 1987), pp. 33–41.

13. 'Why Are There So Few Women Scientists and Engineers?' in *New Society* (21 February 1980), p. 21.

14. 'Mary Ward: Women and Leadership' in *The Way* (Supplement), no. 53 (Summer 1985), p. 59.

15. 'We and They' in *Debts and Credits* (London: Macmillan, 1926), pp. 327f.

16. *Here for Good: Western Europe's New Ethnic Minorities* (London: Pluto Press, 1984), p. 29.

17. See T. D. Moodie, *The Rise of Afrikanerdom: Power, Apartheid, and the Afrikaner Civil Religion* (Berkeley: University of California Press, 1975), *passim*.

18. *West Indian Children in Our Schools* (London: HMSO, 1982), p. 12.

19. See P. L. Selfe, *Sociology* (London: Pan, 1983), p. 233.

20. *Newsweek* (21 March 1987), p. 97.

21. *Faith in the City: A Call for Action by Church and Nation* (London: Church House, 1985), p. xv.

22. *The Brixton Disorders*, op. cit., para. 4.63.

23. R. Hampton, *Sentencing in a Children's Court and Labelling Theory* (Wellington, NZ: Justice Department, 1975), p. 57.

24. 'Women's Liberation in Historical and Theological Perspective' in *Soundings*, vol. 53 (1970), p. 363.

25. See B. Utas (ed.), *Women in Islamic Societies: Social Attitudes and Historical Perspectives* (London: Curzon Press, 1983), *passim*.

26. See L. Adamson (ed.), 'More to Lose than Their Chains', *New Internationalist* (July 1980), pp. 7–11.

27. See J. Phillips, *A Man's Country? The Image of the Pakeha Male: A History* (Auckland, NZ: Penguin, 1987), pp. 288f.

28. See H. Oxley, 'Ockerism, The Cultural Rabbit' in P. Spearitt and D. Walker (eds), *Australian Popular Culture* (Sydney: George Allen & Unwin, 1979), pp. 190–209.

29. See R. R. Ruether, *Women-Church: Theology and Practice of Feminist Liturgical Communities* (San Francisco: Harper & Row, 1985), p. 75 and *passim*.

30. *Dictionary of the Bible* (London: Geoffrey Chapman, 1968), p. 766; see also C. S. Song, *The Compassionate God: An Exercise in the Theology of Transposition* (London: SCM Press, 1982), pp. 127–141.

31. See G. Soares-Prabhu, 'The Unprejudiced Jesus and the Prejudiced Church' in *The Way* (January 1987), pp. 4–13.

32. Ibid., p. 9.

33. 'Declaration on the Relationship of the Church to Non-Christian Religions' in W. M. Abbott (ed.), *The Documents of Vatican II* (London: Geoffrey Chapman, 1966), pp. 666f.

34. See P. E. Grosser and E. G. Halperin, *The Causes and Effects of Anti-Semitism* (New York: Philosophical Library, 1978), *passim*.

35. *The Destruction of Aboriginal Society* (Harmondsworth, Middx: Penguin, 1972), pp. 10f.

36. See 'Racism and Revolution: Response of the Churches in South Africa', op. cit., pp. 13–20; E. Regehr, *Perceptions of Apartheid: The Churches and Political Change in South Africa* (Scottdale, PA: Herald Press, 1979), *passim*.

37. 'Brothers and Sisters to Us', op. cit., pp. 373, 375, 379.

38. See P. I. Rose, *They and We: Racial and Ethnic Relations in the United States* (New York: Random House, 1981), pp. 116–122.

39. See A. Ballara, *Proud to be White: A Survey of Pakeha Prejudice in New Zealand* (Auckland: Heinemann, 1986), pp. 143–146.

40. See information in *Development News Digest* (Sydney) (August 1972), p. 5.

# Chapter 10 Inculturation: migrants and adjustment

1. 'Churches and Immigrants', Research Group for European Migration Problems, *Bulletin*, no. 5 (1961), p. 10.

2. A. Adler and R. Taft, 'Some Psychological Aspects of Immigrant Assimilation' in A. Stoller (ed.), *New Faces: Immigration and Family Life in Australia* (Melbourne: Cheshire, 1966), p. 75.

3. J. E. Ritchie, *Understanding Maoris*, Paper to Wellington Regional Employers' Association, Seminar (24 March 1976).

4. R. Goldfarb, as cited by A. Jacques, *The Stranger within Your Gates: Uprooted People in the World Today* (Geneva: WCC, 1985), p. 80; also 'Asian Migrant Workers: Voluntary Servitude' in *The Economist* (London) (10 September 1988), pp. 25–28.

5. Cited by J. Beckett, 'Aborigines, Alcohol and Assimilation' in M. Reay (ed.), *Aborigines Now: New Perspectives in the Study of Aboriginal Communities* (Sydney: Angus & Robertson, 1964), p. 36.

6. *Fire in the Streets: America in the 1960s* (New York: Simon & Schuster, 1979), p. 311.

7. D. Armstrong, 'This is What it's Like to be Black' in *Sydney Morning Herald* (13 July 1968), p. 15.

8. See 'Aborigines, Alcohol and Assimilation', op. cit., p. 43.

9. *Soul on Ice* (New York: Delata, 1968), p. 14.

10. See 'Contraculture and Subculture' in *American Sociological Review*, vol. 25 (1960), pp. 625–635.

11. Reported in *Listener* (NZ) (10 March 1979), p. 41.

12. *Beyond the Rainbow* (London: Harcourt, n.d.), p. 62.

13. W. Collins, as cited by D. Hiro, *Black British, White British* (London: Eyre and Spottiswoode, 1971), p. 80.

14. Cited by P. Gillman, 'I Blame England' in *Sunday Times Supplement* (30 September 1973), p. 5.

15. See M. Young and P. Willmott, *Family and Kinship in East London* (London: Routledge & Kegan Paul, 1957).

16. Quoted by D. Wilson, *Asia Awakes: A Continent in Transition* (New York: NAL, 1970), p. 56; see also R. and C. Ballard, 'The Sikhs: The Development of South Asian Settlements in Britain' in J. L. Watson (ed.), *Between Two Cultures: Migrants and Minorities in Britain* (Oxford: Basil Blackwell, 1977), pp. 43–47.

17. See R. Johnston, *Future Australians: Immigrant Children in Perth, Western Australia* (Canberra: Australian National University Press, 1972), pp. 246–264.

18. K. Cirtautas, *The Refugee: A Psychological Study* (Boston: Meador, 1957), p. 26.

19. A. Rampton, *West Indian Children in our Schools: Interim Report of the Committee of Inquiry* (London: HMSO, 1981), p. 9.

20. Lord Scarman, *The Brixton Disorders* (London: HMSO, 1981), para. 2.35.

21. See Lord Swann, *Education for All: A Brief Guide to the Main Issues on Education of Children from Ethnic Minority Groups* (London: HMSO, 1985), p. 8.

22. J. S. Coleman *et al.*, *Equality of Educational Opportunity* (Washington: US Dept of Health, Education and Welfare, 1966), p. 22.

23. See S. Tomlinson, *Home and School in Multicultural Britain* (London: Batsford Academic, 1984), *passim*.

24. See M. Kovacs and A. Cropley, *Immigrants and Society: Alienation and Assimilation* (Sydney: McGraw-Hill, 1975), p. 123.

25. *The New Black Presence in Britain* (London: BCC, 1976), p. 16.

26. See I. Crewe, 'Representation and the Ethnic Minorities in Britain' in N. Glazer and K. Young (eds), *Ethnic Pluralism and Public Policy: Achieving Equality in the United States and Britain* (London: Heinemann, 1983), pp. 258–284.

27. See *Te Kaupapa Tikanga Rua*, Report of the Bi-Cultural Commission of the Anglican Church on the Treaty of Waitangi (1986), pp.16–34.

28. *Motu Proprio* and Instruction, *Pastoralis Migratorum Cura* (15 August 1969) (Vatican Press).

29. John Paul II, Address 'The Church and Migrants' (17 October 1985) in *The Pope Speaks* (1985), p. 349.

30. *Faith in the City: A Call for Action by Church and Nation* (London: Church House, 1985), paras 5.54–5.74.

31. *Notes and Reports* (April 1982); see also M. P. Hornsby-Smith, *Catholic Education: The Unobtrusive Partner—Sociological Studies of the Catholic School System in England and Wales* (London: Sheed & Ward, 1978), p. 40.

32. *The Two Catholic Churches: A Study in Oppression* (London: SCM Press, 1986), *passim*.

33. Roman Catholic Bishops of England and Wales, *The Easter People* (Middlegreen, Slough: St Paul Publications, 1980), para. 42.

34. See R. Linkh, *American Catholicism and European Immigrants 1900–1924* (New York: Center for Migration Studies, 1975), p. 192 and *passim*.

35. 'The Hispanic Poor in a Middle-Class Church' in *America* (2 July 1988), p. 11.

36. *A New Australia: Some Reflections on the Impact of Migration on Australian Society* (Sydney: Justice and Peace Commission, Catholic Bishops, 1977), p. 1.

37. See F. W. Lewins, 'Wholes and Parts: Some Aspects of the Relationship between the Australian Catholic Church and Migrants' in A. W. Black and P. E. Glasner (eds), *Practice and Belief: Studies in the Sociology of Australian Religion* (Sydney: George Allen & Unwin, 1983), pp. 74–86.

*Part 3: Inculturation: the pastoral agent*

## Chapter 11 Fostering inculturation: pastoral hints

1. *The Church is a Creator of Culture* (Melbourne: ACTS, 1983), p. 6.

2. *The Anthropological Lens: Harsh Light, Soft Focus* (New York: Cambridge University Press, 1986), pp. 111f.

3. M. Amaladoss, 'Inculturation and Tasks of Mission' in *East Asian Pastoral Review*, vol. 17, no. 2 (1980), p. 125.

4. Paul VI, *Evangelii Nuntiandi* (1975), para. 18.

5. See 'Dogmatic Constitution on the Church' in W. M. Abbott (ed.), *The Documents of Vatican II* (London: Geoffrey Chapman, 1966), pp. 24–37.

6. See G. Egan, 'The Parish: Ministering Community and Community of Ministers' in E. E. Whitehead (ed.), *The Parish in Community and Ministry* (New York: Paulist, 1978), pp. 78f.

7. See D. Steele, *Images of Leadership and Authority in the Church: Biblical Principles and Secular Models* (Lanham, MD: University Press of America, 1986), pp. 23–41.

8. See R. Brown *et al.* (eds), *Peter in the New Testament* (Minneapolis: Augsburg/London: Geoffrey Chapman, 1973), pp. 157–168.

9. *The Testimony of St Paul* (Middlegreen, Slough: St Paul Publications, 1983), pp. 39–49.

10. See R. Gill, *Beyond Decline: A Challenge to the Churches* (London: SCM Press, 1988), pp. 71f.

11. See W. Cohn, *Christian Conversion: A Developmental Interpretation of Autonomy and Surrender* (New York: Paulist, 1986), *passim*, and D. L. Gelpi, 'The Converting Catechumen' in *Lumen Vitae*, vol. 42, no. 4 (1987), pp. 401–415.

12. *Method in Theology* (London: Herder & Herder, 1972), pp. 204f.

13. See E. F. Schumacher, *Small is Beautiful: Economics as if People Mattered* (New York: Harper & Row, 1973), *passim*.

14. Pastoral Letter *The Work of Justice* (Dublin: Veritas, 1977), para. 46.

15. *Faith in the City: A Call for Action by Church and Nation* (London: Church House, 1985), para. 9.72.

16. L. Luzbetak, *The Church and Cultures* (Techny, IL: Divine World Publications, 1970), p. 97.

## Chapter 12 A spirituality for 'refounding the Church'

1. *A Strategy for the Church's Ministry* (London: CIO, 1983), p. 53.

2. *Faith in the City: A Call for Action by Church and Nation* (London: Church House, 1985), para. 3.29.

3. See K. Dyckman and L. P. Carroll, *Inviting the Mystic, Supporting the Prophet* (New York: Paulist, 1981), p. 79.

4. See Y. Congar, *Lay People in the Church* (Westminster, MD: Newman, 1957; repr. London: Geoffrey Chapman, 1985), p. 2.

5. See C. Banana, 'Good News to the Poor' in *Your Kingdom Come: Mission Perspectives—Report on the World Conference on Mission and Evangelism* (Geneva: WCC, 1980), p. 110.

6. See R. L. Sivard, *World Military and Social Expenditures 1982* (Leesburg: World Priorities, 1982), p. 5.

7. *Justice in the World*, Synod of Bishops (1971), para. 48.

8. *International Bulletin of Missionary Research*, vol. 12, no. 1 (1988), p. 16.

9. See John Paul II, Encyclical *Sollicitudo Rei Socialis* (1987), paras 11–26.

10. See L. Doohan, *The Lay-Centered Church: Theology and Spirituality* (Minneapolis: Winston Press, 1984), pp. 90–127.

11. Congregation for the Doctrine of the Faith, *Instruction on Christian Freedom and Liberation* (Vatican City, 1986), para. 63.

12. 'Pastoral Constitution on the Church in the Modern World' in W. M. Abbott (ed.), *The Documents of Vatican II* (London: Geoffrey Chapman, 1966), p. 262.

13. *Justice in the World*, op. cit., para. 47.

14. See G. Gutiérrez, *We Drink from Our Own Wells: The Spiritual Journey of a People* (London: SCM Press, 1984), pp. 19–34.

15. See G. A. Arbuckle, *Out of Chaos: Refounding Religious Congregations* (New York: Paulist/London: Geoffrey Chapman, 1988), pp. 57–62.

16. See W. Brueggemann, *The Prophetic Imagination* (Philadelphia: Fortress Press, 1978), *passim*.

17. See C. Hyers, *And God Created Laughter: The Bible as Divine Comedy* (Atlanta: John Knox Press, 1987), p. 7.

18. See W. Brueggemann, *Hopeful Imagination: Prophetic Voices in Exile* (Philadelphia: Fortress Press, 1986), pp. 32–47.

19. See W. Barclay, *The Mind of Jesus* (London: SCM Press, 1960), pp. 97f.

20. See G. A. Arbuckle, *Strategies for Growth in Religious Life* (New York: Alba House, 1987), pp. 67–87.

21. See *The Screwtape Letters* (New York: Macmillan, 1982), rev. edn, p. ix.

22. See C. Lasch, *The Culture of Narcissism: American Life in an Age of Diminishing Expectations* (New York: Warner, 1979), *passim*.